Mometrix
TEST PREPARATION

I0892935

OAE

Computer Science (054) Secrets Study Guide

DEAR FUTURE EXAM SUCCESS STORY

First of all, **THANK YOU** for purchasing Mometrix study materials!

Second, congratulations! You are one of the few determined test-takers who are committed to doing whatever it takes to excel on your exam. **You have come to the right place.** We developed these study materials with one goal in mind: to deliver you the information you need in a format that's concise and easy to use.

In addition to optimizing your guide for the content of the test, we've outlined our recommended steps for breaking down the preparation process into small, attainable goals so you can make sure you stay on track.

We've also analyzed the entire test-taking process, identifying the most common pitfalls and showing how you can overcome them and be ready for any curveball the test throws you.

Standardized testing is one of the biggest obstacles on your road to success, which only increases the importance of doing well in the high-pressure, high-stakes environment of test day. Your results on this test could have a significant impact on your future, and this guide provides the information and practical advice to help you achieve your full potential on test day.

Your success is our success

We would love to hear from you! If you would like to share the story of your exam success or if you have any questions or comments in regard to our products, please contact us at **800-673-8175** or **support@mometrix.com**.

Thanks again for your business and we wish you continued success!

Sincerely,
The Mometrix Test Preparation Team

Need more help? Check out our flashcards at:
http://mometrixflashcards.com/OAE

TABLE OF CONTENTS

Introduction

Thank you for purchasing this resource! You have made the choice to prepare yourself for a test that could have a huge impact on your future, and this guide is designed to help you be fully ready for test day. Obviously, it's important to have a solid understanding of the test material, but you also need to be prepared for the unique environment and stressors of the test, so that you can perform to the best of your abilities.

For this purpose, the first section that appears in this guide is the **Secret Keys**. We've devoted countless hours to meticulously researching what works and what doesn't, and we've boiled down our findings to the five most impactful steps you can take to improve your performance on the test. We start at the beginning with study planning and move through the preparation process, all the way to the testing strategies that will help you get the most out of what you know when you're finally sitting in front of the test.

We recommend that you start preparing for your test as far in advance as possible. However, if you've bought this guide as a last-minute study resource and only have a few days before your test, we recommend that you skip over the first two Secret Keys since they address a long-term study plan.

If you struggle with **test anxiety**, we strongly encourage you to check out our recommendations for how you can overcome it. Test anxiety is a formidable foe, but it can be beaten, and we want to make sure you have the tools you need to defeat it.

Secret Key #1 – Plan Big, Study Small

There's a lot riding on your performance. If you want to ace this test, you're going to need to keep your skills sharp and the material fresh in your mind. You need a plan that lets you review everything you need to know while still fitting in your schedule. We'll break this strategy down into three categories.

Information Organization

Start with the information you already have: the official test outline. From this, you can make a complete list of all the concepts you need to cover before the test. Organize these concepts into groups that can be studied together, and create a list of any related vocabulary you need to learn so you can brush up on any difficult terms. You'll want to keep this vocabulary list handy once you actually start studying since you may need to add to it along the way.

Time Management

Once you have your set of study concepts, decide how to spread them out over the time you have left before the test. Break your study plan into small, clear goals so you have a manageable task for each day and know exactly what you're doing. Then just focus on one small step at a time. When you manage your time this way, you don't need to spend hours at a time studying. Studying a small block of content for a short period each day helps you retain information better and avoid stressing over how much you have left to do. You can relax knowing that you have a plan to cover everything in time. In order for this strategy to be effective though, you have to start studying early and stick to your schedule. Avoid the exhaustion and futility that comes from last-minute cramming!

Study Environment

The environment you study in has a big impact on your learning. Studying in a coffee shop, while probably more enjoyable, is not likely to be as fruitful as studying in a quiet room. It's important to keep distractions to a minimum. You're only planning to study for a short block of time, so make the most of it. Don't pause to check your phone or get up to find a snack. It's also important to **avoid multitasking**. Research has consistently shown that multitasking will make your studying dramatically less effective. Your study area should also be comfortable and well-lit so you don't have the distraction of straining your eyes or sitting on an uncomfortable chair.

The time of day you study is also important. You want to be rested and alert. Don't wait until just before bedtime. Study when you'll be most likely to comprehend and remember. Even better, if you know what time of day your test will be, set that time aside for study. That way your brain will be used to working on that subject at that specific time and you'll have a better chance of recalling information.

Finally, it can be helpful to team up with others who are studying for the same test. Your actual studying should be done in as isolated an environment as possible, but the work of organizing the information and setting up the study plan can be divided up. In between study sessions, you can discuss with your teammates the concepts that you're all studying and quiz each other on the details. Just be sure that your teammates are as serious about the test as you are. If you find that your study time is being replaced with social time, you might need to find a new team.

Secret Key #2 – Make Your Studying Count

You're devoting a lot of time and effort to preparing for this test, so you want to be absolutely certain it will pay off. This means doing more than just reading the content and hoping you can remember it on test day. It's important to make every minute of study count. There are two main areas you can focus on to make your studying count.

Retention

It doesn't matter how much time you study if you can't remember the material. You need to make sure you are retaining the concepts. To check your retention of the information you're learning, try recalling it at later times with minimal prompting. Try carrying around flashcards and glance at one or two from time to time or ask a friend who's also studying for the test to quiz you.

To enhance your retention, look for ways to put the information into practice so that you can apply it rather than simply recalling it. If you're using the information in practical ways, it will be much easier to remember. Similarly, it helps to solidify a concept in your mind if you're not only reading it to yourself but also explaining it to someone else. Ask a friend to let you teach them about a concept you're a little shaky on (or speak aloud to an imaginary audience if necessary). As you try to summarize, define, give examples, and answer your friend's questions, you'll understand the concepts better and they will stay with you longer. Finally, step back for a big picture view and ask yourself how each piece of information fits with the whole subject. When you link the different concepts together and see them working together as a whole, it's easier to remember the individual components.

Finally, practice showing your work on any multi-step problems, even if you're just studying. Writing out each step you take to solve a problem will help solidify the process in your mind, and you'll be more likely to remember it during the test.

Modality

Modality simply refers to the means or method by which you study. Choosing a study modality that fits your own individual learning style is crucial. No two people learn best in exactly the same way, so it's important to know your strengths and use them to your advantage.

For example, if you learn best by visualization, focus on visualizing a concept in your mind and draw an image or a diagram. Try color-coding your notes, illustrating them, or creating symbols that will trigger your mind to recall a learned concept. If you learn best by hearing or discussing information, find a study partner who learns the same way or read aloud to yourself. Think about how to put the information in your own words. Imagine that you are giving a lecture on the topic and record yourself so you can listen to it later.

For any learning style, flashcards can be helpful. Organize the information so you can take advantage of spare moments to review. Underline key words or phrases. Use different colors for different categories. Mnemonic devices (such as creating a short list in which every item starts with the same letter) can also help with retention. Find what works best for you and use it to store the information in your mind most effectively and easily.

Secret Key #3 – Practice the Right Way

Your success on test day depends not only on how many hours you put into preparing, but also on whether you prepared the right way. It's good to check along the way to see if your studying is paying off. One of the most effective ways to do this is by taking practice tests to evaluate your progress. Practice tests are useful because they show exactly where you need to improve. Every time you take a practice test, pay special attention to these three groups of questions:

- The questions you got wrong
- The questions you had to guess on, even if you guessed right
- The questions you found difficult or slow to work through

This will show you exactly what your weak areas are, and where you need to devote more study time. Ask yourself why each of these questions gave you trouble. Was it because you didn't understand the material? Was it because you didn't remember the vocabulary? Do you need more repetitions on this type of question to build speed and confidence? Dig into those questions and figure out how you can strengthen your weak areas as you go back to review the material.

Additionally, many practice tests have a section explaining the answer choices. It can be tempting to read the explanation and think that you now have a good understanding of the concept. However, an explanation likely only covers part of the question's broader context. Even if the explanation makes perfect sense, **go back and investigate** every concept related to the question until you're positive you have a thorough understanding.

As you go along, keep in mind that the practice test is just that: practice. Memorizing these questions and answers will not be very helpful on the actual test because it is unlikely to have any of the same exact questions. If you only know the right answers to the sample questions, you won't be prepared for the real thing. **Study the concepts** until you understand them fully, and then you'll be able to answer any question that shows up on the test.

It's important to wait on the practice tests until you're ready. If you take a test on your first day of study, you may be overwhelmed by the amount of material covered and how much you need to learn. Work up to it gradually.

On test day, you'll need to be prepared for answering questions, managing your time, and using the test-taking strategies you've learned. It's a lot to balance, like a mental marathon that will have a big impact on your future. Like training for a marathon, you'll need to start slowly and work your way up. When test day arrives, you'll be ready.

Start with the strategies you've read in the first two Secret Keys—plan your course and study in the way that works best for you. If you have time, consider using multiple study resources to get different approaches to the same concepts. It can be helpful to see difficult concepts from more than one angle. Then find a good source for practice tests. Many times, the test website will suggest potential study resources or provide sample tests.

Practice Test Strategy

If you're able to find at least three practice tests, we recommend this strategy:

UNTIMED AND OPEN-BOOK PRACTICE

Take the first test with no time constraints and with your notes and study guide handy. Take your time and focus on applying the strategies you've learned.

TIMED AND OPEN-BOOK PRACTICE

Take the second practice test open-book as well, but set a timer and practice pacing yourself to finish in time.

TIMED AND CLOSED-BOOK PRACTICE

Take any other practice tests as if it were test day. Set a timer and put away your study materials. Sit at a table or desk in a quiet room, imagine yourself at the testing center, and answer questions as quickly and accurately as possible.

Keep repeating timed and closed-book tests on a regular basis until you run out of practice tests or it's time for the actual test. Your mind will be ready for the schedule and stress of test day, and you'll be able to focus on recalling the material you've learned.

Secret Key #4 – Pace Yourself

Once you're fully prepared for the material on the test, your biggest challenge on test day will be managing your time. Just knowing that the clock is ticking can make you panic even if you have plenty of time left. Work on pacing yourself so you can build confidence against the time constraints of the exam. Pacing is a difficult skill to master, especially in a high-pressure environment, so **practice is vital**.

Set time expectations for your pace based on how much time is available. For example, if a section has 60 questions and the time limit is 30 minutes, you know you have to average 30 seconds or less per question in order to answer them all. Although 30 seconds is the hard limit, set 25 seconds per question as your goal, so you reserve extra time to spend on harder questions. When you budget extra time for the harder questions, you no longer have any reason to stress when those questions take longer to answer.

Don't let this time expectation distract you from working through the test at a calm, steady pace, but keep it in mind so you don't spend too much time on any one question. Recognize that taking extra time on one question you don't understand may keep you from answering two that you do understand later in the test. If your time limit for a question is up and you're still not sure of the answer, mark it and move on, and come back to it later if the time and the test format allow. If the testing format doesn't allow you to return to earlier questions, just make an educated guess; then put it out of your mind and move on.

On the easier questions, be careful not to rush. It may seem wise to hurry through them so you have more time for the challenging ones, but it's not worth missing one if you know the concept and just didn't take the time to read the question fully. Work efficiently but make sure you understand the question and have looked at all of the answer choices, since more than one may seem right at first.

Even if you're paying attention to the time, you may find yourself a little behind at some point. You should speed up to get back on track, but do so wisely. Don't panic; just take a few seconds less on each question until you're caught up. Don't guess without thinking, but do look through the answer choices and eliminate any you know are wrong. If you can get down to two choices, it is often worthwhile to guess from those. Once you've chosen an answer, move on and don't dwell on any that you skipped or had to hurry through. If a question was taking too long, chances are it was one of the harder ones, so you weren't as likely to get it right anyway.

On the other hand, if you find yourself getting ahead of schedule, it may be beneficial to slow down a little. The more quickly you work, the more likely you are to make a careless mistake that will affect your score. You've budgeted time for each question, so don't be afraid to spend that time. Practice an efficient but careful pace to get the most out of the time you have.

Secret Key #5 – Have a Plan for Guessing

When you're taking the test, you may find yourself stuck on a question. Some of the answer choices seem better than others, but you don't see the one answer choice that is obviously correct. What do you do?

The scenario described above is very common, yet most test takers have not effectively prepared for it. Developing and practicing a plan for guessing may be one of the single most effective uses of your time as you get ready for the exam.

In developing your plan for guessing, there are three questions to address:

- When should you start the guessing process?
- How should you narrow down the choices?
- Which answer should you choose?

When to Start the Guessing Process

Unless your plan for guessing is to select C every time (which, despite its merits, is not what we recommend), you need to leave yourself enough time to apply your answer elimination strategies. Since you have a limited amount of time for each question, that means that if you're going to give yourself the best shot at guessing correctly, you have to decide quickly whether or not you will guess.

Of course, the best-case scenario is that you don't have to guess at all, so first, see if you can answer the question based on your knowledge of the subject and basic reasoning skills. Focus on the key words in the question and try to jog your memory of related topics. Give yourself a chance to bring the knowledge to mind, but once you realize that you don't have (or you can't access) the knowledge you need to answer the question, it's time to start the guessing process.

It's almost always better to start the guessing process too early than too late. It only takes a few seconds to remember something and answer the question from knowledge. Carefully eliminating wrong answer choices takes longer. Plus, going through the process of eliminating answer choices can actually help jog your memory.

Summary: Start the guessing process as soon as you decide that you can't answer the question based on your knowledge.

How to Narrow Down the Choices

The next chapter in this book (**Test-Taking Strategies**) includes a wide range of strategies for how to approach questions and how to look for answer choices to eliminate. You will definitely want to read those carefully, practice them, and figure out which ones work best for you. Here though, we're going to address a mindset rather than a particular strategy.

Your odds of guessing an answer correctly depend on how many options you are choosing from.

Number of options left	5	4	3	2	1
Odds of guessing correctly	20%	25%	33%	50%	100%

You can see from this chart just how valuable it is to be able to eliminate incorrect answers and make an educated guess, but there are two things that many test takers do that cause them to miss out on the benefits of guessing:

- Accidentally eliminating the correct answer
- Selecting an answer based on an impression

We'll look at the first one here, and the second one in the next section.

To avoid accidentally eliminating the correct answer, we recommend a thought exercise called **the $5 challenge**. In this challenge, you only eliminate an answer choice from contention if you are willing to bet $5 on it being wrong. Why $5? Five dollars is a small but not insignificant amount of money. It's an amount you could afford to lose but wouldn't want to throw away. And while losing $5 once might not hurt too much, doing it twenty times will set you back $100. In the same way, each small decision you make—eliminating a choice here, guessing on a question there—won't by itself impact your score very much, but when you put them all together, they can make a big difference. By holding each answer choice elimination decision to a higher standard, you can reduce the risk of accidentally eliminating the correct answer.

The $5 challenge can also be applied in a positive sense: If you are willing to bet $5 that an answer choice *is* correct, go ahead and mark it as correct.

Summary: Only eliminate an answer choice if you are willing to bet $5 that it is wrong.

Which Answer to Choose

You're taking the test. You've run into a hard question and decided you'll have to guess. You've eliminated all the answer choices you're willing to bet $5 on. Now you have to pick an answer. Why do we even need to talk about this? Why can't you just pick whichever one you feel like when the time comes?

The answer to these questions is that if you don't come into the test with a plan, you'll rely on your impression to select an answer choice, and if you do that, you risk falling into a trap. The test writers know that everyone who takes their test will be guessing on some of the questions, so they intentionally write wrong answer choices to seem plausible. You still have to pick an answer though, and if the wrong answer choices are designed to look right, how can you ever be sure that you're not falling for their trap? The best solution we've found to this dilemma is to take the decision out of your hands entirely. Here is the process we recommend:

Once you've eliminated any choices that you are confident (willing to bet $5) are wrong, select the first remaining choice as your answer.

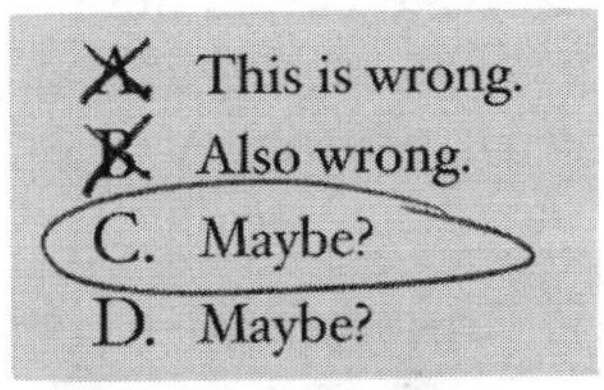

Whether you choose to select the first remaining choice, the second, or the last, the important thing is that you use some preselected standard. Using this approach guarantees that you will not be enticed into selecting an answer choice that looks right, because you are not basing your decision on how the answer choices look.

This is not meant to make you question your knowledge. Instead, it is to help you recognize the difference between your knowledge and your impressions. There's a huge difference between thinking an answer is right because of what you know, and thinking an answer is right because it looks or sounds like it should be right.

Summary: To ensure that your selection is appropriately random, make a predetermined selection from among all answer choices you have not eliminated.

Test-Taking Strategies

This section contains a list of test-taking strategies that you may find helpful as you work through the test. By taking what you know and applying logical thought, you can maximize your chances of answering any question correctly!

It is very important to realize that every question is different and every person is different: no single strategy will work on every question, and no single strategy will work for every person. That's why we've included all of them here, so you can try them out and determine which ones work best for different types of questions and which ones work best for you.

Question Strategies

✓ Read Carefully

Read the question and the answer choices carefully. Don't miss the question because you misread the terms. You have plenty of time to read each question thoroughly and make sure you understand what is being asked. Yet a happy medium must be attained, so don't waste too much time. You must read carefully and efficiently.

✓ Contextual Clues

Look for contextual clues. If the question includes a word you are not familiar with, look at the immediate context for some indication of what the word might mean. Contextual clues can often give you all the information you need to decipher the meaning of an unfamiliar word. Even if you can't determine the meaning, you may be able to narrow down the possibilities enough to make a solid guess at the answer to the question.

✓ Prefixes

If you're having trouble with a word in the question or answer choices, try dissecting it. Take advantage of every clue that the word might include. Prefixes can be a huge help. Usually, they allow you to determine a basic meaning. *Pre-* means before, *post-* means after, *pro-* is positive, *de-* is negative. From prefixes, you can get an idea of the general meaning of the word and try to put it into context.

✓ Hedge Words

Watch out for critical hedge words, such as *likely, may, can, often, almost, mostly, usually, generally, rarely,* and *sometimes.* Question writers insert these hedge phrases to cover every possibility. Often an answer choice will be wrong simply because it leaves no room for exception. Be on guard for answer choices that have definitive words such as *exactly* and *always.*

✓ Switchback Words

Stay alert for *switchbacks.* These are the words and phrases frequently used to alert you to shifts in thought. The most common switchback words are *but, although,* and *however.* Others include *nevertheless, on the other hand, even though, while, in spite of, despite,* and *regardless of.* Switchback words are important to catch because they can change the direction of the question or an answer choice.

✓ Face Value

When in doubt, use common sense. Accept the situation in the problem at face value. Don't read too much into it. These problems will not require you to make wild assumptions. If you have to go beyond creativity and warp time or space in order to have an answer choice fit the question, then you should move on and consider the other answer choices. These are normal problems rooted in reality. The applicable relationship or explanation may not be readily apparent, but it is there for you to figure out. Use your common sense to interpret anything that isn't clear.

Answer Choice Strategies

⊘ Answer Selection

The most thorough way to pick an answer choice is to identify and eliminate wrong answers until only one is left, then confirm it is the correct answer. Sometimes an answer choice may immediately seem right, but be careful. The test writers will usually put more than one reasonable answer choice on each question, so take a second to read all of them and make sure that the other choices are not equally obvious. As long as you have time left, it is better to read every answer choice than to pick the first one that looks right without checking the others.

⊘ Answer Choice Families

An answer choice family consists of two (in rare cases, three) answer choices that are very similar in construction and cannot all be true at the same time. If you see two answer choices that are direct opposites or parallels, one of them is usually the correct answer. For instance, if one answer choice says that quantity *x* increases and another either says that quantity *x* decreases (opposite) or says that quantity *y* increases (parallel), then those answer choices would fall into the same family. An answer choice that doesn't match the construction of the answer choice family is more likely to be incorrect. Most questions will not have answer choice families, but when they do appear, you should be prepared to recognize them.

⊘ Eliminate Answers

Eliminate answer choices as soon as you realize they are wrong, but make sure you consider all possibilities. If you are eliminating answer choices and realize that the last one you are left with is also wrong, don't panic. Start over and consider each choice again. There may be something you missed the first time that you will realize on the second pass.

⊘ Avoid Fact Traps

Don't be distracted by an answer choice that is factually true but doesn't answer the question. You are looking for the choice that answers the question. Stay focused on what the question is asking for so you don't accidentally pick an answer that is true but incorrect. Always go back to the question and make sure the answer choice you've selected actually answers the question and is not merely a true statement.

⊘ Extreme Statements

In general, you should avoid answers that put forth extreme actions as standard practice or proclaim controversial ideas as established fact. An answer choice that states the "process should be used in certain situations, if..." is much more likely to be correct than one that states the "process should be discontinued completely." The first is a calm rational statement and doesn't even make a definitive, uncompromising stance, using a hedge word *if* to provide wiggle room, whereas the second choice is far more extreme.

⊘ Benchmark

As you read through the answer choices and you come across one that seems to answer the question well, mentally select that answer choice. This is not your final answer, but it's the one that will help you evaluate the other answer choices. The one that you selected is your benchmark or standard for judging each of the other answer choices. Every other answer choice must be compared to your benchmark. That choice is correct until proven otherwise by another answer choice beating it. If you find a better answer, then that one becomes your new benchmark. Once you've decided that no other choice answers the question as well as your benchmark, you have your final answer.

✓ Predict the Answer

Before you even start looking at the answer choices, it is often best to try to predict the answer. When you come up with the answer on your own, it is easier to avoid distractions and traps because you will know exactly what to look for. The right answer choice is unlikely to be word-for-word what you came up with, but it should be a close match. Even if you are confident that you have the right answer, you should still take the time to read each option before moving on.

General Strategies

✓ Tough Questions

If you are stumped on a problem or it appears too hard or too difficult, don't waste time. Move on! Remember though, if you can quickly check for obviously incorrect answer choices, your chances of guessing correctly are greatly improved. Before you completely give up, at least try to knock out a couple of possible answers. Eliminate what you can and then guess at the remaining answer choices before moving on.

✓ Check Your Work

Since you will probably not know every term listed and the answer to every question, it is important that you get credit for the ones that you do know. Don't miss any questions through careless mistakes. If at all possible, try to take a second to look back over your answer selection and make sure you've selected the correct answer choice and haven't made a costly careless mistake (such as marking an answer choice that you didn't mean to mark). This quick double check should more than pay for itself in caught mistakes for the time it costs.

✓ Pace Yourself

It's easy to be overwhelmed when you're looking at a page full of questions; your mind is confused and full of random thoughts, and the clock is ticking down faster than you would like. Calm down and maintain the pace that you have set for yourself. Especially as you get down to the last few minutes of the test, don't let the small numbers on the clock make you panic. As long as you are on track by monitoring your pace, you are guaranteed to have time for each question.

✓ Don't Rush

It is very easy to make errors when you are in a hurry. Maintaining a fast pace in answering questions is pointless if it makes you miss questions that you would have gotten right otherwise. Test writers like to include distracting information and wrong answers that seem right. Taking a little extra time to avoid careless mistakes can make all the difference in your test score. Find a pace that allows you to be confident in the answers that you select.

✓ Keep Moving

Panicking will not help you pass the test, so do your best to stay calm and keep moving. Taking deep breaths and going through the answer elimination steps you practiced can help to break through a stress barrier and keep your pace.

Final Notes

The combination of a solid foundation of content knowledge and the confidence that comes from practicing your plan for applying that knowledge is the key to maximizing your performance on test day. As your foundation of content knowledge is built up and strengthened, you'll find that the strategies included in this chapter become more and more effective in helping you quickly sift through the distractions and traps of the test to isolate the correct answer.

Now that you're preparing to move forward into the test content chapters of this book, be sure to keep your goal in mind. As you read, think about how you will be able to apply this information on the test. If you've already seen sample questions for the test and you have an idea of the question format and style, try to come up with questions of your own that you can answer based on what you're reading. This will give you valuable practice applying your knowledge in the same ways you can expect to on test day.

Good luck and good studying!

Algorithmic Thinking and Data Analysis

Transform passive reading into active learning! After immersing yourself in this chapter, put your comprehension to the test by taking a quiz. The insights you gained will stay with you longer this way. Scan the QR code to go directly to the chapter quiz interface for this study guide. If you're using a computer, simply visit the online resources page at **mometrix.com/resources719/oaecompsci** and click the Chapter Quizzes link.

Algorithm Formats

Algorithms

An **algorithm** may be expressed as a formula or as a sequence of instructions that will accomplish a specific task. In computer programming, professionals use algorithms to circumvent the need for long sequences of code. Instead of telling the computer program what to do in every conceivable circumstance, the programmer can write an algorithm that tells the program to do a certain thing if one variable is true, and to do something else if that variable is false. In other words, an algorithm can reduce a near-infinite range of possibilities to a simple "yes or no" choice. Algorithms are also capable of many other functions in computer programming.

An algorithm instructs the computer to carry out an individual task or function. It is a basic unit of a software program. When writing algorithms, programmers must be very precise; any ambiguity can lead to errors and undesired results. One common example of such an error is the **infinite loop**—repetition of a certain task that will go on forever, consuming an infinite amount of resources. To avoid such errors, the programmer must specify the exact amount of resources and the specific length of time the computer should spend completing the task. Algorithms are essentially logical and mathematical solutions to particular problems, solved in the programming language being used.

Function and Purpose

The basic purpose of an algorithm is to detail the steps necessary to perform some task or solve some problem. An algorithm for a programmer can be thought of as similar to a recipe for a chef. The algorithm outlines each task that needs to be performed in order to obtain the expected output. If decisions need to be made, then the algorithm identifies the rules that are required to make such decisions. Algorithms can be very simple, or they can be quite complex. The level of complexity of an algorithm depends directly on the level of complexity of the problem that needs to be solved. Simple algorithms can be created to solve simple problems, while complex algorithms are typically required for complex problems. To extend the recipe analogy, a recipe for toast is rather simple, especially compared to, say, a recipe for lasagna, which would be fairly complex.

Algorithm Design

Algorithms are usually created using certain design techniques, or paradigms, which include the following: divide and conquer, greedy, dynamic programming, backtracking, and branch and bound. Paradigms offer a number of advantages:

- They each lend themselves to particular situations, making it more likely that programmers will have useful templates or approaches for solving any given problem based on the type of problem it is.
- Most high-level languages can translate these paradigms into common controls and data structures.
- They allow for precise analysis of the temporal and spatial requirements of the algorithm.

When analyzing whether or not an algorithm is the one best-suited for handling a given problem, developers usually consider the running time of the algorithm, the optimal performance of the algorithm, and comparisons between the algorithm and another one under consideration.

Divide and Conquer Algorithm Design Paradigm

Divide and conquer is an algorithm design paradigm that utilizes multibranch recursion. In essence, an algorithm designed using the divide and conquer methodology functions by taking the main problem and using a recursive process to break it down into progressively smaller sub-problems. Once the sub-problems are small enough to be solved directly (these states are known as **base cases**), their solutions are combined to provide an answer for the original problem. Popular examples of divide and conquer algorithms include syntactic analysis, sorting programs such as quick sort and merge sort, programs that multiply large numbers, and programs that calculate discrete Fourier transforms. Divide and conquer algorithm design is also capable of condensing a large problem into a single sub-problem, often by using techniques such as **tail recursion**, which uses simple loops. Binary search algorithms are an example of this.

Top-down Approach and Bottom-Up Approach

The **dynamic** programming paradigm can be implemented using one of the following methods:

- **Top-down approach** – This is the most direct method using recursive procedures. Assuming the main problem can be divided into overlapping sub-problems using recursion, the solutions to the sub-problems are stored in a table. Before solving a new sub-problem, the computer will check the table to determine if it has already been solved. If so, the solution in the table is used. If not, a new solution is added to the table.
- **Bottom-up approach** – This is carried out after a problem has been solved using recursion. The sub-problems are then solved from the bottom-up and their solutions are reconstructed into larger sub-problems. Eventually, these are built upon iteratively to reconstruct the main problem. This method is usually carried out in tabular form.

Sharing Algorithms Between Developers

Successful algorithms are frequently shared between programmers because it is much more efficient to reuse a good design than to create a new process from scratch. This sharing can take place even if the programmers are not using the same language to create the code. Remember that an algorithm is not language specific. An algorithm is simply a set of steps that need to be carried out to complete a particular task or process. Once the developer understands the algorithm, then they can convert the steps in the algorithm into code that uses the desired language. For example, the same algorithm can be used to code a process in C#, Java, and Python.

Deciding on the Best Algorithm to Perform a Given Function

Generally many different algorithms may exist that perform the same function, so it is sometimes necessary for a developer to decide for themselves which algorithm should be selected. Several factors should be considered when selecting the most appropriate algorithm. One of these factors is the way in which the data is arranged. Some algorithms require the data to be arranged in a certain manner, while others can work with unordered data. Another factor to consider is the required response time of the application being developed. Oftentimes speed is the most important factor; in many cases the algorithm selected must be able to operate very quickly. Lastly, the developer should consider the machines on which the application will run. Available memory and processing power of the machine that will be running the software can play a large role in which algorithm would be the best choice.

Computational Thinking

At a basic level, computational thinking is the process of learning to "think like a machine." Computational thinking includes both cognitive skills and problem-solving processes. Some models describe various skills associated with computational thinking; common examples of such skills include: breaking a problem down into smaller pieces and solving it incrementally, developing a step-by-step solution to a problem, and finding different ways to express a problem in language so as to find various approaches. The process of creating a step-by-step solution to a problem is sometimes referred to as **algorithmic thinking**. Computational thinking is an important skill for someone in the computer science field because it aids that person in developing computer-based solutions to problems.

Turing Machines

Developed by Alan Turing in 1937, **Turing machines** are theoretical devices that are studied by computer scientists so they can better understand the limits of mechanical computation, CPU function, and complexity theory. A Turing machine is not a practical piece of technology; rather, it is only a thought experiment that can replicate CPU functions and the logic of any algorithm no matter how complex, and whose abstract properties aid the understanding of computer science. According to the **Church-Turing thesis** (developed by Turing and Alonzo Church), Turing machines are capable of giving exact definitions for algorithmic processes or mechanical procedures and informally expressing effective methods in logic and mathematics. There are numerous variations of the Turing machine. A universal Turing machine, or UTM, can replicate the function of any other Turing machine.

Finite-State Machines

A finite-state machine (often referred to as a finite-state automaton, or a state machine) is a theoretical machine consisting of a set of states, actions, and transitions between states. **Finite-state machines** are used to create models of computer behavior. These models are useful in the design of computer programs. A finite-state machine has a finite internal memory, a sequential reading apparatus, and an output apparatus (e.g., a user interface). The machine begins in its start state and then changes state in response to input. The operation is complete when the machine has passed through all possible states. These machines are used in engineering, artificial intelligence, and linguistics programs, in part because they are able to handle multiple problems simultaneously.

Pseudocode

Pseudocode is a way of writing programming code in more general terms, avoiding the syntax of actual programming languages. Writing code this way allows programmers and nonprogrammers alike to analyze and understand the logic behind an algorithm before it is converted into actual programming code. Pseudocode is written between the system specification phase and the coding phase. In other words, it is written once developers know the goals of the program but before they have written a fully functioning program that achieves these goals.

Systems of writing pseudocode vary in how closely they resemble actual programming code. Some pseudocode is useful for helping everyone on a project understand how an algorithm works, while other pseudocode is useful for allowing programmers with different backgrounds to work together without all of them needing to experts in the same specialized programming language. Depending on the purpose of the pseudocode, it may be almost like natural language, or it may be in an agreed-upon or already existing notation that will be almost as stringent as real code.

Number Base Conversion

Binary Number System

Binary code consists entirely of ones and zeros. All the complex and detailed information contained in a computer is stored at the most fundamental level as series of these two digits. The binary system is called a base-2 system because it only has two unique digits. The decimal system, on the other hand, has ten unique digits and is therefore known as a base-10 system). Consequently, a base-10 system has place values that correspond to powers of 10, such as ones, tens, hundreds, and thousands, but the binary number system has place values that correspond to powers of two, such as ones, twos, fours, eights, and so on.

Converting Base-10 Numbers to Binary

In order to convert a number in **base 10** (decimal) to **binary**, we use the place values in the binary number system. Remember that each place value corresponds to a power of 2, as shown below:

64	32	16	8	4	2	1

2^6	2^5	2^4	2^3	2^2	2^1	2^0

Each place value be a 0 or a 1. If a place value is a 1, then that place value is added into the number. If a place value is a 0, then that value is not included. We can perform a conversion to binary by first placing a 1 in the largest place value possible without going above the value of the number to be converted. For instance, if we are converting 7 to binary, 8 is too large, so 4 is the largest place included in the number. Therefore, we place a 1 in the fours column. Since 7 minus 4 is 3, we need to account for the additional value of 3. Repeat the process of adding a 1 to the largest possible place, which in this case would be the twos place. That then leaves a remainder of 1, so place a 1 in the ones place. Therefore, the base-10 number 7 would be written in binary as 111.

Converting Base-10 Numbers into Hexadecimal

One of the easiest ways to convert from base 10 to **hexadecimal** (base 16) is to first convert into binary. It is very easy to then convert from binary to hexadecimal. Once the conversion to binary is done, simply group the binary number into sections of four digits (or **bits**) each, starting from the right. Once the grouping is complete, each group of four bits will represent one hexadecimal digit. If the value of the four bits together is 7, then the hexadecimal digit will be 7. If the value is 13, then the hex digit will be D. Let's look at an example. Consider the number 44. Converted to binary, this number would be 101100. If we start from the right and group the bits into segments of four, we get: 10 | 1100. We look at each group as an individual binary number, so the value of the group on the left would be 2, and the value of the group on the right would be 12. Therefore, the hexadecimal representation of 44 would be 2C. Notice that this requires only two digits, while the binary representation requires six digits.

Number Representation in Computers

Computers use binary to store and work with numbers. Binary notation is a base-2 system, meaning it consists of only two digits, 1 and 0. For instance, the binary representation of the decimal number 14 is 1110. This number has four position holders. The right-most position holder is the ones place. Each subsequent position is twice the quantity of the previous one. Given 16 available digits (bits), you can store any integer value between 0 and 65536. Of couse, the more bits available, the higher the number of possible values.

The occupied spaces are eight, four, and two: 8 + 4 + 2 = 14. By using a **radix point**, binary notation can represent fractional values in the same way a decimal does. The first position immediately following the decimal point has a value of one-half. Each subsequent position is half the quantity of the previous one.

Consider the example 1110.101. The notation represents the number: 8 + 4 + 2 + 1/2 + 1/8 = 14 5/8. There are several forms of the binary notation, including two's complement notation and floating-point notation.

Arithmetic in Binary Notation

Binary notation consists of only two digits, 1 and 0. Adding these digits produces the following values:

0 + 0 = 0

0 + 1 = 1

1 + 1 = 10 (which is expressed as 2 in base 10)

When adding together larger binary values, we can add by columns, much like we do when adding together numbers in a base ten system. Consider the example of adding together 101011 and 11010:

111 1

101011

```
+     011010
     1000101
```

If a column has a sum greater than 1, we drop number in the smaller position into the answer, and carry the larger value to the next position. For instance, in the above example, in the second column from the right, the sum total is 10 (2 in base 10); therefore, we drop the 0 into the answer and bring the 1 to top of the next column. In the fifth column, the total is 11 (3 in base 10); therefore, we drop the 1 in the ones column (the second 1 in the binary number 11) and carry the 1 in the twos column (the first 1 in the binary number 11). Addition in **two's complement notation** is done in a similar manner, with one exception: Every number, even the answer, must be truncated to the same length.

Hexadecimal Number System

In digital devices, data can be stored efficiently as 1's and 0's because these correspond to "on" and "off" states. However, for larger numbers, very long binary numbers are required. This is where the hexadecimal number system comes in handy. If you think of each digit in a binary number as a bit, then you can see that the hexadecimal system allows for the representation of four bits in a single digit. The hexadecimal system uses a **radix** of 16. This tells us that each digit can be represented by up to 16 individual single characters. Since 0 through 9 gives us only ten characters, the hexadecimal system uses letters A through F to represent the decimal numbers 10 through 15. If you have ever run across a strange looking number in computer code or elsewhere, like 0F3A1C, chances are it is actually a hexadecimal number.

Octal Number System

As the prefix implies, the octal number system uses a radix of 8. The value of each position in an octal number is based on a power of 8. So, from right to left, the value of positions in an octal number would be ones, eights, sixty-fours, five hundred twelves, etc. Each digit can be represented by the numbers 0 through 7, signifying the number of times that a particular place value is included in the number. For example, the decimal number 24 would be represented in octal as 30, while the decimal number 65 would be represented as 101 in octal. The octal number system is not used as frequently as binary or hexadecimal, but it is used often enough that a basic familiarity with it is necessary.

Radix

The term "**radix**" is synonymous with the term "**base**" when referring to number systems. The radix is the number of digits available in any one position of the number. Let's look at an example using the most common number system, the decimal system, also referred to as the base-10 system. In this system, there are ten digits available at each position, 0–9. In the binary number system, or base 2, there are only two digits available at each position. Those two digits are 0 and 1. So in these two examples, the radices for these number systems would be 10 and 2, respectively. Theoretically, a number system could be created with any radix, although it may be difficult to identify single unique characters to use as digits as the radix gets larger.

Algorithm Analysis

Creating Overly Complex Algorithms

Overly **complex algorithms** can have many adverse effects.

- One of the most obvious is **slow performance**. If the execution of a task contains unnecessary steps and takes a longer path than necessary, then the application that uses this algorithm will take longer to execute actions than it should.
- Another adverse effect is the **excessive use of computer resources**, such as memory and processor capacity. Carrying out the extra and unnecessary steps uses more memory and CPU processing than is needed.

- Finally, overly complex algorithms can be **difficult to troubleshoot and debug**. The more steps a process contains, the more difficult it is to troubleshoot. An overly complex algorithm likely also contains unnecessary steps, so troubleshooting is not only difficult but ultimately unnecessary.

Polynomial Problems

A **polynomial problem** is any problem in $O(f(n))$ where $f(n)$ is a polynomial or is bounded by a polynomial. The expression **P** represents the entire population of polynomial problems, which include the problems of sorting lists and searching lists. If a problem falls within class P, it can be solved in polynomial time using a deterministic algorithm. This is an important distinction in computer science. Problems that do not fall within P often have excessive execution times for only moderately sized inputs; therefore, if a problem cannot be solved in polynomial time, it may not even have a practical solution. If a problem does not fall within P but is theoretically solvable regardless, it may still have such a large time complexity that it is practically unsolvable. These types of problems are described as **intractable**. Class P establishes a boundary between practical and intractable problems.

Exponential Problems

Exponential problems are any problems that are not bounded by a polynomial; therefore, they are not included in class P and tend to have very long execution times. Consider the polynomial expression $f(n)$ and the exponential expression 2^n. As n increases, the values of 2^n will become much larger than the values $f(n)$. Consequently, algorithms that have complexities $\Theta(f(n))$ are usually much more efficient than algorithms that have complexities $\Theta(2^n)$. This is because the latter is not bounded by any polynomial, and solving it becomes exponentially more time-consuming as n increases. Problems often become exponential due to the size of their output. However, problems can be exponential even if their output is merely a yes or no answer. One such example is truth statements regarding the addition of real numbers.

Computational Problems That Cannot Be Solved in a Timely Manner

One of the most famous problems that computers cannot solve in a reasonable amount of time is the **halting problem**. The halting problem consists of asking the question, "Will this program stop at some point (halt), or will it continue to run forever?" Determining if a simple problem will halt is simple, but when you introduce more complex programs the solution becomes much more complex and, for many, impossible. One technique is to run the program for a certain number of steps and see if it halts. This number of steps may take an hour, a day, or even a year. However, if it doesn't halt there is no way to determine with certainty if it will eventually halt or run forever.

When problems cannot be solved in a reasonable amount of time, they should be solved using the **heuristic approach**. A heuristic approach to problem solving often involves a shortcut that develops a solution that may not be perfect. When using a heuristic approach, it is usually more important to be fast than exact. An example of a heuristic approach in computer science is a search engine algorithm. The search engine values speed over absolute correctness, so even if it hasn't found the perfect match for the keywords that a person has entered, it returns what it has found in a reasonable time. In this case the person is more satisfied with a quick answer than the most complete or perfect one.

Traveling Salesman Problem

The traveling salesman problem is one of the most famous unsolved problems in computer science. In this problem, a **traveling salesman** must visit clients in several different cities while staying within his travel budget (i.e., not exceeding a certain mileage total). In solving this problem, we must systematically examine all possible paths through the cities, and find one that does not exceed the mileage total. This method poses difficulty because it is not bound by a polynomial. As a consequence, the solution cannot be found in polynomial time, and solving the problem using this method becomes impractical as the number of the cities increases. Therefore, in order to reach a viable solution, we need a more efficient solution, which can be found using a **nondeterministic algorithm** that takes the following steps:

- Find one path through the cities and calculate its total.
- If the total distance is below the total allowable mileage, declare success. If the distance is higher, declare nothing.

In the above algorithm, the computer must rely on its creative capacity when deciding on a path because it receives no instruction on how to do so. The traveling salesmen problem is one of many nondeterministic polynomial problems that have no deterministic solution. The solution can only run in polynomial time using nondeterministic algorithms.

Deterministic vs. Nondeterministic Algorithms

Nondeterministic algorithms require a device to exercise some type of creative ability. **Deterministic algorithms** have no such requirement. Consider, for instance, the following instructions:

Deterministic: Perform function A if X > Y, or function B if X<=Y.

Nondeterministic: Perform function A or function B.

There is no set course of action prior to executing the instructions, and the instructions take far different approaches. The first instruction provides a specific set of directions. The second instruction requires the device to exercise its own judgment. From a purely functional standpoint, a deterministic algorithm will always produce the same results if it receives the same input data. A nondeterministic algorithm, on the other hand, could very well produce different results even when receiving the same input data. From a purely technical standpoint, nondeterministic algorithms are not true algorithms.

Nondeterministic Polynomial Problems

A nondeterministic polynomial problem, also known as an **NP problem**, includes any problem that has a polynomial time solution when executed by a nondeterministic algorithm. Consider, for instance, the traveling salesman problem, which is an NP problem because it currently can be solved only by a nondeterministic algorithm. As the number of cities that the salesman must visit increases, the solution time required by even a nondeterministic algorithm increases at a relatively slow rate. Both the time necessary to choose a path through the cities and the time necessary to compute the distances of those paths are proportional to the total number of cities. Because the time necessary to compare those distances to the salesman's maximum allowable mileage total does not depend on the number of cities, the problem is bound by a polynomial. The drawback of the nondeterministic algorithm is its reliance on guessing. All problems in class P also fall under class NP.

NP-Complete Problems

NP-complete problems are a special class of problems within class NP. Their purpose is resolving the longstanding issue of whether or not all class NP problems are also class P problems. We already know that all class P problems fall under class NP, but we do not know if the inverse is true. However, if just one **NP-complete problem** could be solved in polynomial time using a deterministic algorithm, we can conclude that class NP is the same as class P because the same algorithm would be capable of solving all NP problems. The traveling salesman problem is an example of an NP-complete problem. If a deterministic solution were discovered for class NP, the consequences could be dire because many encryption systems rely on the current inefficiency of solving such problems. An efficient solution would compromise the integrity of these methods of encryption.

Deductive Reasoning vs. Inductive Reasoning

Deductive reasoning and inductive reasoning are both based on propositional logic; however, there is at least one key difference between the two. **Deductive reasoning** allows an inference to be drawn that can be accepted as total truth due to the truth of the propositions used to make the inference. For example, all dogs bark. Fido is a dog. Therefore, Fido barks. This is an example of deductive reasoning. If the first two statements are accepted as true, then the inference must also be true. **Inductive reasoning**, however, allows an inference to be reached based on observations of patterns. The inference is likely true but cannot be proven to be an absolute truth.

Measuring Algorithm Efficiency

There are several ways that the efficiency of an algorithm can be measured. Two of the most common measurements are the **time it takes the function to run** and the **amount of memory required**. These both are straightforward measurements that allow developers to better plan overall systems. Some applications have requirements that they must operate within certain time limitations. Being able to measure the efficiency of an algorithm by the amount of time it takes to run allows the developer to know early in the design of the program whether a particular algorithm can possibly be used. In some cases, certain algorithms are immediately eliminated because it would be impossible to fit them within the specifications of the design.

Calculating the Running Time of an Algorithm

When determining the running time of an algorithm, we must first count the number of basic operations the algorithm performs under a **worst-case input**. Examples of basic operations include assignments, variable comparisons, and arithmetic operations. Consider the following example:

```
// get is a function that returns a user-entered integer
repeat
    b ← get()
    a ← a * 2
until(b == 16 or a == 16)
```

The worst-case input for the above algorithm is x iterations, meaning four iterations. The worst-case input varies according to the type of algorithm, the basic operations it performs, and the input size:

- **Sorting algorithm**: Algorithm that performs the basic operation of comparison. The number of items to be sorted is x, the worst-case input. Put another way, if every item needs to be moved, then x items need to be moved—the worst case.
- **Multiplication algorithm**: Algorithm that performs the basic operation of single-digit arithmetic. The worst-case input, x, is the total number of digits in both variables being multiplied.
- **Graph-Searching Algorithm**: Algorithm that searches a graph. The worst-case input, x, is the number of graph edges or number of graph nodes.

Determining Which Algorithm Is More Efficient

Determining the better of two algorithms is quite subjective; there is no way to get an absolutely correct or objective answer. However, analysis and observation help to provide more information, in turn allowing developers to know which algorithm is a better fit for a specific use case. Certain implementations may require that speed be the deciding factor without regard for resource requirements. In other cases, memory may be a limiting factor, even if it means that the application is somewhat slower. In order to select the better algorithm, the developer should first know the constraints under which the system is operating. Is speed or memory usage more important? Once the details are known, the algorithms can be compared to determine which is the better fit in that specific case. It may even be possible to code each algorithm and run them at the same time in a head-to-head competition to see which performs better.

Importance of Algorithm Efficiency Analysis

Algorithm analysis is a very important piece of the software design process. Far too often, this piece of the process is overlooked. This can lead to slow performance and high resource usage. It is very important that a developer perform a thorough analysis of the algorithms being used to get an idea of the speed at which the application will run, as well as how much memory may be required for the application to function appropriately. This is generally not an issue for small programs that are developed for teaching purposes. However, in real-world development of very large applications, algorithm efficiency can make or break a project.

Creating Efficient Algorithms

It is not only important to create an accurate algorithm, but it is also important to create an efficient one. Inefficient algorithms needlessly use computing power and memory. They also use more time, causing the whole application to perform slower than it should. Efficient algorithms operate quickly, using minimal amounts of processing power and memory. An efficient algorithm is also much more likely to be reused in other applications. When one developer discovers an efficient way of performing some task, other developers are quick to reuse the process.

Inefficient Algorithms

Speed and efficiency are always becoming more and more important in today's world, to the extent that technology may be widely perceived as already quite fast and efficient. This could lead some to believe that inefficient algorithms are no longer in use. However, the reality is quite different. Inefficient algorithms still exist and are still in use in many cases today. The reasons for this vary. In some situations, an inefficient algorithm was used when an application was developed, and it would simply be too costly or time consuming to make a large update to change the algorithm. In other cases, a developer may not realize that a more efficient algorithm is available to perform a task. Finally, there are instances where an inefficient algorithm is the only way to accomplish a task. Consider a linear search algorithm. On average, it is one of the least efficient of all the search algorithms. However, depending on the data being searched, it may be the only algorithm available that can perform a reliable search.

Improving Inefficient Algorithms

Remember that an algorithm can give the correct result and still be inefficient. Consider creating an algorithm to get ready for work in the morning. Imagine if the algorithm were as follows: turn off the alarm clock, run around the bedroom ten times, eat breakfast, get in the car, drive around the block, brush your teeth, take a shower, get dressed, get undressed, get dressed, and leave for work. This might seem like a silly example, but it illustrates the point that the desired result is produced. If one follows this algorithm, they will be ready for work by the end of it. However, the algorithm is obviously very inefficient because it includes unnecessary steps that will cost a lot of time and effort. Running around the bedroom ten times, driving around the block, getting dressed an extra time, and getting undressed could all be eliminated in order to make this algorithm efficient. The result would be the same, but a lot of time and energy would be saved.

Types of Algorithm Analysis

Best-case scenario, average-case scenario, and worst-case scenario are the minimum, average, and maximum lengths of time, respectively, that an algorithm requires to perform a function. Consider, for instance, a situation where we need to sort a list with 10 entries using an insertion sort algorithm. The analysis for the insertion sort would go as follows:

- **Best-case scenario** is calculated using the formula $n - 1$ where n is the length of the list. This assumes that, each time the computer selects a new entry as the pivot entry, it is already in the correct place.
- **Worst-case scenario** is calculated using the formula $(\frac{1}{2})(n^2 - n)$. This assumes that the list is arranged in reverse order, and each pivot entry must be compared to all previous entries.
- **Average-case scenario** is calculated using the formula $(\frac{1}{4})(n^2 - n)$. This assumes that each pivot entry must be compared to half of the previous entries.

Time Complexity

The **time complexity** of a problem is determined by the time required to execute its solutions. We should note that in computer science, algorithms are used to formulate solutions to problems; therefore, when determining a problem's complexity, we examine the simplest possible algorithm that can be used to solve the problem.

From the machine's perspective, complexity is not a function of the number of instructions an algorithm must run. Rather, complexity is function of the number of times an algorithm must execute instructions. Consequently, an algorithm with 30 instructions, each of which is executed only once, is considered less complex than an algorithm with only one instruction that is executed 200 times. This is because the latter algorithm requires longer execution time. The time complexity of an algorithm is inversely proportion to its efficiency. Time complexity is expressed in big O notation.

Space Complexity

Space complexity measures the complexity of a problem according to its storage space requirements rather than its time requirements. The storage space requirement is simply the total amount of storage space necessary to solve the problem. Consider, for instance, that the problem of sorting a list with n entries has a time complexity of $O(n \log n)$. This identical problem has a maximum space complexity of $O(n + 1) = O(n)$; the computer must store the list itself (length n) and one additional entry for temporary storage. A problem's space complexity never grows faster than its time complexity; as the list grows, the time complexity increases more rapidly than the space complexity. If a program solves problems using information stored in a table, space complexity is a better measure than time complexity. However, if a program relies on data compression, time complexity is the better measure because the problem requires additional time to compress and decompress information.

Big O Notation

Big O notation is used to express our current understanding of a problem's time complexity, and is a variation on **big-theta notation**. This variation is due to the problem that we often have difficulty being certain that we have an accurate set of bounds for n. Consequently, we use **big O** (pronounced "big-oh") **notation**, which looks at the worst-case scenario given n inputs. One compares the graphs of competing algorithms $f(n)$ and $g(n)$ as n approaches infinity, and chooses the algorithm with better worst-case performance.

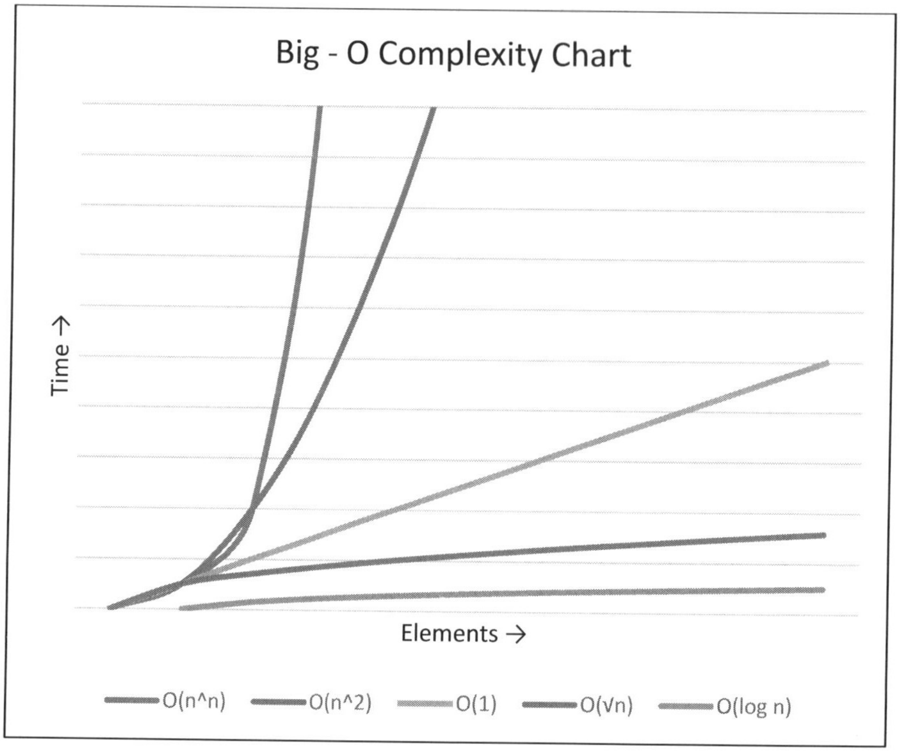

Parabolic and exponential formulae tend toward asymptotes parallel with the time axis, reflecting the likelihood of a rapid increase in time cost at some point as n increases. Logarithmic and square root formulae, however, tend towards an asymptote parallel with the dependent variable n, resulting in a decreasing growth of time cost as *n* goes to infinity. Therefore, in a worst-case scenario, time complexities in the format O(*log n*) are superior to those of O(n^2). Big O notation is inferior to big-theta notation; however, big-theta notation requires adequate bounds, which are often difficult to determine, so big O notation is popular as a fast litmus test.

Searching and Sorting Algorithms

A countless number of algorithms exist today to perform all kinds of functions. Some of the most common types of algorithms are **search algorithms** and **sort algorithms**. Searching and sorting of data are performed frequently for various reasons, so a wide assortment of algorithms have been developed to perform these functions. Searches look through a set of a data and find the item that matches the search key, or the item the program is looking for. Sort algorithms take a set of data and sort it into a defined order, such as numerically ascending, alphabetically descending, etc. Sort functions are very useful because many other functions require data to be sorted in a particular manner before they can work properly.

Common Search Algorithms

Two of the most popular search algorithms are the linear search and the binary search. A **linear search** is very straightforward. It simply takes a list of items, and it searches one by one through the list until it finds the item that matches the search key. As the number of records being searched increases, the time required to perform this type of search increases proportionately. The **binary search** is much more efficient. However, the data must be sorted before a binary search can be performed. A binary search effectively cuts the number of items to be searched in half at each step by determining whether the search key is larger or smaller than the item in the middle of the list. Some other search algorithms include exponential searches and hashing.

Other Available Search Algorithms

Although linear and binary searches are two of the most common search algorithms, there are many other search algorithms that are used in some cases. One of these is the **interpolation search**. An interpolation search is similar to a binary search in that the list being search must be sorted in advance. But an interpolation search has an extra requirement that the elements must be equally distributed. This allows the interpolation search algorithm to narrow down the list even further and reduce search time below that of the binary search. There are other more specialized or advances searches, such as the jump search, the exponential search, and the **Fibonacci search**. These are not used as commonly, but they may be beneficial in certain situations.

Time to Perform a Linear Search and Number of Elements in the List

The time required to perform a linear search is a direct function of the number of elements in the list. This is often represented as O(*n*), where *n* is the number of items in the list. This representation is an example of big O notation, and it means that, in a worst-case scenario, the search will require *n* iterations to complete. For a linear search, each item added to the list adds a potential iteration to the search, because linear searches go through lists one item at a time, comparing each item to the value being searched for (sometimes called the **key**). For small lists, this increase is negligible. If a list has five entries, the greatest possible number of comparisons will only be five. But imagine a list that contains exactly one million items. In this case, *n* would be 1,000,000. If the key is in the last spot in the list or not in the list at all, the search will have to make one million comparisons. This is very time consuming, especially relative to a binary search, which would immediately skip half of these. For this reason, linear searches are not often use in real-world applications.

Deciding on the Best Search Algorithm in a Given Situation

The efficiency of most common search algorithms is readily available. Remember that efficiency can be simply stated in big O notation. To decide on the best search algorithm for a situation, the developer must identify the input data and how it will be structured. This may limit the number of search algorithms available for use. After narrowing down the possible algorithms, the developer can then compare the efficiency of each one. Some quick calculations can be done based on the number of elements in the data and the efficiency expectations of each algorithm as described in big O notation. This will allow the developer to determine which algorithm is likely to perform the best given the nature of the data. These two steps will be an effective guide to the developer in choosing which algorithm to implement.

Sequential Search Algorithms

A **sequential search algorithm** is designed to scan a list of values and find a specific entry. It looks at values in order one at a time. The benefit is that the items do not need to be sorted; the search will check each value regardless. The downside is that, the longer a list is, the more inefficient the algorithm will be.

In pseudocode, a sequential search that finds one number in a list of numbers could be written as follows:

```
/* size( int[] ) returns the size of the array as an integer.
IsEmpty( int[] ) returns TRUE if the array has no values and FALSE
otherwise. */

int[] List ← {22, 6, 9, 17, 13, 10, 12, 40}
Search( List, 10 )
bool Exists ( List, TargetValue )
   if( IsEmpty( List ) )
      return false
   else
      for( int i ← 0; i < Size( List ); i ← i + 1)
         if( List[i] == TargetValue )
            return true
         end if
      end for
      return false
   end if
end search
```

This sequential search algorithm will search `List` for the value of `TargetValue`. If it finds a value in `List` that is equal to `TargetValue`, it will return `true`. On the other hand, if `List` is empty or if the algorithm does not find a value equal to `TargetValue`, it will return `false`.

Efficiency of Binary Searches vs. Linear Searches

In most cases, a binary search is far more efficient than a linear search. A linear search must step through each item in the list one by one in order to find the search key. When the key is located at the end of the list or is not in the list at all, a linear search must search through every single item in the list. A binary search cuts the list in half repeatedly, each time searching only the half that will contain the key, if it is there. Therefore, in the case above, where the key is at the end of the list or not on the list, a binary search saves time by not even needing to look in one half of the list. This remains true each time the list is halved. By eliminating half of the elements at each iteration, the binary search greatly reduces the time required to find the key.

Binary Search Algorithms

The binary search algorithm is **recursive**. To understand how binary searches work, consider the following list of numbers: 1, 3, 5, 7, 9, 11, 13, and 15. If we wanted to search for the value 11 in the list, we could use the following binary search algorithm:

```
/* IsEmpty( int[] ) returns TRUE if the array has no values and FALSE
otherwise.
IsOne( int[] ) returns TRUE if the array contains only one value and
FALSE otherwise.
FindMiddle( int[] ) returns the value at the middle index. If the
array has an even number of members, the function returns the value at
the second of the two middle indices.
```

```
FirstHalf( int[] ) returns the first half of the array as an array. If
the input array has an odd number of members, the middle index will be
included in the returned array.
SecondHalf( int[] ) returns the second half of the array as an array.
If the input array has an odd number of members, the middle index will
not be included in the returned array. */

int[] List ← {1, 3, 5, 7, 9, 11, 13, 15}
Exists( 11, List )
bool Exists ( TargetValue, List )
   int TestValue
   if( IsEmpty( List ) )
      return false
   else if( IsOne( List) )
      TestValue ← List[0]
      if( TestValue == TargetValue )
         return true
      else
         return false
   else
      TestValue ← FindMiddle( List )
      if( TestValue == TargetValue )
         return true
      else if( TestValue < TargetValue )
         return Exists( TargetValue, SecondHalf( List ) )
      else
         return Exists( TargetValue, FirstHalf( List ) )
      end if
   end if
end Exists
```

`TargetValue` is 11, and the program will begin searching the list at the middle value, 9, which becomes `TestValue`. (Note that there is no middle value in this particular list because the number of list items is even. To account for this common situation, the `FindMiddle` method should be written to select the first value in the second half.) Once the function arrives at the else if statement appropriate for 9 by finding that 9 is less than 11, it will call itself to now search the second half of the list (the half with values greater than 9). The second time the function runs (as a step in the first function), 13 will be `TestValue`. Since 11 is less than 13, the function will call itself yet again, this time using only 9 and 11 as the list. In performing this third running of the function, 11 will be the test value, and since it is also the target value, the if statement will finally be true, the program will finally identify `TargetValue`.

Situation to Perform a Linear Search Rather Than a Binary Search

As a general rule, a binary search is faster than a linear search. However, remember that the data must be sorted in order to perform a binary search. Various sorting algorithms exist that will sort a list of unordered data. Depending upon the data itself, some of these sorting algorithms can take a long time to execute. When working with unsorted data, a developer must closely examine the data and the algorithms being used to sort and search. There are some cases where the data is difficult to sort; in these situations, a binary search can take longer than a linear search.

Sorting List Items Before Performing Binary Searches

First, it is important to recall how a binary search is performed. Binary searches effectively eliminate half of the list at each iteration of the search, based on whether the item being searched for is more or less than the middle element in the list. It is imperative that the list is ordered when performing this type of search. If the list were out of order, then the correct element could be mistakenly eliminated from the search and never found. Consider the following example:

Find the element "4" in the following list:

1	5	3	7	6	4	2

The first iteration compares the middle element 7 with 4, the value being searched for. A binary search algorithm works by eliminating the first half of the list if the search value is greater than the midpoint value, and elimination the second half of the list if the search value is less than the midpoint value. In this situation, the algorithm would eliminate the second half of the list. It would then search only the first half of the list:

1	5	3	7

Notice that 4 is not contained in this new list even though it was in the original list. Thus it is critical for the elements to be in order when performing a binary search.

Common Sorting Algorithms

There are many algorithms used today to perform various tasks on data. The majority of these require data to be sorted beforehand. Because data is usually unordered when it is received, it must be sorted before work can begin. Fortunately, many sorting algorithms are available that can quickly and efficiently sort data. Some of the most popular sorting algorithms are the **merge sort**, the **insertion sort**, and the **bubble sort**. The merge sort tends to be one of the most efficient methods. It works by breaking the list into smaller and smaller lists, and then merging these lists back together in the desired order, resulting in a new, sorted list.

Selection Sort Algorithm

The **selection sort** is one of the simplest sort algorithms that is used in modern programming. The selection sort begins by searching through the entire list and finding either the smallest or largest item, depending on whether the sort is done in ascending or descending order. If the goal is to sort in ascending order, the selection sort algorithm finds the smallest item in the list and then creates a new, sorted list. Next, it removes the smallest item from the original list, the one being searched. This process is repeated until all elements have been sorted into the new list and the original list is empty. Selection sorts are not very efficient, particularly with larger lists.

Insertion Sort Algorithm

An **insertion sort algorithm** is an iterative structure capable of sorting a list. To understand how insertion sorts work, consider the following list of numbers: 9, 3, 5, 1, and 7. Using an insertion sort algorithm, a computer can sort this list from lowest to highest. An insertion sort will make use of a **pivot entry**, which is a temporary storage space that is separate from the list. As the program runs, it sets each list value as the pivot entry in order to create a blank entry (or hole) in the list. This hole allows the values within the list to be moved around. Consider the following pseudocode:

```
/* Size( int[] ) is a function that takes an array of integers and
returns the size of the array as an integer.
Swap( int, int ) is a function that takes two integer variables and
switches their values. */

int[] NumberList ← {9, 3, 5, 1, 7}

void Sort ( NumberList )
   int n ← Size( NumberList )
   for( int Pivot; Pivot < n; Pivot ← Pivot + 1)
      x ← Pivot
      while( x > 0 and NumberList[x] < NumberList[x - 1] )
```

```
            Swap( NumberList[x], NumberList[x - 1] )
            x ← x - 1
        end while
    end for
end Sort
```

The above algorithm is a loop within a loop. The "outer" loop (the for loop above) maintains the pivot entry's location in the list. The "inner" loop (the while loop above) moves each pivot entry's value into the correct location by swapping it with the previous value whenever the previous value is greater. Another way to look at this swapping is to see the algorithm as moving the hole earlier in the list until the appropriate place for the pivot entry's value is found. `Pivot` and `x` are variables denoting the original and final positions of the pivot entry in the list. This algorithm eventually sorts the list into ascending numeric order.

Merge Sort Algorithm

The **merge sort** is slightly more complicated or advanced than the selection sort and insertion sort. In a merge sort, the original list is first broken down into smaller and smaller list, until each resulting list is a single element. A list with only a single element is considered to be sorted. The actual sorting happens when these lists are all merged together again. This is done in such a way that the resulting list is sorted in the desired order. A merge sort typically operates more efficiently than the basic selection sort or insertion sort. One drawback to the merge sort is the amount of memory required during execution. Since the merge sort creates so many new lists—one for each element of the original list—it can require significant amount of memory, particularly when dealing with large lists. When considering the efficiency of a merge sort for a particular application, the merge sort's time efficiency must be balanced with its space inefficiency.

Quicksort Algorithm

A **quicksort algorithm** is one of the most efficient sorting algorithms in use today. Its actual implementation is somewhat complicated. Note that a quicksort is utilized on an array and not a list. While the difference is subtle, it is worth noting. The algorithm works by selecting **pivot elements** within the array and then reordering based on comparisons of other elements with the pivot element. The quicksort can operate significantly faster than other common sorting algorithms.

Using Sorting Algorithms in Conjunction with Search Algorithms

A sorting algorithm is rarely used in isolation. Most of the time, a sorting algorithm is used to sort data because another function requires the data to be sorted before the function can operate correctly. This is generally the case with search algorithms. While there are search algorithms that can search unsorted data, they tend to be inefficient. On the other hand, efficient search algorithms typically need the data to be sorted. This is when a sort algorithm would be used in conjunction with search algorithm. First the sort algorithm efficiently sorts the data, and then the search algorithm can efficiently find an element within the sorted data. This way, two efficient algorithms are used rather than one inefficient algorithm.

Recursive Algorithms and Randomization

Recursion

In computer science, **recursion** is the use of a function that calls itself. Such a technique is useful when a large problem can be solved by finding solutions to many small versions of itself. For example, in order to solve a maze, one can simply find the first intersection and explore each corridor that branches off from it. If another intersection is encountered in one of the corridors, one can explore each corridor of this intersection. This simple process of exploring each corridor at each intersection can be repeated until the exit is found.

The universality of recursion makes it an integral part of computer science. The majority of high-level programming languages support recursive procedures. In these languages, functions can call themselves; it will not, in itself, cause an error in compiling or running. While imperative languages may also use while loops and for loops to perform repeated actions, recursion may be more efficient in certain applications. Functional programming languages perform recursion by calling code repetitively. According to **computability theory**, a recursive-only language is mathematically identical to imperative language. In other words, it can solve similar types of problems as imperative languages, despite not having any looping structures. Recursion is effective because it uses a finite set of operations to describe a potentially infinite set of calculations.

RECURSIVE ALGORITHMS

An algorithm is classified as recursive when it contains a function that calls itself. This can obviously get complicated very quickly. One way to visualize this is by imagining yourself looking into a mirror when there is a mirror behind you. You can see your appearance reflected again and again; each reflection of your appearance is like a step deeper into a recursive algorithm. In practice, a recursive function calls itself, creating a nested function. This function will start another function. The series of nested functions will continue until the newest function reaches the **base case**; this will be the deepest level of the recursion. When this function finds that it is at the base case, instead of calling itself yet again, it will return a value. Then the function in the layer above it will receive this returned value and return a value. Then the layer above this layer receives the value and returns a value. This series of returns continues back up the chain of recursions to the original function.

INFINITE LOOPS

A recursive algorithm does not generally create an **infinite loop** because sooner or later a base case will be reached. The base case is reached when the function returns a value rather than calling itself again. Once a base case is reached, the deepest function is completed, its **parent function** is in turn completed, that function's parent function is completed, and so on back up to the original function. In some cases, a recursive algorithm can create an infinite loop, if there is no base case, or if recursion is being used to find multiple base cases but there are actually infinite base cases. Various measures can be taken to prevent situations like these or at least ensure that the recursion stops at a given point.

RECURSIVE ALGORITHM EXAMPLE

One of the classic examples of a recursive algorithm is the use of exponents. Raising a number to a power is a problem that can be solved using a recursive algorithm. Imagine a function called `power` that takes a number *x* and raises it to the *y* power. A sample call of that function may look something like this: `power( 3, 3 )`. The details of the function itself may look something like this:

```
int power ( x, y )
   if( y == 0 )
      return 1
   else
      return x * power( x, y - 1 )
   end if
end power
```

Notice that for any value of y other than 0, the function calls itself. Let's now step through each call of `power (3, 3)`:

```
power( 3, 3 )           // original call
   power( 3, 2 )        // 1st recursion
      power( 3, 1 )     // 2nd recursion
         power( 3, 0 )  // 3rd recursion
         return 1
      return 3        //  3 = 3 * 1 = 3 * power( 3, 0 )
   return 9           //  9 = 3 * 3 = 3 * power( 3, 1 )
return 27               // 27 = 3 * 9 = 3 * power( 3, 2 )
```

Identifying the Equivalent Iterative Algorithm Example

Identify the equivalent iterative algorithm for the following recursive algorithm:

```
int add(int x)
    if( x == 0 )
        return 0
    else if( x > 0 )
        x ← x + add( x - 1 )
        return x
    end if
end add
```

This recursive method will repeatedly sum all the numbers up to and including the parameter that is passed to it. For example, if the call statement is `add( 3 )`, we will get 3 + 2 + 1 + 0 = 6. In order to create this using an iterative algorithm, we could use a for loop. Keeping the input variable name as `x`, the following could be used:

```
int add( int x )
    int ans ← 0
    for( int i ← 0; i ≤ x; i ← i + 1 )
        ans ← ans + i;
    end for
    return ans
end add
```

This for loop continuously adds the current value of `i` to the accumulator, which is named `ans`. The last iteration occurs when `i` is equal to `x`, as in the next iteration `i` will no longer be less than or equal to `x`. This algorithm is equivalent to the recursive method.

Recursive Structures

A **recursive structure** is a programming algorithm that repeats a set of instructions until a certain task has been completed. Unlike iterative structures (i.e., loops), recursive structures repeat the instructions as subtasks of themselves, interrupting their execution to begin a new subtask. In this way, all parent tasks are left unfinished until the whole task has been completed. For example, consider a person conducting research on house construction. As he reads one article, he notices that it makes a distinction between homes with concrete foundations and homes with pier and beam foundation. Because he doesn't understand the difference, he reads a new article on foundations. Only after reading this article does he return to the original article. But in both cases, he is reading an article. This is similar to a recursive process in computing. One instruction sets off a subsequent, identical instruction, and the first one cannot be finished until the subsequent one is finished. Binary search algorithms are often recursive.

Control of Recursive Processes

Recursive processes use the following means of control, just as loops do:

- **Initialize**: set an initial value that will be passed to each recursion
- **Modify**: alter the value that is being passed
- **Test**: check if the termination condition has been met

Common examples of recursive procedures include computing a factorial, computing the Fibonacci sequence, finding the greatest common divisor, and binary searching of sorted data. The factorial of a positive integer, for example, can be computed with recursion as follows:

```
int factorial ( n )
    if( n == 1 )
        return 1
```

```
    else
        return ( n * factorial ( n - 1 ) )
end factorial
```

Note that the program will execute the method inside of itself repeatedly until `n` has a value of 1. Then each method will return its value to the one that was called before it, up the chain of execution until the final number is returned to where the `factorial` method was initially called.

Calling a Recursive Method in a Base Case

Calling a recursive method in a base case is never acceptable. The base case is the necessary step that is used to stop the recursion and return execution to the calling function. You can liken the base case in recursion to the stopping condition of a loop. Once it is true, the loop ends, and **control flow** moves to the statement after the loop. If the loop is not properly written to stop at the end condition, iteration will continue infinitely. Similarly, for recursion, if in the base case we continue to call the recursive function, there will be no way to end the execution of the recursion, and we will then have infinite recursion. There must be a clear separation of the recursive section of the method and the base case. This is often done by using separate decision statements.

Parts of a Recursive Algorithm

A recursive algorithm has two main parts: the **general case** (or the **recursive case**) and the **base case**.

The base case is the case that stops the recursion and returns execution to the calling method. If the base case is never reached, the method will be called forever, causing infinite recursion. Eventually the compiler may detect this and stop, or the program will run until all available memory is used up and the compiler will crash.

The recursive case must contain a recursive call to the function it is a part of. This recursive call must alter the input to the function so that it gets closer to the base case. For example, if the base case occurs when x is 0, the recursive part of the method should make sure that eventually the value 0 is passed into the method as the x variable. For example, each time the recursive part of the method runs, we might pass $x - 1$ to recursive function. This would result in x having a value of 2 in the initial function, a value of 1 in the first recursion, and then finally a 0—the base case—in the second and final recursion.

Stack Overflow

Remember that a recursive algorithm continues to call itself until it reaches a base case. The base case is when the function returns a value rather than calling yet another function. Each time a function is called, the function call is stored in temporary memory in a structure known as the call stack. In recursion, this temporary storage serves an important purpose, as the return of each function can be stored separately to provide accurate returns all the way back up to the original function call. If it takes too long to reach the base case, a **stack overflow** will occur, and the program will crash. Only so much temporary memory is allocated to the program, so the call stack does not have infinite space. If there are too many intermediate function calls and return values that need to be stored, then the stack will run out of space. When any additional items need to be stored but the stack is already full, a stack overflow occurs. Either the algorithm will need to be revised before being run again, or more memory will need to be allocated to the program.

Random vs. Pseudorandom Numbers

The definition of **random** is "made, done, or chosen through chance." There is no way to predict a random event. The physical tossing of a coin or rolling of dice is said to be random because the outcome cannot be predicted. If you wanted to choose a random number from 1 to 9, we could write these numbers on pieces of paper, place them in a container, and pick one out. However, if we wanted a computer to create a random number, we would be facing an impossible task because computers are deterministic systems—meaning they cannot generate an output that isn't determined in part by some type of input. Computers can therefore only create **pseudorandom numbers**. These numbers are created through a deterministic process; however, the input is usually something that is very hard to predict, like the current time in milliseconds of according to the

CPU clock. If a person could know what number this was at the millisecond that a pseudorandom number was generated by a computer, and they also knew the algorithm for generating a pseudorandom number using the time in milliseconds as a **seed**, they could accurately predict the number. However, since the generation happens very quickly, uses a seed that changes every millisecond, and likely uses a complicated calculation in conjunction with this seed, it is virtually impossible for people to predict the number. The number is therefore acknowledged as being almost as "random" as a genuinely random number.

Digitalization, Data Encryption and Decryption, and Computational Tools

Digital Systems vs. Analog Systems

The distinct difference between **digital** and **analog systems**. Digital systems use numbers to represent all information. They developed this way because electrical signals can be used to encode information by switching the signal on and off. As long as we have these two values, "on" and "off," we can represent any data with them. Analog systems, however, do not use clearly defined data values. There is no universal "on" state or "off" state that every analog system can have; rather they have a nearly infinite number of states. One everyday example is a radio tuner. Most radios today have digital tuners that specify exact numbers for frequency and amplitude. However, analog radio tuners have an electrical component that changes the frequency and amplitude on a sliding scale. With a standard analog radio tuner, there is normally no way to ensure that the tuner is set to an exact frequency or amplitude—we just turn the knob and use our hearing to find the clearest signal.

Converting Analog Data to Digital Data in Musical Recordings

Digital music files are created with the use of an analog-to-digital converter, which translates sound waves into binary code. In other words, a converter translates analog data into digital data. When the music file is played on a computer, the digital data is converted back into analog waves. An electronic converter records tiny samples of the music and then arranges them in order, so close together that the human ear cannot hear the gaps. In fact, a compact disc contains approximately 44,100 audio samples per second. A similar process is used in the conversion of photography and moving images from analog to digital and back.

Digital Representation of Words and Letters

On a computer, all information is represented digitally as ones and zeros. This includes all of the information used in arithmetic operations, as well as letters, symbols, and numerals. These latter three types of information are known collectively as character data. Though appearing complicated to the human eye, binary code is the easiest way for a computer to store and communicate data. Computers use several different styles of code for character data, including ASCII, which represents each character as a seven-bit sequence, extended ASCII (or EASCII) styles, which represent every character as an eight-bit sequence, EBCDIC (Extended Binary-Coded Decimal Interchange), used formerly by IBM mainframes, and Unicode styles, the most common of which, UTF-16, represents every character as a sixteen-bit sequence.

Storing Sound and Images in Bits

In order to be stored, images and sounds have to be digitized. Images are subdivided into pixels, each of which is assigned a binary number depending on its color. Sounds, on the other hand, are broken down into wave components. Samples taken from various points along the wave are converted into digital values. In order to represent a specific sound in sufficient detail, a computer must digitize thousands of wave samples every second.

Record of Deleted Items on a Digital Device

There are many businesses today whose main service is recovering data from digital devices. In many cases, a person believes they have deleted data from a device. That may be true, but a simple deletion does not actually erase the data from the device in most cases. When someone deletes a piece of data from a digital device, that location of that data in the device's memory is marked by the operating system as available for use. So the data that was stored there does not actually get erased. It still exists in the same spot, but the spot itself is marked as empty. Using specialized tools, a computer technician is still able to access that memory location and recover the data.

Binary Encoding Schemes EBCDIC, ASCII, and Unicode

The abbreviation "EBCDIC" stands for "Extended Binary Coded Decimal Interchange Code." EBCDIC is a binary encoding standard developed by IBM in the 1960s for use on mainframes. In this standard, every character is represented as a sequence of eight bits (i.e., one byte). "ASCII" is short for "American Standard Code for Information Interchange." It is a binary encoding standard for microprocessors that represents characters with seven bits. At one time, ASCII was the most widely used encoding standard in computers, and many modern coding schemes have been derived from or influenced by it. There are several coding schemes classified as "extended ASCII," and these use eight bits rather than seven to represent characters. Eight bits allows for 256 characters, which is not enough for some languages. Unicode, or the Unicode Standard, is broad standard that includes several coding schemes. It was published in the early 1990s as the product of an attempt to create a character set that included every existing written character. The eight-bit form of Unicode, UTF-8, replaced ASCII as the most widely used encoding standard in computers, and the sixteen-bit form, UTF-16, allows for 2^{16} (or 65,536) character codes.

Code Examples

Example 1

In ASCII (American Standard Code for Information Interchange), the decimal number that represents A is 65. Knowing this, what ASCII character is represented by the byte 01001101 in binary?

In order to calculate this, we first need to convert 01001101 to decimal. We can do this by labeling the place value of each digit, as below:

Decimal	128	64	32	16	8	4	2	1
Binary	0	1	0	0	1	1	0	1

Every place value that has a 1 in it is considered "on," and we can add the place values that are "on" to find the equivalent decimal number. Therefore, we have 64 + 8 + 4 + 1 = 77. We then take note that 65 represents the character *A*. We only need to know that, in ASCII, the capital letters of the Roman alphabet are in alphabetical order and count upward from the value for *A*. In other words, if 65 is *A*, then 66 must be *B*, 67 *C*, and so on. Counting like this to the number 77, which we converted to decimal from the binary number in the byte we were given, we find that we have the ASCII encoding for the uppercase letter *M*.

Example 2

If a character can be represented by eight bits, how many kilobytes would it take to hold 108,000 characters?

Because there are 8 bits in 1 byte, and 1024 bytes in 1 kilobyte, we can divide 108,000 characters by 1024 bytes. This gives us 105.46875 KB. Characters are often stored using 8 bits because of the ASCII table. This is a table that maps a set of characters to numbers. Some of these characters are visible, such as letters, numbers, and symbols. Other characters are nonprintable characters, such as the carriage return.

Data

In computing, **data** can be described as a stream of symbols. These symbols are a code that can be interpeted to form information. The format in which data is stored is known as data representation. On modern computers, data can be used to represent numbers, text, images, music, and more. Data is either analog or digital. **Analog data** is usually in the form of a wave, such as a sound wave or light wave. Such data can, in the case of sound, be interpreted into speech, music, and so on, by humans. Likewise data in the form of light waves can be interpreted into colors, brightness values, shapes, etc. **Digital data**, on the other hand, consists entirely of ones and zeros, a system known as binary code. Data in this form can be interpreted by a computer. All the information on a computer, including text, images, and sound, is stored on the hard drive as a series of ones and zeros.

Computer Operation Using Binary Code

The reason that computers operate using binary code is because computers use electrical signals to encode data. Since the two basic states of an electrical circuit are "on" or "off," streams of "on" and "off" signals can be used as code, which allows information to be sent or stored using the signals. Binary code is perfect for this use, because it uses only ones and zeros. Each one or zero, referred to as a "bit," signifies either "on" or "off." The bits are sent and stored in various ways in different parts of a computer and in different types of storage. They may be represented by the presence or lack of electrical current in a microprocessor, or they may be represented by positive or negative polarity, as they are on a hard disk. Other number systems, such as octal or hexadecimal, allow for multiple bits to be represented in a single digit; however, at the microprocessor level, the code is still in binary.

Lossy and Lossless Compression

Lossy compression is a type of compression that is achieved by removing information that is not necessary for the overall quality of the information to be maintained. One example of this is image compression. In order to compress images, redundant information or small details that are difficult to see can be removed. This results in less information being stored, and the size of the file containing the data is therefore smaller. If the comprehension algorithm is effective, the image will still be able to serve its intended purpose but will take up less memory space. Another example of lossy compression being used is the storage of a music. Recorded sound can be compressed into an MP3 file, a sound file that uses lossy compression to save space without compromising too much sound quality. One part of such lossy compression might be to remove sounds that are at frequencies high or low enough to be outside the range of human hearing. This reduces the file size without much discernible difference.

Lossless compression is a type of compression that can be reversed to recreate the original data exactly. No data is lost when using this type of compression. This is best for data such as text, where leaving out information would not work. One technique that may be used in lossless compression of text is to use a dictionary that counts commonly used words or phrases. The most common words and phrases can then be identified and replaced with a shorter unique form. For example, if the word "the" is used many times in a text file, it could be replaced with a single character when it is compressed.

Compression and the Relationship of Speed and Space

Information is generally compressed for two reasons.

- The first is to save space. When a file is compressed, it takes up less space on storage media, such as a hard drive. This allows the user to store more information on those devices than they could have with the original file. For example, if a file is compressed to 10 percent of its size, you could hold 10 of those files in the space that would have comprised a single version of the original.
- The second reason files are compressed is so that information can be transferred at greater speed over a network. Files that are smaller contain less data; less data takes less time to pass through a network cable. In the previous example, where a file was compressed to 10 percent of its size, if that file were to be transferred instead of stored, it would transfer 10 times faster than the original file.

Encoding vs. Encryption

Encoding is the process of changing data from one format to another. An example of encoding is the ASCII table of characters. This table provides a set standard by which each textual character has its own number value. Computers need to work with all information in the form of numbers, and this table allows the computer to work with characters as numbers. Encoding is not used to hide information, but instead to provide a standard by which information can be converted into one format and reverted into its original format as necessary.

Encryption is a way of changing data so that it is no longer readable to anyone who does not have the encryption key. It is used for security purposes, to ensure that data will only be used or read by the entities for which it is intended. One method of encryption is public-key encryption, which is used to transfer information securely over the Internet.

Simulation and Modeling

Benefits of Performing Simulations to Solve Problems

Simulations can be very useful for solving problems and thoroughly testing solutions. A simulation is a way of recreating a real event in order to observe probable outcomes. For example, when designing a bridge, an engineer can hardly hope to build a few experimental bridges first in order to test different materials or structures. This is a case where a simulation would be very helpful. A simulation would allow the engineer to build any number of virtual bridges in an application. It would be relatively easy to change materials, dimensions, loads, the environment, and any other factors the engineer would like to experiment with. An engineer would be able to find the most viable designs for the project with minimal effort and expense. Simulations are also useful in many other fields, including meteorology, astronomy, medicine, aviation, and many more. With current advances in computing technology, simulations continue to evolve into more advanced and accurate depictions of real scenarios.

Examples

Example 1

Summarize how you might simulate a person shooting a basketball towards a hoop using computer code.

To start building a simulation, we should consider what the required input and output values are. In the case of someone shooting a basketball, the height of the person, the force they put on the ball, the ball's angle of departure, and the spin would all be useful inputs for this simulation. Each of these would change based on the person who is shooting and the particular shot they take. The algorithm would take all this information and calculate a vector (i.e., a direction in three-dimensional space and an initial velocity). Based on the relative position of the hoop, the algorithm can determine whether the ball would land in the hoop or somewhere else. In cases where the ball lands in the hoop, the output should show that the shooter scored. For cases where the ball doesn't land in the hoop, it would be good to have an algorithm that can calculate where the ball lands, taking into account bounces off the rim and backboard. This way, the output could offer some detail about the outcome of the shot or how close the shot was.

Example 2

Given the following code, explain what is being simulated.

```
//generateRandom(int x) generates a random number between 0 and x

int randomNumber
int horse1 ← 0
int horse2 ← 0
int horse3 ← 0
while( horse1 < 10 && horse2 < 10 && horse3 < 10 )
   randomNumber ← generateRandom(9)
   if( randomNumber < 3 )
```

```
      horse1 ← horse1 + 1
   else if( randomNumber < 6 )
      horse2 ← horse2 + 1
   else
      horse3 ← horse3 + 1
   end if
end while
```

This code simulates a horse race where the horses, horse1, horse2, and horse3 (represented by integer variables of the same names), have different odds of reaching 10 first. Each time the while loop executes, a random number from 0 to 9 is generated. If the number is 0, 1, or 2, horse1 "moves ahead" (i.e., its value increase by 1). If the number is 3, 4, or 5, horse2 moves ahead, and if the number is 6, 7, 8, or 9, horse3 moves ahead. Therefore, the odds of horse1 winning are 3 out of 10, the odds of horse2 winning are also 3 out of 10, and the odds of horse3 winning are 4 out of 10 (or 2 out of 5).

EXAMPLE 3

Identify the missing code in the coin-flip simulation below.

```
//generateRandom(int x) generates a random number between 0 and x

int total ← 0
int randomNumber
while( total < 50 )
   randomNumber ← generateRandom(1)
   if( randomNumber == 0 )
      heads ← heads + 1
   else
      tails ← tails + 1
   end if
end while
```

This code is meant to simulate 50 flips of a coin, as we can see from the fact that the while loop condition is `total < 50`. With each iteration, a 0 or 1 will be generated randomly. If a 0 is generated, the if statement takes effect, and `heads` increases by 1. If a 1 is generated, the else statement takes effect, and `tails` increases by one. This simulation could be experimented with and used for fun, or it could also be useful for testing the randomness of a random number generator. However, a critical mistake has been made in the writing this code. The while loop condition is `total < 50`, as we have mentioned, and `total` has been initialized to 0. The glaring problem is that there is no statement in the loop to increment `total`, so the loop will run infinitely. This can be fixed by adding the code `total ← total + 1` or simply `total++` between `end if` and `end while`.

EXAMPLE 4

Explain how too little data in a dice rolling game can show that the odds are greater for a certain number.

Having too little data about a particular situation can lead to incorrect conclusions. For example, if I were to take a survey of all the people in New York asking them what their favorite baseball team was, I could not then use that to determine the favorite baseball team of the entire USA. The sample was heavily biased due to geography. This holds true for rolling dice. Because a die has six sides, each with a different number from 1 to 6, the chances of rolling any one number should be 1 in 6, or approximately 16.67 percent. If we rolled a die 10 times, and the die showed the number 2 on 5 of those throws, we might be tempted to see this as evidence that for that die, there was 50 percent chance of rolling a 2 every time. The data does not actually support this, however. Because we rolled the die only 10 times, our sample size is too small. The more times we roll, the larger our sample will be, and the stronger our data would get for supporting any conclusions. If we rolled 100 more times, we might see the frequency of 2s move back toward a number we expected. Therefore, using the appropriate amount of data for the given situation is just as important as the data values themselves.

Data Storage and Management

File Types

The term "**file type**" refers to the format a file is saved in. On the programming level, the format of the file is important, because applications are designed to write and read files only in a specific format or set of formats. It is the file format that determines how the actual binary data is organized and how a piece of software will interpret the data. One can normally identify the format of a file by looking at the **file extension**, or the letters that appear after the dot in the filename. Some common file types are executables (.exe), JPEG images (.jpg or .jpeg), and MP4 media files (.mp4). A file type may be **proprietary**, meaning it was made by a certain company for use with that company's software. Proprietary file formats may sometimes be opened for royalty-free use. Some well-known examples of proprietary file formats are Microsoft Word documents (.doc and .docx), Microsoft Excel workbooks (.xls and .xlsx), and Adobe's Portable Document Format (.pdf).

Common Graphics File Formats

- **Bitmaps** (.bmp) were developed by Microsoft for users to create and store images on personal computers using basic applications like Microsoft Paint. Bitmaps tend to take up a lot of storage space.
- The **Graphics Interchange Format** (.gif) uses compression to store images efficiently for sharing over a network. Widely known as "GIFs" or "gifs," files of this type are common across the internet, in part because they can store animations as well as still images.
- The **JPEG** file (.jpg or .jpeg) format takes its name from the group that first developed it, the Joint Photographic Experts Group. This format is very common because it can store images in a very small file, thanks to its lossy compression.
- **Tag Image File Format** (.tif or .tiff) was developed with graphic design and desktop publishing in mind. It is widely used for printing and scanning, and it uses lossless compression to maintain image quality.
- The **Portable Network Graphics** (.png) format, like the GIF, is intended to allow users to store images and share them over a network—most commonly the internet. One distinctive feature of this format is the inclusion of an alpha channel, which allows parts of the image to be transparent.

Sound Files

A **.wav file** is a sound file that is used by sampling aptitudes and frequencies of audio over a set of time. The more samples that happen, better the quality of the audio, but also the larger the file. All .wav files include every part of the sound, even parts that are inaudible to human hearing. With **.mp3 files**, the original .wav files are compressed. This is done by removing tones that humans cannot hear as well as using inexact approximations of data so that it is "good enough" for a human to not recognize any difference from the original file.

Executable Files

An **executable file** is a file that runs a script or program on your computer. This type of file can be easily identified by its file extension, .exe. Whereas general data files are normally opened or read, executable files are run. Executable files are powerful and pose a security risk because they can make changes to the computers they run on. When a person installs a program on their computer, the installer is an executable file. Furthermore, any executable file that is run could potentially make changes to the computer. Operating systems may warn the user if a program is trying to execute an administrator-level task, but it is nevertheless prudent to avoid opening executable files unless they are from trusted sources. The task that it executes could be malicious, and it could do harm to the computer.

Converting Text to Graphics vs. Converting Graphics to Text

Text is created through font sets. Font sets have specific representations for each character in a list of all possible characters. For example, the letter 'A' is just a set of pixels that is oriented in a particular way to show the symbol representing that letter. In order to convert this to graphics, the computer just needs to process where the pixels are located and combine them into a graphical format. To convert graphics back to text is much more difficult because there is no set way that the graphics are laid out. The graphical image may be from a picture that was taken that happened to have a sign with text on it. In order to parse that sign, patterns must be extracted from the graphical information to attempt to match it to a particular font set. Once that match is made, particular letters and symbols must be determined, and there is large room for error because the image may contain elements that prevent the correct detection of the font set, including images being too bright or dark, color variations in the text, and obscured parts of the image.

Sampling in Digital Graphics

Sampling in digital graphics refers to the process of taking an analog image and mapping it to a set of discrete values. This process is known as digitization. Because an analog image from the real world has no specific perceivable number of colors or areas that represent it, it can be difficult to represent this in a computer that has finite, or digital, data. When an image is sampled, it is broken down into many small areas called pixels. Each pixel contains a mix of color values from red, green, and blue that with enough bits can accurately represent almost any color. The number of pixels in a picture defines its resolution, often written as the number of pixels wide by the number of pixels tall that a picture is. For example, a picture that is 1024 x 768 contains 786,432 pixels. The more pixels a picture has, the higher the sampling rate and the better the quality of the image.

Sampling in Digital Audio

Audio sampling is the process of taking measurements of the amplitudes of a sound wave over time. The more samples that are taken, the better the representation of the sound. For example, if we took a sound clip that was one second long and sampled it 100 times during its duration, and then took the same clip and sampled it 1000 times during that same duration, the sound file with 1000 samples will sound much clearer. This is because during that time more accurate information was kept about the sound, so the computer will be able to represent the playback of the sound more closely to the original analog sound.

Types of Files Processed by Procedural Languages

There are two types of files that procedural programming languages can process. Both are featured prominently in mainframes that perform batch processing. These two types of files are:

- **Sequential files**: These are best suited for storing information that is processed routinely. The computer must access the entire file before it can process any of the records contained therein.
- **Random files** (also known as direct access files): These allow the computer to process any individual record without accessing the entire file. In order to access the record, the user must have a record key, which is normally a unique number or designation. An example is an invoice number or a shipping number.

Directory Structure

Files are stored on a computer in what is called a **directory structure**. A directory structure is a hierarchy of folders that contain all the files on the computer, including programs themselves. This structure helps the user keep track of files. Think of the directory structure as a digital file cabinet. The cabinet itself could be the hard drive, the drawers in the cabinet could be folders, and the folders inside the drawers could be subfolders. The documents that are stored in the cabinet would be the individual files in the directory structure. Modern directory structures are easily maintained and intuitive; files and folders can named almost anything the user specifies, and there is effectively no limit on the number of folders the user can create.

Importance of File Naming Conventions

File naming conventions are important because they help users find and retrieve information quickly and easily. Using a standard organization method helps companies stay organized and limits time spent searching for information. One simple method for file organization is to give files the following attributes:

- Unique names that are succinct and meaningful.
- Include what the file contains as part of the name.
- Include the date and place it was created.
- Have consistency among those who are going to use and create files.

If this simple convention is followed, files will be easy to find and utilize, and valuable time will not be used searching for or recreating files that are lost.

Managing Files

There are two basic kinds of files: data files and program files. Data files include spreadsheets, text documents, music files, and images. Program files include word processing programs, spreadsheet programs, games, and media players. An operating system allows users to organize files into hierarchies of folders. Every file has a name so that it can be easily found and identified.

Spreadsheets vs. Databases

While **spreadsheets** and **databases** are similar in many ways, there have some major differences as well.

- The basic structure of the two is very similar. They are both laid out in a row and column format. Typically, column headers are used in both to categorize data, while rows are used in both to represent individual records that have data in each of the columns. Both can contain multiple tables, but a spreadsheet generally has sheets that can be freely formatted, and ranges of data can be designated as discrete tables. A database, on the other hand, is a collection of tables that have well-defined relationships with each other.
- Furthermore, both spreadsheets and databases are used for storing, manipulating, querying, and presenting data, but they do so differently. Spreadsheets usually have simple interfaces with powerful tools that give the user a lot of freedom. Databases are more rigid to work with. The user must generally know how to create forms for entering data and reports for showing data.
- Finally, both spreadsheets and databases can import and export data, but it is difficult to do this seamlessly on a large scale with spreadsheets. In contrast, databases are widely used in data connections. Most websites that store dynamic data utilize a database in some form. The website code can perform searches in the database and display the information that is returned as part of the page.

Spreadsheets

A **spreadsheet** is organized into rows and columns, and each data point is referenced by its column and row index. Typically, columns use letter indices and rows use numerical indices. For example, the uppermost and leftmost point may be referred to as A1, with A being the column and 1 being the row. The data points in a spreadsheet are normally called "cells." Accordingly, the same data point mentioned above could be referred to as the value in cell A1. Cells in a spreadsheet can contain many different types of data, such as text, numbers, dates, times, and currency. One of the most common spreadsheet applications used today is Microsoft Excel. An example of how a spreadsheet could be used is for keeping track of the grades of each student in a class. Each class member's name could be listed in column A, the scores from tests 1 through 3 could be shown in columns B, C, and D, and the student's grade average could be calculated in column E. Spreadsheet software can generally perform calculations using data in the spreadsheet and fill other cells with the resulting values.

USEFUL SITUATIONS

Spreadsheets have innumerable uses, and they vary greatly in complexity. A basic example of a situation for which a spreadsheet would be well-suited is keeping track of the grades of students in a class. Students' names could be listed down the page in column A, with the header for column A reading "Student." The other column headers could then be the names of the tests and assignments that the class had. For example, column B could be Exam 1, column C Exam 2, column D Quiz 1, and so on. With such a spreadsheet, the grade for each student on each item could be entered manually. A column named "Average" could be added. In this column, a function could be written in the first cell—corresponding to the first student on the list—that calculates the average of all the scores for that student. This function could then be filled down to the bottom of the column, with each instance of the function referencing only the grades in its row. Much more could be done with the grade data. For example, class average for each test could be calculated, which might be useful for determining whether the class as a whole struggled more with a particular topic. A student's average could be tracked over time. With more data on the individual students, average grades not just of the students or the whole class but of specific groups (e.g., freshmen) could be found. Any of the data in the spreadsheet could also be plotted in a graph to visualize the data and make analysis or presentation of the data much easier.

DATABASES

A **database** stores large quantities of information, all of which relates to a specific topic or subject. It also allows for easy retrieval and updating of stored information through a database management system, or DBMS. Databases and DBMSs far exceed the capabilities of other methods of storing data. A DBMS enables users to create, maintain, and use database contents, and in most cases it includes features for sorting information and grouping reports. Typically, a DBMS includes a data dictionary, which gives names and descriptions of every data record type and defines the relationships between them. There are six primary types of database models: hierarchical, network, relational, distributed, object-oriented, and hypermedia. DBMSs are designed to work with each of these models.

DATABASE SOFTWARE

Database software, or database management system (DBMS) software, is used to generate and manipulate the contents of a database. Examples of common consumer database software are Microsoft Access and Claris FileMaker. For servers, the common database software packages include Oracle and MySQL. These database management programs allow users to compile and integrate large amounts of data, which prevents redundancy and proliferation of documents. Effective databases also allow the user to compare records quickly.

HOW DATABASES STORE DATA

Databases are made up of records, which themselves are made up of fields containing individual pieces of data. For instance, a database of the customers for a business might contain separate records for each individual customer. Within each record, there will be different fields for the customer's name, address, phone number, etc. Records are typically presented horizontally in a database, so that one horizontal row will contain an entire record. With this format, each vertical column contains all the data values under a specific category of data. For instance, one column might contain all the customer phone numbers.

LOCATING DATA WITH QUERIES

Because it is not efficient to examine an entire large database to find a particular piece of information, database management programs have developed query languages that enable users to quickly find and edit data. The best-known example of such a language is SQL, or Structured Query Language, which enables the user to enter queries in a format that is similar to natural language questions. Another well-known query language is QBE, or Query by Example, in which the user effectively performs a short fill-in-the-blank exercise that helps the program locate the desired piece of information.

Using the Results of a Database Search

Once a database search has been completed, the user can save the results to a hard drive or disk. In addition, the results of the search could be converted into HTML format and published on the internet, exported to another program on the computer, or sent to another computer over a network. In many cases, data can be exported directly into a spreadsheet where it can be analyzed, used to create a graphs or other visuals, or exported again. Sometimes, the user will want to take the data and use it to generate a text document which can be easily read and understood by his or her audience. Finally, the results of a database search can be transferred to another database.

Relational Databases

In a **relational database**, there are multiple tables containing overlapping sets of data. Relational databases get their names from the fact that every table in such a database contains data that relates to data in another table in the same database. For example, a database used by human resources may have a table for employees and a table for pay schedules. Then, in the table for employees, a single employee record could have an employees name, ID number, and pay schedule. The data point showing an employee's pay schedule could be linked to that pay schedule's record in the pay schedule table. With this kind of database, change made to the information in one table will be reflected in the other tables. Thus, relational databases eliminate the need for users to enter the same data in multiple places. A table in a relational database must have a key, which is a data field that serves as a unique identifier of each record. For example, in the human resources database scenario just mentioned, the employee ID number would be a good key. Whereas two employees could have the same name, each employee ID number is unique to that employee.

Entering Records into a Database

When creating a database, a user can enter records into forms or into tables. If a form is used, the user must first design a form that includes all the data fields that exist in one record of the table where the data will go. Once the form is designed, it can be used for data entry. Normally there must be data of the proper format in every field before the record can be saved. Database management software typically requires certain types or formats of data to be entered in fields. For instance, it may have a built-in phone number that, when used in a table, will only accept phone numbers, and only in a specified format. Data can also be entered directly into tables. Doing this is much like filling out a spreadsheet; the arrow keys and perhaps the tab key or enter key can be used to navigate around the individual fields. The user can fill in fields by entering information into blanks in a new record. The restrictions that apply to entering data through a form also typically apply when entering data in a table; only one new record can be made at a time, because a record cannot be added to the table unless every field has data in it.

Hierarchical Database Model

A **hierarchical database model** arranges information in the form of a tree-like structure, much like a family tree. At the top of the hierarchy sits a general subject, such as the United States of America. This subject is then divided into a group of related topics, such as the individual states that comprise the USA. These topics can be further divided into even smaller topics, such as the counties in every state.

Hierarchical databases are often described as using one-to-many relationships because one elemental can have several child elements. Furthermore, because of this structure, any given data element has one parent, except for the single, overarching topic, to which every element can be traced. Additionally, all related data elements reside on the same level in the hierarchy. The hierarchical model is very useful for nesting information, and it was used frequently in early databases. However, since then, it has been surpassed by the relational database model, though it is still widely used for certain applications.

Relational Database Model

The **relational database model** is the basis for modern database design. It represents database information in two-dimensional tables, and allows for relationships between the columns of these tables. A relational database has three basic parts: relations, attributes, and domains. **Relations** are represented by tables with columns and rows. The columns are known as **attributes**. Each attribute has a name and a corresponding data type. All the data values in a given column must be of the appropriate data type, and they must be valid. The entire set of values that are valid for a column is known as a **domain**. Rows are called **records** (or, more formally, **tuples**), and each row represents a unique item on the table and its attributes. Rows are often identified using a unique identifier called a **key**. An attribute that is not the key may take its values from another table through a **relationship**. Consider the following example:

Instructors		
Instructor ID	**Instructor Name**	**Department**
00232	Paul Wilson	English
00234	Mary Smith	Math
00235	Jessica Miller	Math

The above is part of a table that lists instructors. Another table in the same database could list departments. In this case, there would be a relationship between the Department attribute in the above table and the records in the Departments table.

STRUCTURED QUERY LANGUAGE

Structured query language, or SQL (pronounced like the word "sequel"), helps manage information within relational databases. Based on relational algebra, SQL allows users to query (or "interrogate") databases and extract useful information. Additionally, SQL facilitates the process of updating information, changing schemas, and controlling access to data. SQL consists of the following elements:

- Clauses – optional parts of statements that determine the range the statement applies to
- Expressions – generate values or tables containing information
- Predicates – define the conditions that SQL will use when finding data
- Queries – retrieve specific information from the database.
- Statements – manipulate schemas and data

DATA WAREHOUSING

A **data warehouse** facilitates the reporting and analysis of information and, thereby, aids the process of management decision making. **Data warehouses** use relational database management systems, but they tend to store data differently than operational databases. Most data warehouses include tools for managing data dictionaries, tools for retrieving, changing, and loading information into a repository, business intelligence tools, and metadata management functions. There are three primary design methodologies in data warehousing:

- **Bottom-up**: Data marts are created that analyze and report on business processes. The data marts are connected to create the warehouse.
- **Top-down**: All organizational information is stored in a centralized data warehouse. Data marts are created to process information specific to a department.
- **Hybrid**: The speed of bottom-up design and the consistency of top-down design are combined.

DATA MINING

Data mining is a method of examining information and extracting trends or forecasts that had gone unnoticed beforehand. Data mining uses data warehouses and data marts as sources. It is very useful in marketing, scientific research, and surveillance. In most cases, data mining is not performed on all available data but rather on a sampling of that data; consequently, the accuracy of the trend or forecast depends entirely on how well the sample represents the data as a whole. Data mining consists of four basic tasks:

- **Classification**: arranging data elements into groups that the user defines
- **Clustering**: grouping data elements by similarity instead of by predefined groups

- **Regression**: modeling data according to the function that is least error-prone
- **Association**: rule learning – examining variables for relationships

Measuring Memory Capacity

For the sake of convenience, main memory systems are designed such that the total number of cells equals a power of two. For instance, early computers had 2^{10} (1,024) cells. Consequently, one **kilobyte** is equal to 1,024 bytes, two kilobytes is equal to 2,048 bytes, and so on. Later computers had greater memory capacity, so the prefixes "mega" and "giga" came into common use. One **megabyte** is 1,048,576 (1024^2) bytes, and one gigabyte is 1,073,741,824 (1024^3) bytes. There is a problem with these prefixes, however. Outside the computer industry, they only apply to powers of ten, not powers of two. In other words, "kilo" corresponds to 10^3, which is exactly 1,000, but operating systems equate 1 kilobyte to 1,024 bytes, not to 1,000 bytes. This discrepancy grows larger as the amount of memory being measured gets bigger. It can cause confusion for consumers, as a hard drive might be advertised as 1 terabyte because it does actually offer 1,000,000,000,000 (i.e., 1 trillion) bytes of storage. However, that number of bytes is really only 931 gigabytes. To an operating system, which is measuring memory in powers of 2, it takes 1,099,511,627,776 bytes to make a terabyte. To remediate this problem, industry experts have suggested that the prefixes "kilo," "mega," and "giga" be replaced with prefixes for powers of two: "kibi" (kilobinary), "mebi" (megabinary), "gibi" (gigabinary), "tebi" (terabinary), etc.

Storage Requirements Necessary for a Completely Redundant System

A **redundant system** has the ability to continue working without data loss when there is a catastrophic hardware failure. The easiest way to create a redundant system is to have an exact copy of all the data in the system stored at a different location and being updated in real time. This would require that the system make changes in two different places for each single change. If this type of redundancy is used, the system requires twice the amount of storage as a nonredundant system, because there is a one-to-one copy of all information. In a more complex redundant system, the secondary storage can be compressed, which results in less total data. The drawback of this system is speed. Whenever information needs to be written, it first needs to be compressed. Also, if a catastrophic failure of the main system occurs, the backup data needs to be decompressed before it can be used as normal.

Data Manipulation

Transforming Data in Order to Make It More Useful

One way to transform data to make it more useful is through the use of **filters**. Filtering is a method of transforming data where the only records shown are those with a given datapoint that matches specific criteria. Consider a team that is viewing a list of customers, but for the moment only wants to see customers age 65 years or older. A filter could be used so that only customers whose "age" datapoint was greater than 65 would be shown in the list. Such a filter would make the desired information much more visible, compared to looking at the whole list and reading the age of every customer to check whether they are part of the group being considered.

Removing Data for a Data Set to Be Useful

With some data sets, removing certain pieces of data can cause the data set to be of more use. One type of data that must be removed is the **outlier**. Outliers are data values that are radically different from the other data. If outliers are left in a data set, the data will be skewed. Outliers are often caused by malfunctioning equipment or human error. Another example of data that needs to be removed are zeros. In some cases, zeros are true readings. However, except in certain situations, a zero is more likely to be an erroneous value or evidence that the real value wasn't entered, and it will skew the data. Lastly, sometimes data is only considered valid if it is within a certain range. In these cases, data outside of this range must be removed in order for the data to be used as intended.

Working with Publicly Available Data Sets

The major benefit of working with publicly available data sets is that all the data is transparent. It encourages research through the reanalysis of existing data and allows more people to review the data for accuracy. Because the data is open, it can be mined more easily, and relationships between data sources that would otherwise be inaccessible can be found. Furthermore, with public data, analysis does not have to be filtered through or associated with an organization; it can be viewed and used by any group or individual. Open data should follow three key requirements. First, it should be available in its entirety. Next, it should be publicly accessible for download on the Internet in a format that is readily recognizable and modifiable. Lastly, data must be provided in a form that is redistributable and reusable for future research.

Nature of Data That Surveys Generate

Survey data is the result of collecting data from a groups of survey respondents. The data from a survey is influenced by a variety of factors, including the method of giving the survey, how often the survey is repeated, and who the respondents are.

The method of surveying has many variables. Surveys could be online, face to face, over the phone, or on paper forms that are collected. Because people may write their opinion differently than they would say it, or voice certain opinions online that they would not in person, the medium of a survey always has some influence. Likewise, survey methods can vary in how they ask for opinions. They could use agree-or-disagree statements, multiple choice questions, or short answer questions, to name a few. Therefore, the method of the survey should be taken into consideration when analyzing the resulting data.

Next, we must note how often the survey is given. If the survey contains data that is less likely to change over a short period of time, like people's favorite sports, then surveys can be given at longer intervals. However, for a topics like political elections, where public opinion constantly fluctuates and the data is relevant for only a limited time, surveys should be given more often.

Lastly, the sampling of the respondents has a tremendous effect on the validity of a survey. A sample must be sufficiently large and sufficiently random. Imagine a survey about whether or not college is important. If only 20 people take the survey, the resulting data will not be useful for determining public opinion, because the sample size is too small. Likewise, if only college professors are given the survey, or only college students, or only the residents of a particular area, the sample will not be sufficiently random. Furthermore, voluntary participation can make a sample less random, as the participants will all be people who want to share their opinion. A large and truly random sample can be difficult to obtain, but it is essential for accurate survey data.

Crowdsourcing and Citizen Science

Crowdsourcing is a way to solve a problem, gather data, or complete a task by making participation in the effort open to anyone. It is generally done through the Internet. An example of crowdsourcing would be an app that allows people to upload their location when they see an accident while driving. As more and more people report the accident, the app can more reliably verify that there is indeed a car accident there, and it could then report the accident or display its location on a map so that drivers know to avoid it. The data in this scenario comes entirely from a large number of participants, and it would be difficult the same data so quickly and reliably through other means.

Citizen science is scientific research or data collection that is done by members of the general public rather than exclusively by scientists. For example, in order to keep track of the migration of lantern flies (an invasive species in North America, first spotted there in 2014), people have created websites where sightings can be reported. The information from these websites can be used by scientists to learn more about lantern flies and determine best courses of action. Citizen science is typically done by amateurs and enthusiasts. Like crowdsourcing, it has become far more widespread and practicable due to the internet.

Chapter Quiz

Ready to see how well you retained what you just read? Scan the QR code to go directly to the chapter quiz interface for this study guide. If you're using a computer, simply visit the online resources page at **mometrix.com/resources719/oaecompsci** and click the Chapter Quizzes link.

Programming Concepts

Transform passive reading into active learning! After immersing yourself in this chapter, put your comprehension to the test by taking a quiz. The insights you gained will stay with you longer this way. Scan the QR code to go directly to the chapter quiz interface for this study guide. If you're using a computer, simply visit the online resources page at **mometrix.com/resources719/oaecompsci** and click the Chapter Quizzes link.

Extensibility, Modifiability, and Reusability of Code

Programs

In computing, a **program** is a set of instructions that use a processor and memory to solve a problem or complete a task. Programming is a five-step process.

1. The first step is identifying the problem that the computer program is going to solve or task it will perform.
2. The second step is coming up with a solution to the problem.
3. The third step is composing program code in the appropriate syntax.
4. The fourth step is testing.
5. The fifth and final step is the comprehensive and detailed documentation of the program. Documentation is needed both for developers and testers who will work with the code later and for users as guidance on how to use the program effectively.

Coding a Computer Program

The activity of writing a computer program is called **coding**. There are different programming languages in which coding can be performed. Most applications for public use are developed with **high-level programming languages** like C++ and Java. One programming language might be better suited to a particular type of program than another language. Every language has its own **syntax**, though languages of the same type tend to be similar. In the case of computer programming, the term "syntax" refers to the expected format of written lines of code. Just as the words in an English sentence only make sense in a certain order, with certain other words to modify them, and so on, the commands, functions, control structures, and other items that make up programming code must be written in a certain way, according to the rules of the applicable programming language.

Necessity for the Correct Order of Steps in Algorithms

Any process must be done in the correct order to obtain the correct result. A process performed by a computer program is no different. When developing an algorithm, developers must walk through the process one step at a time and ensure that each step is properly defined and uses the correct rules. If the steps are out of order, unexpected results will likely occur. Remember that an algorithm is a set of steps and rules necessary for completing a process. Imagine the following steps being performed to prepare dinner: place the pan in the oven, mix the ingredients together, cool the dish for five minutes, remove the pan from the oven, and set the oven to 350 degrees. That would not result in a very appetizing dinner! The same is true for an algorithm used to create a computer program. The steps must be performed in the correct order to obtain the desired result.

Code Writing Examples

Example 1

Assume the variable `x` *equals 0.*
Also assume we currently have a loop set to run while `x < 5`*.*
Also assume we have a counter variable that begins at 0 and is incremented by 1 during each iteration of the loop.

If we changed the end condition so the loop will run while `x ≤ 5`*, how many more iterations would occur?*

A while loop will continue to execute while its condition is true. Because the counter variable is initialized to 0 and incremented by 1 each time the loop executes, the counter variable will begin at 0 and count up until it becomes 5. When the counter is 5, the condition `x < 5` that keeps the loop going now becomes false. The code in the loop will have executed five times, for the numbers 0 through 4. If, however, we change the end condition to `x ≤ 5`, we gain one more iteration because the loop will execute the numbers 0 through 5. Therefore, changing the condition from "less than" to "less than or equal to" extends the loop by one full iteration.

Example 2

Write code to determine if the area of a rectangle is bigger than the perimeter of a rectangle and print the result. All lengths are integers.

We know that the area of a rectangle is its length times its width ($A = LW$), and that its perimeter is two times its length plus two times its width ($P = 2L + 2W$). Therefore, it would be good practice to first store the area and perimeter in variables in order to compare their values later.

```
int area ← length * width
int perimeter ← 2 * length + 2 * width
```

Once these values have been computed, we now can compare them.

```
if( area > perimeter )
   print "Area is larger."
else if( perimeter > area )
   print "Perimeter is larger."
else
   print "They are equal."
end if
```

It is important to include the else statement that occurs when the area and perimeter are equal. If we did not have this step, equal areas and perimeters would display nothing.

Example 3

Given the following method, what is one possible input for `a` *and* `b` *so that the output is 2?*

```
int myMethod( int a, int b )
   if( a > b )
      a ← a - b
      return a % 4
   end if
   return 0
end myMethod
```

To determine the output, we must first understand what types of inputs are required. Two integers must be entered, and `a` must be the first input, while `b` must be the second. The if statement `if( a > b )` must be true in order to get the required answer, because if that doesn't happen, the method will default to `return 0`. Once values are inputted in which `a` is greater than `b`, we then subtract `b` from `a`, and this becomes the new value of `a`. Whatever that value is will then have the **modulo** operator applied to it. Modulo division returns the remainder after division. One possible answer would be when `a` is 8 and `b` is 2, a function call of `myMethod( 8, 2 )`. In this case, `a` is greater than `b`, so the statements within the if statement occur. The variable `a` then has 8 – 2, or 6, stored in it. `6 % 4` gives you 2, because that is the remainder after division.

EXAMPLE 4

Given an array of integers named `myNums`, write a method to find and return the highest number.

For this method to work, we will need to have an output value that is an integer, which will contain the highest number. We will also need to input the array and the total number of elements in that array. We will need this because we will be using a loop to iterate through all the elements in the array looking for the highest number. Every time a number is found that is higher than the current highest number, the current highest number will be replaced by that value.

```
int findHighest ( int[] array, int length )
   int highest ← 0
   for( int i ← 0; i < length; i ← i + 1 )
      if( array[i] > highest )
         highest ← array[i]
      end if
   end for
   return highest
end findHighest
```

EXAMPLE 5

For a program that finds the square root of x – y, identify a necessary precondition that would ensure the program finds a valid number.

Functions and programs may have preconditions, which are conditions that must be met before a method executes so that there will be no unhandled exceptions. Examples of preconditions include that the input must be an integer, that the input must be a positive integer, that the input must be within a certain range, and so on. In this case, it is important that the value put into the program is not a negative number. Trying to find the square root of a negative number will result in an imaginary number, which is a number that cannot be computed. This can be prevented with a precondition that $x \geq y$. This will ensure that the subtraction before the square root is taken will result in a positive number or 0, either of which would enable the square root function to properly calculate and return a valid number.

EXAMPLE 6

Compare the decision statements "!X or !Y" and "!(X and Y)" and determine whether they are equivalent.

The statement "!X or !Y" could be phrased in natural language as "X is false or Y is false." On the other hand, "!(X and Y)" could be phrased as "X and Y together are false." Note that this is different from saying that X is false and Y is false ("!X and !Y").

This question is can be answered using **De Morgan's laws**. These laws are a set of logical rules first described by Augustus De Morgan, a 19th-century British mathematician. De Morgan's laws can be summarized as the following:

"!A or !B" is equivalent to "!(A and B)."

"!A and !B" is equivalent to "!(A or B)."

Since the laws clearly include the two decision statements mentioned in the question, we can easily see that the statements in the question are equivalent. We can also check that this is true using a truth table. As you can see, the values in the "!X or !Y" column and the values in the "!(X and Y)" column are the same.

X	Y	!X	!Y	!X or !Y	X and Y	!(X and Y)
T	T	F	F	F	T	F
T	F	F	T	T	F	T
F	T	T	F	T	F	T
F	F	T	T	T	F	T

Syntax Errors vs. Runtime Errors

Syntax errors and **runtime errors** are both errors that prevent code from producing the expected results. Both types of errors must be corrected in order for the program to work. While they are similar in that respect, the two types of errors have different causes and different resolutions. **Syntax errors** prevent the code from compiling—being converted into machine language—so the code will not even be able to run. This type of error is similar to a grammatical error in that it is merely a rule of structure, spelling, formatting, etc. that has not been followed. The code may be missing a semicolon, or there could be a parenthesis out of order. **Runtime errors**, on the other hand, occur as the program is actually running. The program can be compiled and run, but the desired results are not produced, or the program crashes. Runtime errors could be caused by faulty logic, referencing an invalid space in memory, or numerous other mistakes. In summary, syntax errors prevent the code from running, and runtime errors occur as the code runs. Either way, the error must be fixed for the code to work properly.

Discovering Syntax Errors

Syntax errors can be thought of as the grammatical errors of the programming world. A syntax error occurs when the rules of the programming language in use are not followed. It could be something as simple as a missing comma or semicolon, or it could be something more complex, such as attempting to use a keyword as a variable name or not properly ending an if statement. Most syntax errors are caught and corrected easily, because compilers will identify them out of necessity and report them upon failing to compile. Compilers generally give information about such errors, including specific line numbers, to help the programmer find and correct them. Furthermore, many modern **integrated development environments (IDEs)** use color-coded text so that the programmer can immediately see how the compiler will interpret the code. **Keywords** (words that cannot be used as variable or function names because they are built into the programming language) can be shown in specific colors or styles. For example, all built-in commands may be one color, while programmed functions are another color, variables another color, and operators another color still. The IDE can also help the programmer avoid common errors by making suggestions or automatic changes. For example, it may help in properly setting off code blocks (such as in loops or if statements) by automatically indenting to the correct level or automatically adding a closing brace. The most user-friendly IDEs have tooltips or other popups to highlight possible missing semicolons or remind the programmer what the arguments of a function should be, all as the programmer types.

Logic Errors

Logic errors prevent pieces of code from producing the expected results. Logic errors are most often caused by faulty human thinking. Computer code does not think for itself. It only does what it is told to do by the programmer. When the programmer assumes that a problem can be solved one way, but their assumption is incorrect, logic errors can occur. Logic errors can be very simple. For example, the code may be set up for addition of numbers when subtraction is needed. It may assign a value to one variable when the value should be assigned to a different variable. Logic errors can also be more complex. Logic errors may occur inside nested if statements, or the programmer may set the program to loop through a series of steps without providing a way to exit the loop. Because logic errors do not necessarily cause crashes or wildly incorrect outputs, they can be difficult to notice and find. Regardless of the cause of the logic error, it is something that must be corrected before the code will work as intended.

Classification of Logic Errors

Logic errors are classified as runtime errors. A logic error does not prevent the code from running, but rather causes the code to produce incorrect or unpredictable results. Remember that syntax errors occur when the rules of the programming language are not followed. Code that contains a syntax error will not run. Code that contains a logic error and no syntax errors will run and produce results. Often, logic errors are some of the hardest errors to find and correct. The compiler is not able to give the programmer any indication of where the error is occurring because, according to the compiler, the code is working correctly. However, the code is not performing the action that the programmer intends, and the programmer is likely to notice this only when the program is running. Therefore, although logic errors may not be obvious, as by causing a crash, they fall under the category of runtime errors.

Correcting Logic Errors in a Piece of Code

When attempting to correct a logic error, a programmer may often need to step through a piece of code line by line to examine what is happening at each step. This process is called "**debugging**," and most IDEs provide a debugger that allows the programmer to step through each line of code manually, step into called functions, step through those functions one line at a time, etc. An IDE also will typically provide a variable tracker, which allows the programmer to see the values stored in variables and how they change with each line of code. These features are very useful tools for correcting logic errors, because programmers can use these tools to pinpoint where the variable changes to an unexpected value. Another way to correct logic errors can be to draw out a map of the process or logic on paper, and then compare the code to the process map to ensure that the correct logic is being followed throughout the entire program. Logic errors can sometimes be difficult to trace, and correcting them can be a tedious process. However, following a methodical process to step through the code is generally the best approach.

Identifying Stack Overflow Causes and Preventing Them

A **stack overflow** occurs when an attempt is made to push an additional item onto the call stack when it is already full. A stack overflow and causes the program to crash. Remember that the stack is the memory space used for temporary storage of data during the running of an application. One way to prevent stack overflows is to allocate more memory to the application. If the size of the stack is increased, then more data can be stored there, which might allow recursion to run as deep or long as it needs to, or a particular necessary algorithm to be used. Another way to avoid a stack overflow is to store fewer data items on the stack during the running of the program. Use other storage methods instead of pushing the data onto the stack. This will take up less room on the stack, and the likelihood of a stack overflow will decrease.

Code Example

Look at the following code:

```
float calculateValue ( int x, int y )
   return x / y
end calculateValue
```

A student finds that when they use an odd number for `x` *and the number 2 for* `y`*, their answer is not correct. Why?*

When two numbers of data type int are divided in a computer program, integer division is performed. This means that any decimal values that are part of the answer are removed, as the number must be truncated into an integer (i.e., a whole number). Therefore, if we were to divide 5 by 2, under normal mathematical circumstances we would get the quotient 2.5.

However, in programming, since both 5 and 2 are integers, I would instead get the truncated version of 2.5, which is only 2. The ".5" portion is left off of the answer, because integers cannot store decimal points or numbers to the right of the decimal point. In the above method, although the return data type is a float, the actual calculation is done using integers. In order to force the computer to execute decimal division, at least one of the values being divided must be a data type that stores decimal fractions. Changing the method header to `float calculateValue ( float x, float y )` would be the best solution, although only one value (`x` or `y`) must be a decimal.

Characteristics of Robust Software Design

In software design, **robustness** encompasses many different aspects of a piece of software. Characteristics of robust design include modularity, efficiency, and exception handling—to name a few. **Modularity** means that the software is broken down logically into pieces that function by themselves as part of the larger application. Modular software can be maintained and improved more easily. Robust software is also efficient. It makes good use of the computer's resources, and it does not perform unnecessary tasks. Last, and perhaps most synonymous with the traditional meaning of the word, robust software handles errors and exceptions with minimal destabilization and crashing. Software that constantly crashes or that could crash easily with only a minor mistake by the user would not be considered robust. Such software would need to be modified to handle exceptions more gracefully before we could call it robust.

Effect of Robust Design on Software Reliability

Software reliability is very important to today's users. Software that is reliable consistently performs as expected and required. A robust design allows software to be more reliable. Robust software by definition handles exceptions without crashing or becoming unstable, and robust software can expected to handle any situation it may encounter. Therefore, robust design is a major key in reliability. Providing a solid, robust design that allows software to be very reliable is a deliberate process that must be planned and executed well.

Effect of Robust Design on Software Maintenance

Software maintenance cannot be avoided if a piece of software is expected to be in operation for any length of time. Maintenance can sometimes account for as much as 80 percent of a piece of software's lifecycle. Beginning with a robust design can make the maintenance process much easier. A robust design usually includes modular programming, which means that different pieces of functionality in the code are broken into separate modules. When software is made this way, maintenance is easier because it can be performed on a single module. There is no need to touch the other modules or the main module. Contrast this with software that isn't modular; such software has most or all of its code lumped together in a very long chain of statements. Finding the section of the code that needs the update—not to mention all the other places in the code that may be affected if this portion is changed—can prove to be an extreme challenge.

Effect of Robust Design on Easier Software Expansion

Many pieces of software need to be **expanded** at some point in their lifecycle, to add more features or functionality for example. The robustness of the original software can directly affect how easy or difficult the expansion is. If the original design was very robust, then expansion is usually much easier. Robust design ensures that software is developed in a manner that makes adding features easy. Modularity is one way that this is accomplished. New features can be coded as new modules and then be incorporated into the existing code. Without a robust design, adding new features can require rewrites of large sections of code, which is unnecessarily time consuming and expensive.

Correlation Between Robust Design and Software Efficiency

Robust software should operate **efficiently**. It should be designed so that it does not unnecessarily use memory or perform unnecessary operations. Inefficient design can cause the software to run slower than it should. It can also cause software to use more memory and system resources than are necessary. Such problems lead to higher overall costs of using the software because they create higher performance demands on hardware. Designs should be robust so that the software performs as expected while using as few operations as possible to accomplish what is needed.

Relation of Software Validity to the Robustness of Its Design

A user always expects the software being used to produce the correct output. By using a robust design, a programmer can help ensure that users are confident in the validity of the software. Through robust design, the programmer can make certain that all the required rules are followed so that the output produced is the correct one. Thorough error and exception handling also increases the validity of software because the code is able to handle errors as they arise without a full crash. Debugging and testing of the code is also made easier through robust design, so the programmer can perform thorough testing of the software to ensure that it functions as expected before releasing it. Thorough testing ultimately serves to increase users' confidence in the validity of the software.

Making Troubleshooting Easier with Efficient and Robust Design

No developer wants to have errors in their code, but they are almost inevitable as code is developed. When errors do arise, it is important to be able to identify them quickly in order to facilitate a prompt resolution. By implementing a robust and efficient design, a developer makes it easier to troubleshoot code and resolve issues when they arise. Efficient code does not contain unnecessary steps, and efficient code typically contains as few lines as possible. Just as inefficient code compounds problems by creating a need for troubleshooting when there otherwise would not be, efficient code avoids not just the unnecessary operations but the unnecessary troubleshooting as well. Robust code also uses **modular design**, which allows the developer to test specific pieces of code individually, without needing the whole application to work. In this approach, the code that needs to be searched for the error can be narrowed down to a small section, making it much easier for developers and testers to find and correct the error in a timely fashion.

Types of Code Reuse

Two common types of code reuse are **opportunistic reuse** and **planned reuse**.

- Opportunistic reuse occurs when a team discovers that pieces of existing code can be reused in a new way. They take advantage of that opportunity and reuse the code in order to save development time and effort.
- Planned reuse occurs when a development team intentionally creates code in pieces that they know will be useful later. Often, this is done in the case of creating generic functionality will be necessary in other applications or other parts of the application. Developers create modules of this generic code and can then easily include the modules into other applications as needed.

Repurposing Code and Possible Redundancy Issues

One method of repurposing code is to simply copy portions of code that are needed from one application and paste them into another application. This creates exact duplicates of the same pieces of code in different places. As that code is reused again and again, it ends up being used in many different places. Consequently, any update to the code is very difficult to implement. If an update is needed, then the same update must be made in every place where the code is used—creating a redundancy. Tracking all the places the code is reused and keeping it all up to date can become quite an overwhelming task.

Creating Methods vs. Copying, Pasting, and Editing Code

When you create an algorithm or piece of code that needs to be reused, the best way to allow it to be reused is to create a method. Beginning programmers who do not know how to use methods may copy, paste, and edit code to fit specific use cases. This practice presents several problems, however:

1. First, reuse by copying and pasting makes the file size larger unnecessarily. Although there may be little difference when programs are small, in larger programs, where code is reused hundreds of times, the difference can be quite significant.

2. Second, if the algorithm that is being copied and pasted changes at all during the software development cycle, a programmer must then find every place where the code is pasted change it. The result is a lot of wasted time and possibly some errors where code was accidentally left unchanged or was not changed properly.
3. Lastly, if the method is designed correctly, it will be able to accept many types of inputs without necessitating any coding changes.

The method will be versatile, and there will be less tedious work for programmers, who can focus on development tasks. These benefits are lost when no method is created.

PRELOADED INPUTS VS. INPUTS PROVIDED AT RUNTIME

Preloaded inputs are those that are loaded into a program prior to its running, while inputs provided at runtime are fed to the program as it runs. Most programs today rely on inputs provided at runtime to accomplish their functions. In most cases, the inputs come directly from a user, and since those inputs can change each time the program runs, it is necessary to provide them at runtime because there is no way to preload inputs that are constantly changing. Some other items are more often preloaded, however, such as libraries or individual functions. Preloading these types of items increases performance speed because the program does not need to perform the loading of all these items as it runs.

CODE EXAMPLE

A student is writing a method to calculate the number of roots that a quadratic equation has. What inputs must the student acquire?

In order to determine the number of roots of a quadratic equation, the student must use the discriminant, calculated by the equation $b^2 - 4ac$, where the quadratic equation is in the format $ax^2 + bx + c$. Thus the method created to determine the number of roots will need floating-point inputs for a, b, and c. The output will be an integer because the possible number of roots of a quadratic equation can only be 0, 1, or 2. When the discriminant is negative, there are 0 roots, when it is 0, there is 1 root, and when it is greater than 0, there are 2 roots. The method header would look something like this:

```
int roots
double a
double b
double c
```

IMPROVING EXISTING CODE

First, the programmer needs to understand the changes that need to be made. Once the programmer is comfortable with the desired end product, then they need to examine the current code to determine the best way to make the necessary changes. Depending on the complexity of the changes, a total rewrite may be more efficient than modifying existing code. Assuming that the programmer moves forward with an edit, they then need to get a copy of the code into a development environment to begin making the edits. Editing code in the production environment is never recommended, as any mistake will affect a live system, potentially causing major problems. The programmer should make the edits in the development environment and then begin thorough testing of the changes. Users need to be consulted during the testing to ensure that all required functionality is included. Once testing is complete, the new version of the code can be placed into production so that all users have access to the updates.

CHANGING EXISTING CODE

There are many reasons why a piece of existing code may need to be changed. The most obvious reason is due to a bug or defect. If the code does not function as intended, then it must be updated so that it produces the correct results. Another reason that code may need to be changed is to add additional features. The needs of users typically change over time, so it is necessary to keep code updated so that it performs the actions that the users need it to perform. As work processes change, the way a system needs to operate changes as well. There could be a need to add more features or perhaps change the way that certain features behave. It is also possible that changes to one system cause changes in other systems to be required. Many applications today must integrate with other applications. Thus they may rely on other systems for data, or they may pass data to other applications. They may also need to interact with each other in real time. A change in the way that any integrated application operates could require changes in the applications it is integrated with.

DIFFERING SYNTAX BETWEEN PROGRAMMING LANGUAGES

Each programming language has its own syntax that must be followed. The syntax of a programming language is similar to the grammar of a human language. Just as the grammar of English is different from that of Spanish, so the syntax that must be used in Java is different from the syntax of C++. One language may require that every statement end in a semicolon. The other may not have any character to end lines but may instead use indentations to signal new lines. One language may use the keyword "float" to refer to a floating-point decimal number data type. The other may use the keyword "real." One language may require that every function return a value. The other may allow for functions that do not return values.

Furthermore, **constructs**, the building blocks that make up a program, such as built-in functions and control structures, may be similar from one language to another but use different syntax. For example, two languages may both use for loops, but one may require a separate iteration counter variable to be declared, while the other may require the number of iterations to be written in the for statement.

In any case, it is difficult to learn all the syntax of even one programming language, let alone many different ones. Therefore, it is more useful to simply be aware that syntax exists and that each programming language has its own. A programmer may often need to remind themselves of syntax they do not use regularly or need to learn syntax that they have never used.

Programming Control Structures

LOOPS

A loop is a structure in which the program executes the same set of instructions until a certain termination condition has been met. The following are the three primary loop structures:

while (condition is true) **do** (set of instructions)

repeat (set of instructions) **until** (condition is true)

for (number of iterations) **do** (set of instructions)

While statements are considered **pretest loops** because the condition is checked before the set of instructions is executed. If the condition is not true, the instructions will not execute. Repeat statements are considered **posttest loops** because the set of instructions is executed before the condition is checked. If the condition is not true, the instructions while have already executed, but they will not be executed again.

Controlling a loop involves three elements:

- **Initialize** – create an initial value that will be used as the loop runs
- **Modify** – alter the value so that eventually the termination condition will be reached
- **Test** – use the value to determine if the loop should continue running

Consider the following while statement:

```
int value ← 2
while( value < 20)
```

```
    value ← value * 2
end while
```

This loop will execute four times. After the fourth iteration, `value` will no longer be less than 20. Now consider the following posttest loop:

```
int value ← 2
repeat
    value ← value + 2
until( value == 9 )
```

The above loop will never end because `value` will never equal 9. In order to make this a valid loop, we would need to change the condition or change the way `value` is modified.

There is also a third primary loop structure, known as the **for** loop. This is a controlled loop in which the developer sets the loop to run a specific number of times.. Consider the following pseudocode:

```
for( int value ← 2; value ≤ 5; value ← value + 1 )
    print value
end for
```

The loop will run four times, printing the numbers 2 through 5 to the user.

While Loops

While ... end while statements instruct the computer to perform a repetitive function. A conditional statement will follow the word "while." The subsequent instruction or set of instructions will repeat until the condition after the word "while" is false. Consequently, during the course of a while loop, the value being tested in the codition must change. Otherwise, the loop will repeat into infinity. Consider the following example:

```
x ← 100
while( x > 20 )
    x ← x - 30
end while
```

Before the while loop starts, `x` is given a value of 100. With each repetition of the loop, the value of `x` is reduced by 30. Once `x` is less than 20, the loop will end, because `x` being greater than 20 is the test condition. The value of `x` at the end of the final iteration of this loop will be 10.

Result of Leaving the Counter Out of a While Loop

There are a few necessary components for a while loop to complete successfully. First, you must have a variable that has a starting value. Next, you need a condition. Once this condition is met, the loop will end. Finally, you need a variable that will eventually make that condition true. This variable is sometimes known as a **counter**. The counter should be changed in each iteration of the loop, and this is often done by **incrementing** (increasing) or **decrementing** (decreasing) the counter. During a loop's execution, the change to the counter variable value should eventually lead to a value that will make the loop's stopping condition true, ending the loop. If this counter is left out of the body of the loop, the condition will never become true. This mistake will result in an infinite loop, a loop that cannot be stopped except by "brute force" or by a lack of resources such as memory.

Conditional Loops

A **condition-controlled loop**, or conditional loop, tests for a certain condition and, if the condition is true, carries out the instructions within the loop. The condition is typically a simple variable comparison, such as `x < 10`. The computer will continue to perform the instructions as long as the condition is true. It will only stop once the condition becomes false. Conditional loops may be signaled by various keywords depending on the programming language, but they most commonly use the terms "while," "do ... while," and "repeat ... until." Consider the following example:

```
int a ← 10
while( a < 100 )
    a ← a * 2
end while
```

The above loop will run four times—initially when `a` is 10, again when `a` is 20, again when `a` is 40, and a final time when `a` is 80. After that, the value of `a` will be 160. Therefore `a < 100` will be false, and the computer will move to `end while`. Now consider this example:

```
int a ← 10
do
    a ← a * 2
while( a < 100 )
```

The above loop will also run four times. After the fourth iteration, when `a` is 160, the condition while be false and the loop will end. Note that in the while loop, the condition is checked before the loop runs, whereas in the do while loop, the condition is checked afterward. Finally, consider this example:

```
int a ← 10
repeat
    a ← a * 2
until ( a ≥ 100 )
```

Again, the above loop will run four times. After the fourth iteration, when `a` is 160, the condition while be false. However, note that the condition is different in this loop. For repeat until loops, the loop will not run again if the condition is true. Contrast this with do while loops, which will not run again if the condition is false.

Nested Loops

Very simply, a **nested loop** is a loop inside another loop. Though the theory seems simple, nested loops can become very complex in practice. Nested loops can be useful when there are multiple levels of loops that need to be performed. For example, imagine writing two-digit numbers vertically down the length of a page, starting at 00 and ending at 99. The second digit, on the right, would go in a sequence from 0 to 9, and then the digit on the left would increment, from 0 to 1. This is an example of a nested loop. The outer loop (the left digit) begins at 0, and the nested loop (the right digit) increase by 1 for each of its cycles, so it increments in a sequence from 0 to 9. Once the nested loop completes 9 cycles, the outer loop moves to its next cycle, by changing from 0 to 1. This causes the nested loop to start over again at 0 and increase by 1 for each of its cycles. When it reaches 9 again, the outer loop will change to 2. This is a very simple example, but it is a useful way visualize a nested loop.

Counted Loops

A **count-controlled loop**, or counted loop, executes a set of instructions a certain number of times by defining a counting variable prior to entering the loop. The counting variable determines how many times the instructions will be carried out. Counted loops may be signaled by various keywords depending on the programming language being used, but they most commonly use the terms "for" and "for ... next." Consider the following example:

```
for( int a ← 1; a ≤ 10; a ← a + 1 )
    x = x / 2
    y = y * 2
    z = ( z + 1 ) / 2
end for
```

The above counted loop will be carried out ten times. The counting variable is `a`, which starts at 1 and increases by 1 with each iteration `(a ← a + 1)`. The loop will not continue if `a` is greater than 10 `(a ≤ 10)`. As a result, the loop stops after running a tenth time.

INFINITE LOOPS

An **infinite loop** (also known as an endless loop) has no means of ending itself. It executes a set of instructions, but no mechanism is in place to control the loop, so it repeats the instructions again and again. The loop will only stop if the program crashes or a "brute force" method is used, such as killing the process or powering down the computer entirely. Consider the following example:

```
a ← 5
while( a > 4 )
   a ← a + 1
end loop
```

The above loop will never stop because the condition will always be true. The stopping condition would be `a ≤ 4`, but `a` starts at 5 and increases by 1 with each iteration.

Although in most cases infinite loops occur due to a mistake in the code and result in the program crashing, they are occasionally used intentionally. In such cases, an if statement inside the loop can test for a stopping condition and then break out of the loop.

IF STATEMENTS

Using **if statements**, computers can perform logic tests on data. The exact structure and syntax of an if statement will vary by programming language, but generally, as the name implies, it will begin with the keyword "if" and a condition. If the condition is true, the computer will carry out the statement sequence after condition. (In many programming languages, this sequence will be set off with braces to denote that it is a block of code.) If the condition is false, there are three basic possibilities: if there are no further statements, the computer will simply proceed past the if statement; if "else if" is used, the computer will test that condition; if "else" is used by itself, the computer will execute the code this else statement contains.

To make the best use of if statements, a programmer is often well served to understand the **logical operators** and **relational operators** of the language they are programming in. Operators can be **binary operators**, meaning they require two terms (one on either side of the operator), or they can be **unary operators**, meaning they require one term. Common logical operators include:

`and` – A binary operator that returns "true" if both operands are "true"; can often be written `&&`

`or` – A binary operator that returns "true" if either operand or both operands are "true"; can often be written `||`

`not` – A unary operator that returns "false" if the operand is "true," and "true" if the operand is "false"; can often be written `!`

Common relational operators include:

`=` – Binary operator "equal to," which may be `==` in languages where `=` is an assignment operator

`≠` – Binary operator "not equal to," which may be written `!=`

`≤` – Binary operator "less than or equal to," which may be written `<=`

`≥` – Binary operator "greater than or equal to," which may written `>=`

< – Binary operator "less than"

> – Binary operator "greater than"

Else Statements and Else If Statements

When the logical test in an if statement comes back "false," the computer will not execute the code in the if statement. Instead, will procee to any **else** or **else if** statements that have been included in the if statement.

Else statements provide alternative instructions for the computer to execute if the test condition is false. Care must be taken with else statements, as they will be true in every case that is not true for the original if statement; it is possible that these cases should be handles in specific ways, and not in a "one size fits all" else statement.

Because some cases may cause the if condition to return "false" but still require special handling, it is helpful to have else if statements in mind. An else if statement is like an else statement in that it will only execute if the if statement is false. However, it is like an if statement in that it can test for a condition. Consider the following examples:

```
if( age < 18 )
   print "Under 18"
else
   print "18 or older"
end if
```

In the above example, the program will output the text "Over 18" and go to `end if` in any case where `age` is less than 18—including if `age` is a negative number.

```
if( age ≥ 0 and age < 18 )
   print "Under 18"
else if( age ≥ 18 )
   print "18 or older"
else
   print "Invalid age"
end if
```

In the above example, the program first checks if `age` is both greater than or equal to 0 and less than 18. If both of these are true, the program will output "Under 18" and then go to `end if`. Otherwise, the program will check if `age` is greater than or equal to 18. If so, it will print "18 or older" and then go to `end if`. If `age` is a negative number or some other value that does not satisy the if condition or the else if condition, the program will execute the catch-all else statement and output "Invalid age."

If ... Then ... Else ... End If ... Statements

If ... then ... else ... end if statements instruct the computer to engage in decision branching. A conditional statement follows the initial keyword "if." If the condition is true, the computer will carry out the statement sequence contained in the subsequent code block:

```
if( x < y )
   // code here will be executed if x is less than y
```

Depending on the programming language, the keyword "then" maybe be necessary to signal this code block:

```
if( x < y ) then
   // code here will be executed if x is less than y
```

If the condition is false, the computer will skip the code block under "if" (or the code block under "if ... then") and instead carry out the statements after the else clause. Once it has executed one of the clauses, the computer will move to the end if statement. Consider the following example:

```
if( x < y ) then
   smaller ← x
else
   smaller ← y
end if
return smaller
```

If `x` is less than `y`, the computer will set `smaller` to `x`. If `x` is not less than `y`, the computer will set `smaller` to `y`. After one of the clauses is executed, the `smaller` value is returned.

Case Statements

A case statement (also known as a **select statement** or a **switch statement**) is used when an if statement would be cumbersome because of the number of conditions that need to be tested for. A **case statement** provides a separate set of instructions for each possible condition. In many cases, each condition corresponds to a possible value of a variable. Consider the example below, in which `bases` is an int and its value determines what output is printed:

```
switch( bases )
   case 0
      print "Out!"
   case 1
      print "Single!"
   case 2
      print "Double!"
   case 3
      print "Triple!"
   case 4
      print "Home run!"
end case
```

In the example above, it would be awkward to write separate else if statements for each case. We would have to write `else if ( bases ==` at least four times. Using a case statement, we assign a number of specific outcomes based on the value of a variable without having to test the variable repeatedly using a relational operator.

Iterative Structures

An **iterative structure** is a control structure (i.e., a special statement that has specific syntax and forces the program to proceed in a specific way) where a set of instructions is repeated. There are several types of algorithms that may necessitate the use of iterative structures, such as sequential searches and insertion sorts.

Control Statements

A **control statement** is a type of imperative statement that manages the sequence of program execution. An example is the goto statement, which directs program execution to a different location marked by a name or number. Control statements are often misused, resulting in branching structures that are overly complex, poorly written, and unreadable by other people. To avoid this problem, programmers rely on a method known as structured programming, which seeks to make the most efficient, accurate, and readable use of control statements. Most modern programming languages use control statements capable of representing complex branching structures in a single lexical statement. These include if-then-else statements, while statements, and switch or case statements. When choosing the most appropriate statement, programmers should work to achieve the best possible design while maintaining readability.

CONTROL STRUCTURES

In computer programs, the order that execution follows is known as the **control flow**, because control (of the computer) passes from statement to statement according to this order. Control structures are constructs that direct control flow. They contain instructions and include statements that determine which of those instructions will be executed and in what order. The normal order in which a program proceeds is known as sequential execution. When a computer program follows sequential execution, it executes instructions in the order in which they appear in the code. A control structure manipulates this order of execution—the control flow. Statements in a control structure may be executed only on certain conditions, executed repeatedly, or executed whenever they are called by a statement elsewhere in the code.

DECISION MAKING AND CONDITIONAL CONTROL STRUCTURES

Programs typically execute in a sequential fashion, starting at line 1 and progressing through the code in sequential order. There are points in the flow of a process where a decision needs to be made. Conditional control structures allow the program to make a decision at this point. Instead of progressing sequentially through the code, the program may potentially skip certain code sections based on some condition. If the specified condition is met, then that particular section of code will be executed. If the condition is not met, then the code performs some other action. This is very basic decision making, and the decisions are generally based on true-false conditions.

RELATIONSHIP OF BOOLEAN DATA TYPES TO CONDITIONAL CONTROL STRUCTURES

Remember that a variable of the **Boolean data type** is assigned a value based on logical expressions. The value in a Boolean can only be either "true" or "false," though these may be represented in different ways in memory. For example, some languages use a 1 to represent true and 0 to represent false. Boolean data types are related to conditional control structures because these control structures require a condition to be met in order for the code within the structure to execute. The Boolean value is used to determine whether a specified condition has been met. Let's imagine a Boolean value called `isDaytime` that stores a "true" or "false" value based on whether the current time is during the daytime or the nighttime. A conditional control structure could then be created that uses this Boolean to perform some action when it is daytime. An if statement, for example, executes the code block it contains if the expression it is passed evaluates to true. In this case, if `isDaytime` held the value "true," the statement `if( isDaytime )` would execute the code block it contains.

EXAMPLE SCENARIO

Conditional control structures allow computer programs to make logic-based decisions. Based on whether some condition is true, the program will either execute or skip over certain code sections. Consider a video game developer who is creating a new basketball video game. The developer has created a routine that will add points to a team's score based on the scoring method. The developer may use conditional logic to determine how many points to add. For example, if the team scores a three-pointer, the program will add three points. If the team scores a regular two-point goal, then two points will be added. If the team scores a free throw, then one point will be added. This is a very high-level example, but it shows how conditional logic can be used in programming.

ITERATIVE CONTROL STRUCTURES

Iterative control structures allow developers to create sections of code that can be repeated many times. Each time that code section executes is called an **iteration**. Iterative control structures, also known as loops, are useful because there are many instances when code sections may need to be executed over and over again. The alternative would be to copy and paste that entire section of code as many times as it is needed. Not only would this be an inefficient way to write code, but it would also not allow for situations where the programmer did not know in advance how many times the code would have to be repeated. Iterative control structures are an efficient and clean way of executing many repetitions of a single code section.

Types of Iterative Control Structures

Iterative control structures can be divided into two types. One type allows a section of code to be repeated a specified number of times. This could be a specific number of times (e.g., five times), or it could be a number of times represented by a variable (e.g., *x* times). The other type of iterative control structure allows a section of code to be repeated as long as a condition is true or until a condition becomes true. In these types of iterative structures, the structure will contain a test, either at the beginning of the loop or at the end. Each time the test is done, the program determines whether or not to repeat the section of code.

Example Scenario

Remember that an iterative control structure allows a developer to execute the same section of code repeatedly while a condition is true, repeatedly until a condition is true, or a specific number of times. Imagine a developer who is working on the control system of a robot. The robot could have a sensor to detect whether the path ahead of it is clear. If the path is clear, the robot could receive a command to walk, which would involve taking repeated steps. In this case, a loop could be made where each iteration is a step. The condition for stopping would be if the sensor detects an obstacle directly ahead. In such a case, the loop would stop, so the robot would not take another step.

Example of an Iterative Algorithm

Remember that an iterative algorithm is an algorithm that repeats specific steps a certain number of times or until some condition is met. Consider a very simple iterative algorithm that counts to 100 and displays the numbers as it counts. The process would start at 1 and display 1. It would then check for a certain condition—whether or not the current number is greater than 100. If not, then the number would increment by one, and the process would be repeated. As soon as the current number became greater than 100, the process would stop, and the flow would continue on to the next steps in the program.

Sequence Control Structures and Goto Statements

A sequence control structure rearranges the control flow, or the order in which a computer processor performs instructions. It uses a **goto statement**, which tells the processor to proceed to another place in the instruction sequence. A goto statement usually consists of the keyword "goto" followed by a reference to the instruction that should be executed next. Once this sequence control structure has been entered, the computer skips over all the code between the goto statement and the referenced instruction.

Selection Control Structures

Selection control structures are structures that consist of if statements, else if statements, and else statements. These statements set up conditions and contingencies for the computer program to follow. A selection control structure establishes that, if a certain condition is true, the computer should follow a corresponding set of instructions, but if that condition is not true, the computer should follow a different set of instructions (in the case of an else statement) or check for yet another condition (in the case of an else if statement). In other words, the selection control structure sets a fork in the path of the program; depending on a simple true-false test, the program will select one of two paths. These control structures are fundamental to programming in most languages, because they allow programmers to create programs that behave differently in different situations instead of performing the same action all the time.

Assignment Statements

An assignment statement is a type of statement that assigns a value to a variable (i.e., a specific location in the computer's memory). In effect, **assignment statements** tell a program to store a certain value in a variable. The value could be another variable, in which case the value of that variable would be copied. Consider the following example:

```
A ← B + C
```

The above is a basic assignement statement. It uses an arrow ("←") as the assignment operator, but this varies from language to language, with equals signs and colons ("=" or ":") being common. This statement tells the computer to store the value of the sum of `B` and `C` in the variable `A`. Assignment statements can involve mathematical expressions of greater complexity than above, such as the following:

```
x ← 2 * ( 7 + 3 ) - 4
```

In calculating the value to store in `x` in the above statement, the program will follow the rules of **operator precedence**. In general programming, P-E-MD-AS (parentheses, exponents, multiplication and division, addition and subtraction) is followed. However, care must be taken to know operator precedence of the laguage one is working in, particularly when working with operators that are less familiar; for example, modulo division (or remainder division) would have the same level of precedence as multiplication and ordinary division, in most programming languages. Also note that many programming languages will still perform operations left-to-right if the operators have the same level of precedence.

Assignment Statement Example

If we pass in the value 6 for the variable `a` in the following assignment statement, what will be stored in `result`?

```
result ← 4 + a - a ^ 2 + 2 * a + ( 4 / 2 + 3 )
```

The **order of operations** in computer programming is generally the same as in mathematics. It follows P-E-MD-AS (parentheses, exponents, multiplication and division, addition and subtraction). This is the order in which the computer will execute all operations. To find what will be stored in `result`, the first step is to substitute the variable `a` with 6.

```
result ← 4 + 6 - 6 ^ 2 + 2 * 6 + ( 4 / 2 + 3 )
```

The computer would calculate `( 4 / 2 + 3 )` next because it is in parentheses. The division here will be first, and since 4 divided by 2 is 2, and 2 plus 3 is 5, the whole expression would be:

```
result ← 4 + 6 - 6 ^ 2 + 2 * 6 + 5
```

The exponentiation would be next.:

```
result ← 4 + 6 - 36 + 2 * 6 + 5
```

There is only one case of an operator that has the level of precedence that multiplication and division do, so the multiplication of 2 times 6 would be next:

```
result ← 4 + 6 - 36 + 12 + 5
```

Lastly, the addition and subtraction will be done from left to right because addition and subtraction have the same level of operator precedence. Thus, in this line of code, the computer would assign the value of -9 to `result`.

Nested If Statements vs. Else If Statements Functionality

As a reminder, if statements are a way of telling the program to perform some action when a certain condition is true. Using else if or else statements causes the program to check for more than one condition. Nested if conditions allow the programmer to check whether one condition and another condition are both true. Else if statements allow the programmer to check whether one condition is true and another is false (as distinguished from both being true or both being false). With a nested if statement, the program must decide that both conditions are true in order to the point of execution to reach the line of code inside both if statements. With the else if statement, when the program encounters any true condition that is true, then the action will be performed, and no else if or else conditions will be checked. Most programming languages will allow layering of multiple else if conditions so that the code can check many different conditions. A final else statement is sometimes used as a catch-all. If none of the conditions are true, then the action contained in the code block after else will be performed.

EXAMPLE 1

Write code that uses nested if statements to check if a person is old enough to vote (assuming a minimum voter age of 18) and subsequently if that person is registered to vote.

A nested if statement is an if statement that is inside the block of code in another if statement. A nested if statement can be useful when a question about data only applies in some cases. For example, if a person is not old enough to vote, there is no need to know if they are registered to. The question of whether they are registered only applies if they are old enough. Therefore, the code could be written with nested if statements as follows:

```
/* userAge is an int containing a user-input value for their age in years.
isRegistered is a bool that is TRUE if the user has indicated they are registered and FALSE otherwise. */

if ( userAge ≥ 18 )
   if ( isRegistered )
      print "You can vote!"
   else
      print "You must register in order to vote."
   end if
else
   print "You are too young to vote."
end if
```

In these statements, the computer first checks to see if `userAge` is greater than or equal to 18. If it is not, the computer instantly goes to the else statement that prints that they are too young to vote. You will notice that the nested if statement is not executed because it is within the block of code that only executes when `userAge` is greater than or equal to 18.

If `userAge` is greater than or equal to 18, the computer then goes to the nested if statement, which checks to see if the person is registered. Since `isRegistered` is already a bool, we do not need a logical operator to compare values and generate a bool. If `isRegistered` is `false`, the statement printing that they can vote will not be executed, and the else statement will be. Then the computer will go to `end if` for the nested if statement, and finally to the `end if` for the parent if statement.

EXAMPLE 2

Modify the following code so that the **`and`** *operation is not used and an else statement is used. Note the precondition that* `grade` *is not less than 0 and not greater than 100.*

```
/* grade is a user-inputted int. Validity checks ensure the value is between 0 and 100, inclusive. */

if( grade > 80 and grade ≤ 100 )
   print "Excellent"
else if( Grade > 50 and Grade ≤ 80)
   print "Average"
else if( Grade ≥ 0 and Grade ≤ 50)
```

```
   print "Below Average"
end if
```

In this question, we have a precondition that `grade` is between 0 and 100 (inclusive). This means we need only check values that are in this range. Values outside this range will not be accepted; therefore we do not need an else statement that will catch all values not suited to our purposes, such as negative numbers or numbers greater than 100. We can use the functionality of else statements, however, to simply the code, as follows:

```
if( grade ≤ 50 )
   print "Below average"
else if( grade ≤ 80 )
   print "Average"
else
   print "Excellent"
end if
```

Because we can assume that the value in `grade` will be 0 or greater and 100 or less, we can filter out the numbers that are 50 or less using `if( grade ≤ 50 )`, then filter out the numbers that are 80 or less using `else if( grade ≤ 80 )`, and finally leave the remaining numbers using `else` . Because we know `grade` will be 0 or greater, we don't need to set a lower bound. Likewise, because we know `grade` will not be greater than 100, we don't need to set an upper bound.

Example 3

Modify the code to use a logical operator instead of using a nested if statement.

```
if( hungry )
   if( money ≥ 3.50 )
      print "Get a sandwich"
   end if
end if
```

Nested ifs can sometimes be rewritten as compound if statements. A compound if statement is an if statement where the whole condition includes two or more conditions and uses logical operators (such as **and** or **or**) to combine them in desired ways. The first if statement in the question checks if `hungry` is true. If `hungry` indeed contains the value `true`, the code block inside this if statement is executed. The code block contains another if statement, the nested if, which checks to see if `money` is greater than or equal to 3.50. When this is the case, the relational operator ≥ will return `true`, the subsequent code block will be executed, and the string "Get a sandwich" will be printed. Because the code only checks if both conditions are met, it can be rewritten in a simpler way that uses the **and** operator. The **and** operator is logical operator that takes the Boolean value on its left and the Boolean value on its right and returns `true` if both values are `true`. Therefore, the replacement code could be as follows:

```
if( hungry and money ≥ 3.50 )
   print "Get a sandwich"
end if
```

Example 4

A program has been written for an online cupcake store. Each cupcake costs $1, but there is also a 6% tax applied. The user is able to enter how many cupcakes they want to order, and the system will show them their total cost including the tax. A programmer has written the algorithm out, but the steps are out of order:
1. Display total cost
2. Calculate tax
3. Add tax
4. Calculate cost of cupcakes
5. User enters in number of cupcakes they would like to purchase
Place the statements in appropriate order.

The general order in which information flows through a program is: input, calculate, display. Using this as a guide, we can see we will first need to get the input for how much cupcakes the user wants, make a series of calculations to find the cost, and finally show this cost to the user. Therefore, the steps of the algorithm should be rearranged as follows:

1. User enters in number of cupcakes they would like to purchase. (Input)
2. Calculate cost of cupcakes. (Calculate)
3. Calculate tax. (Calculate)
4. Add tax. (Calculate)
5. Display total cost. (Display)

Operators, Data Types, and Variables

Boolean Algebra vs. Standard Algebra

One of the main differences between standard algebra and Boolean algebra is the fact that standard algebra uses variables to represent numbers, whereas Boolean algebra uses variables to represent true or false values. Just as standard algebra follows certain rules, Boolean algebra also has a set of rules that must be applied. While standard algebra uses arithmetic operators like addition and subtraction, Boolean algebra uses logical operators like AND and OR. Boolean algebra can be used to prove the equivalence of propositional statements, just as standard algebra can be used to prove the equivalence of mathematical expressions.

De Morgan's Laws and Propositional Logic

De Morgan's laws are two expressions of one principle. They are important to propositional logic because they provide rules on which inferences can be based. They allow unions and intersections of sets to be expressed in terms of each other through the use of the negation operator. The laws read as follows: "The complement of the union of two sets is the same as the intersection of their complements, and the complement of the intersection of two sets is the same as the union of their complements." In terms of propositional logic, it may be easier to understand these laws expressed as logical statements:

NOT (A OR B) = (NOT A) AND (NOT B)
NOT (A AND B) = (NOT A) OR (NOT B)

Their application in Boolean algebra and working with sets is generally easiest to comprehend by seeing the laws expressed with Venn diagrams.

Venn Diagrams of De Morgan's Laws

De Morgan's laws can be represented with **Venn diagrams**. In each case, the resultant set is the set of all points in light blue (light gray for print readers).

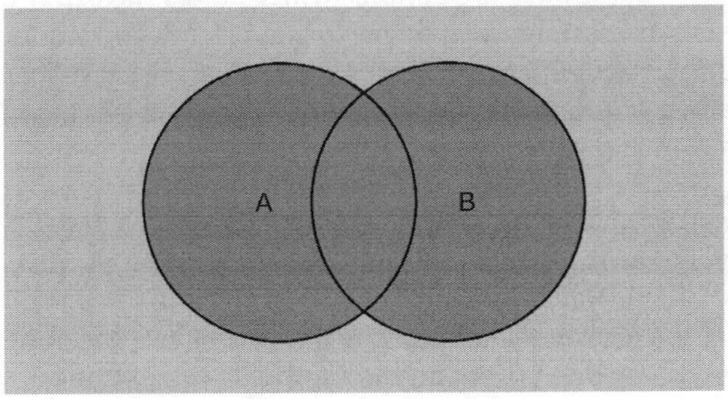

$A \cup B$
$\overline{A \cup B} \equiv \overline{A} \cap \overline{B}$

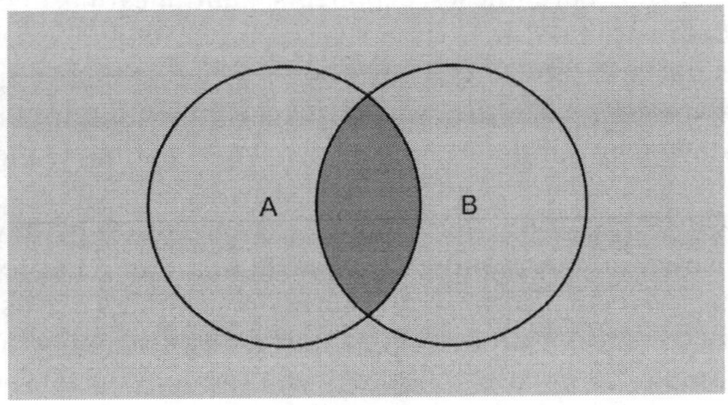

$A \cap B$
$\overline{A \cap B} \equiv \overline{A} \cup \overline{B}$

Example

A student is writing a program but doesn't remember what the AND operator is in the current programming language. The student decides to try to express (NOT A) AND (NOT B) without using AND, where A and B are Boolean variables. Write the logical expression that the student should use.

In order to solve this problem, we should remember De Morgan's laws. These laws provide equivalent Boolean expressions, including those that the student need. Recall that these laws can be stated in logical expressions as:

NOT (A OR B) = (NOT A) AND (NOT B)
NOT (A AND B) = (NOT A) OR (NOT B)

Therefore, the student can write NOT (A OR B) instead of (NOT A) AND (NOT B).

Including Arithmetic Functionality in Code

The inclusion of arithmetic functionality is actually quite simple because, in most cases, mathematical operators are already included in the programming language. Nearly every language that programmers would code in has basic arithmetic functionality built in. There is no need to identify or include any additional libraries or routines. A programmer can write mathematical expressions directly in code, as long as they follow the syntax of the language. In many cases, more advanced mathematical functions can be used as well by including a math library, which is a library of functions that are not included in a program by default, but that can be included using a statement.

Basic Arithmetic Operators

Arithmetic operators perform very basic mathematical calculations. Most of these require little or no explanation. These include addition, subtraction, multiplication, and division. Another operator included in most languages is the **modulo operator**. This operator returns the remainder of integer division rather than the whole number quotient. For example, 6 "mod" 3 is 0, because 6 divided by 3 is 2 with a 0 remainder. However, 7 mod 3 would be 1, because there is a remainder of 1 when this division is performed. Most arithmetic operators perform their operation on two values, given on either side, called operands. In the code `7 % 3`, the modulo operator `%` will perform its operation using the operands 7 and 3. More complex mathematical calculations, like square root, sine, and cosine, are not considered arithmetic operators.

ORDER OF OPERATIONS

The **order of operations** used in most programming languages is the same as the order of operations used in mathematics. Some people use the mnemonic "PEMDAS" to help themselves remember the correct order. This stands for "parentheses, exponents, multiplication, division, addition, subtraction," which states the order in which arithmetic operations will be performed. The first operation that will be performed is any operation inside parentheses. Some expressions even contain multiple sets of parentheses as well as parentheses inside other parentheses to ensure that specific actions are carried out first. Next, any exponents will be evaluated, followed by multiplication and division, and finally, addition and subtraction.

It can be important to remember that in math generally, as well as in most programming languages and software, multiplication and division share the same level of priority, and addition and subtraction share a lower level of priority. If an expression contains one use of multiplication and one use of division, these will be processed from left to right in most cases—meaning that the multiplication may be done after the division. For example, the code `10 / 5 * 2` will result in the division being done first and the multiplication second, yielding 4.

CODE EXAMPLE

Express the result obtained from the expression `2 * 2 + 1` *and identify a way to change the expression to obtain a different result.*

The result of this expression is 5. This is due to the order of operations, in which multiplication is performed before addition. The first operation to be performed is 2 times 2. This yields a result of 4. The addition 4 plus 1 is then performed, which generates the result of 5. By adding parentheses, a different result could be obtained. Examine the same expression with parentheses added:

```
2 * ( 2 + 1 )
```

In this case, the operation inside the parentheses, 2 plus 1, will be performed first, yielding 3. Then the multiplication will be carried out, with 2 times 3 producing 6.

IMPORTANCE OF THE ORDER OF OPERATIONS

The order of operations is very important when evaluating mathematical expressions because, depending on the order of operations, the resulting value may be different. For example, look at the expression `2 + 3 * 2 + 4`. As written, this expression would produce a result of 12 in most programming languages. Due to the order of operations, the multiplication 3 times 2 would be performed first, then the addition 2 plus 6, and then finally 8 plus 4. However, the expression could have been carelessly written and intended to be evaluated left to right—2 plus 3 first, then 5 times 2, then 10 plus 4, yielding 14. Furthermore, the programmer could have wanted to perform the calculation `(2 + 3) * (2 + 4)`. In wanting to avoid left-to-right evaluation but confusing the order of operator priority, they could have written an expression where the multiplication would be done first rather than last, though last was intended. In many cases, developers may add parentheses as reassurance that an order will be followed or as a way of structuring an expression visually so as to make it more readable.

OPERATOR PRECEDENCE

In the absence of parentheses, **operator precedence** determines the order in which a computer evaluates program expressions. This order, from highest to lowest, is as follows:

1. **Exponentiation**, or numbers that have been raised to a certain power
2. **Multiplication** and division in the order in which they appear from left to right
3. **Addition** and subtraction in the order in which they appear from left to right

When parentheses are present, they are evaluated before any other expression. The innermost parentheses are evaluated before the outermost parentheses, and the expressions inside parentheses are evaluated in the order of operator precedence. For instance, consider the following expression:

```
100 / (A * (B - C))
```

First, the computer would deal with parentheses. Finding that the outer set of parentheses has another set of parentheses inside it, the computer would evaluate `B - C`, the expression inside these inner parentheses. Then, it would multiply the resulting value by `A`. Finally, it will divide 100 by the resulting value.

In most programming languages, other operators figure into operator procedence as well. Examples of such operators include logical operators, like `AND` and `OR`, and unary operators (operators that use only one operand) like `++` and `--`. Programmers are well-served to be aware of operator precedence, to know when to double-check operator precedence, and know how or where to double-check it.

Relationship of Syntax Rules to Mathematical Expressions

Mathematical expressions must follow certain syntax rules. Operators must be in the correct place, and the correct number of inputs, or operands, must be provided. If these syntax rules are not followed, then an error will be produced. If the code must be compiled, the compiler will generate a syntax error that must be corrected before the code can run. Examples of valid expressions are as follows:

```
2 + 3 + 5 - 7
2 * 3 + 4 - 1
```

Remember that expressions may also include variables, such as:

```
2 * x + (a / 5)
```

An example of an invalid expression is:

```
3(4 + 8 -
```

Note that there is no closing parenthesis in the above expression, and that the subtraction operator is missing an input. This expression would generate a syntax error.

Data Types

Data types are categories for data. In computing, data is stored in memory as binary code, and data types provide a way for one kind of data (for example, integers) to have its own rules for being stored in memory and operated on, as compared to another kind of data (for example, text). Common data types include real numbers, Boolean variables, integers, characters, alphanumeric strings, and floating-point numbers. The data type determines the possible operations within a value set, the possible values within the set, and the storage method for the set. Data types also place constraints on the interpretation of data within a system and, thereby, enable the system to evaluate the correctness of computer algorithms. All programming languages incorporate data types—though the terminology may differ from language to language. Often, programmers may also create their own data types and associated operations. In most cases, new data types combine characteristics of existing data types.

Integer Data Type

Just as in mathematics, an **integer** in computing is a positive or negative whole number. Many languages refer to it as an **int**. Fractions or decimals cannot be included as part of an integer. The range of integers that can be used depends on the amount of memory or storage size for the integer itself. Typically, an integer is allocated either 2 or 4 bytes for storage. The use of 2 bytes allows for a range of integers from -32,768 up to 32,767. Increasing the storage to 4 bytes drastically increases the range. Using 4 bytes allows for the use of integers from roughly negative 2 billion up to positive 2 billion. Some examples of integers are 3, 24, -67, and 1431.

Numbers that are not considered integers include those with values to the right of the decimal point, such as 2.5, and "mixed numbers" (or numbers with fractions) such as 12 ½.

Floating-Point Data Type

The floating-point data type, or simply **float**, is used to represent numbers that have a decimal component. This could also include numbers with fractions, though the fractions would be represented in a decimal format. If there is any chance that calculations performed during the running of the program could lead to a result that includes a decimal point, then a floating-point type should be used to avoid losing the data after the decimal point. Some languages may also include a floating-point type called a **double**. Such a data type is used to represent a floating-point number with more precision. To accomplish the higher precision, languages allocate more memory for doubles—often double the amount of memory, and thus the name "double." Thanks to the additional memory, double can store many more **significant digits**. In other words, they store numbers that are more precise because there can be more digits on either side of the decimal point. Examples of floating-point numbers include 3.14, 6.73, and 1.25368474.

Boolean Data Type

The Boolean data type, or simply **bool**, has only two possible values: "true" and "false." Some languages actually store the words "true" and "false" to represent a Boolean value, while others may use the number 1 (usually to indicate "true") and the number 0 (usually to indicate "false"). It should be noted that not every programming language explicitly contains a Boolean data type. Boolean data types are generally used in logical expressions, and when logical operators (such as AND) or relational operators (such as ==) are used, they usually return a value of the Boolean data type. For instance, in the conditional test `7 > 5`, the "greater than" operator would return the Boolean value "true," while `3 == 6` would return the Boolean value "false." In programming, this type of logic is used very frequently to allow the program to make decisions during its processing. For example, in many languages, an if statement checks for the Boolean value "true," while the operators in the condition itself provide this value. Even languages that do not explicitly include a Boolean data type still allow for this kind of conditional testing.

String Data Type

The **string data type** is used to store text. Information that is considered "text" in this case includes not only letters and numerals, but also spaces, non-alphanumeric characters (such as punctuation), symbols or special characters, and formatting characters such as line breaks. Strings are often stored as arrays of characters, with each character occupying one position in the array. There are many operations that can be performed on strings. Some examples include concatenation, splitting, and joining. String parsing is another function that is commonly performed. This involves searching through a string to find desired text by looking for known text that occurs before or after the text that is needed. Some examples of strings include "string," "this is a string," and "Strings can even be complete sentences." When a string value (like "this is a string") is written in code, it generally needs to be set off with characters such as double quotation marks, so that the compiler does not try to interpret it as a function or variable. Remember that when strings are joined, spaces must be accounted for. For example, joining the strings "join" and "string" results in the string "joinstring." If a space is needed, it must be added as well.

Character Data Type

A **character data type** (often written as **char**) is, as its name suggests, a single character. The character may be a letter, number, or any other single piece of text. In most programming languages, the character data type is not used very often. Furthermore, some languages use an implementation of the character data type where a character is either a fixed-length string or a variable-length string. In languages that treat a character type as one single character, multiple characters may be joined together to create a string.

Primitive Data Types

Primitive data types are the building blocks for all other types of data structures. A primitive data type is a basic data type which only holds values of one kind. Some examples include integers, characters, and Booleans. For example, the integer data type is primitive because it holds a single value that can only be an integer. That integer may be 2, -5, 91, or -23,545, but it will never be anything other than an integer. A character data type is primitive for the same reason. A variable of that data type will never hold anything other than one single character value. Depending on the language, there are generally somewhere between four and eight primitive character types. The most common types are integer, character, Boolean, and floating point.

Speed of Primitive Data Type Operations

Operations on primitive data types run very quickly because primitive data types are relatively small, with most only requiring two to four bytes of memory. Because the value stored requires only this low number of bytes, there can be a one-to-one relationship between variables and blocks of memory. Therefore, data can be managed and accessed very quickly. Their small size also means primitive data types require a low number of CPU operations, sometimes as little as a single operation—and modern CPUs can run billions of operations every second. In summary, operations on primitive data types run very quickly because these data types require minimal memory, basic units of memory, and minimal processing power.

Reference Data Type

Reference data types can be a bit tricky for a new developer to understand. Reference data types contain information about a location in memory (i.e., a **memory address**) rather than the data itself. Consider the string "This is a string." If strings in this programming language are a reference data type, the string variable does not actually contain the value "This is a string." Rather, that value is stored in some location in memory. The string variable instead stores the address of this memory location. When the value of the string is needed, then the system goes to this location in memory and pulls the value from that location.

Primitive vs. Reference Data Types

One of the main differences between primitive and reference data types is the size and physical location of the data that is being dealt with. Primitive data types are small, often either two or four bytes. These data types can be stored completely within the **register** of the CPU. This is one reason why operations on primitive data type operations can often be performed within a single cycle of the CPU. Reference data types, however, may contain much larger pieces of data. Because of this, a reference data type stores only a memory address, and the data itself must be stored somewhere in the computer's memory system.

Object Data Type

An **object data type** forms the very basis of object-oriented programming. Objects can contain large pieces of data. An object is a reference data type because it uses a reference to a location in memory rather than storing the entire value. Objects are so large that they even contain **routines**. These allow a developer to perform specific functions within the object itself, offering a way for the developer to manipulate the data inside the object. The developer be confident that the results will be consistent because the functionality is built into the object and does not have to be written with separate code in the main program.

What Makes an Item an Object Data Type

An object data type allows for the storage of much larger pieces or collections of data than a traditional primitive data type. Primitive data types are typically single items, such as integers or characters. Object data types, however, are collections of data, such as lists or arrays. An object data type is not simply stored in a small, single space in memory. Rather, it occupies more space in memory and is accessed by reference. This means that the memory address of the first item in the object is the actual value, and that first item is linked to the other items in the collection. An object is also classified by the functions that may be performed on the items in the data collection. Each object data type has a set of specific functions that may be performed on that data.

Object Data Types vs. Abstract Data Types

Data types allow a computer program to operate on pieces of data differently depending on the intended use of each piece of data. Object and abstract data types both require some level of abstraction (i.e., both involve rules and operations that the user and developer do not directly observe or control). Most modern programming languages do not actually provide any real implementation of abstract data types. In fact, abstract data types are often considered more an academic concept than a real data type that can be implemented in code. Object data types, however, are implemented very frequently and are quite common in all modern programming languages.

Abstract Data Types

An **abstract data type**, or ADT, is a data type whose definition remains constant between different programming languages. In essence, when two or more programming languages use an ADT, they will have similar semantics for it. In other words, a few rules or implementation details regarding the data type may be different from language to language, but the overall concept of that data type will be the same, and the same operations will likely be available, and are even likely to be called the same thing. For example, one language may have an implementation of stacks that is slightly different from that in another language, but the stack will still be essentially the same data structure, and its associated operations, such as pushing and popping, will be available.

Common ADTs include stacks, queues, priority queues, strings, containers, lists, deques (double-ended queues), maps, multimaps, multisets, trees, and sets. ADTs are used to describe abstract algorithms in simple terms, assess data structures, categorize data structures, and provide formal descriptions for programming languages. Although they are mostly theoretical and conceptual constructs, ADTs do appear in formal specification language. They can be implemented in the form of modules that include procedures for ADT operation. As conceptual tools, ADTs are important in object-oriented programming languages.

Importance of Choosing the Correct Data Type

A computer can interpret what appears to be the same value very differently depending on what data type is used. Take for instance the value "14235" as a data type of integer. In this case, the value is treated as the number fourteen thousand two hundred thirty-five (14,235). A developer could perform mathematical operations on this value, such as addition or subtraction. Contrast this with the same value "14235" being represented as a string data type. In this case, the value would be treated as the characters one, four, two, three, and five. Mathematical operations could not be performed on this value. However, additional characters could be appended to the value, or some characters could be removed from the value. These are just a couple of examples of how a value that is read one way by humans can be read differently by computers according to its data type.

Variables

A **variable** is a single location in the computer's memory capable of storing one value. Variables are given names by the programmer, but the name is just a human-readable reference to a memory location. Such locations provide temporary storage for multiple types of data, including numbers and characters. Program algorithms will later take values for variables in as inputs, process them, and generate output. There are two broad classifications for variables:

- **Global variables**: These are considered "in scope" throughout the entire program, including in functions and subroutines. In other words, any statement anywhere in the program can make use of these variables.
- **Local variables**: These are considered "in scope" only in part of the program, such as a specific function or subroutine. Only statements in the function where the variable is in scope may use these variables. For instance, if an integer variable were declared in both an object and a function which is defined inside of the object, and the programmer referenced the variable from within the function, the local copy of the variable (that is, the copy within function) would be that which is resolved, as it shares a scope with the code being executed. Variables belonging to objects can be referenced outside of those objects by specifically naming the object to which they belong, as long as they are not defined as private. Variables defined inside of functions or subroutines only exist while the method is executing. They are thus always inaccessible from outside of the method.

Scope

The **scope** of a variable defines sections of a program in which the variable exists, can be used, or can be known to exist. Scopes can nest programming elements or be nested within programming elements, and contain various types of information, such as declarations, definitions of identifiers, and statements and expressions that define executable algorithms. The type of scope dictates program semantics, and the relationship between scope and semantics varies between programming languages. Scope also determines **information hiding**, which is the program's ability to "see" and access variables. Consider, for instance, a **namespace**, which is a type of scope that uses a single identifier to group several related identifiers logically. A variable declared within a procedure only exists within that procedure, and its scope is thus that procedure. Once the procedure has completed, the variable is destroyed. A variable that is a member of an object can share the same name as a variable that is a member of another object, as their scopes are different. For example, if ObjectA and ObjectB each have a variable named ObjName, from within ObjectA, ObjName will resolve only to ObjectA's version, and likewise for ObjectB. However, if outside the scope of either of these objects, one has to reference the object in order to reference the variable (e.g., ObjectA.ObjName). ObjName is thus a **member** of ObjectA, and is limited by the scope of its parent (ObjectA). This allows a program to be organized logically and for common names to be reused without conflict.

How Variables Operate

The concept of a variable is a very important one to understand in programming. Without variables, developing anything other than very simple, single-use programs would be very difficult. Variables can be thought of as containers for values. Variables are given names so they can be easily identified by the programmer. Imagine needing to add two numbers together and save the value for later use. You have no way of knowing what the sum will be until the program runs. Using a variable, you can store the sum and refer to it later in the code—and even name the variable `sum` to indicate what it contains. The value of `sum` may be different each time the program runs, but the program will still perform the same operations each time. Think of variables like containers into which values can be placed. When programs can be written to use these containers rather than constant values, programs can be used again and again without the need to manually change values in the code.

Constants vs. Variables

The difference between a variable and a constant is fairly straightforward. A variable is a placeholder for a value that can change at any time. Variables may change many times as a program runs. Constants, however, cannot change once they are established. A constant retains its original value throughout the entire running of the program. There are some cases where a constant is necessary because the developer may need to use a value that should never change. By using a constant, the developer can ensure that the value will stay the same throughout the entire program. In most programming, variables are used much more frequently than constants.

Lists

A **list** may sound simple in theory, but it can become quite complicated in its implementation. A list is a sequential grouping of data items that are all linked together. The specific details of the linking depend upon which type of list is being implemented. One of the most common implementations is a single **linked list**. In this type of list, each element within the list contains that element's value, as well as a **pointer** to the location of the next item in the list. There are a number of operations that can be performed on lists, although they are not detailed here. Because lists can grow quite large, and because each item points to the memory location of the next item, a list is considered a reference data type.

Common Types of Lists

A list is a basic abstract data structure that arranges data entries sequentially. The first entry in a list is called the **head**, and the entry at the end is called the **tail**. Data in lists can generally be searched, rearranged, and changed. There are two basic types of lists: stacks and queues.

Stacks

One of the most common and simple abstract data types is a **stack**. Its name comes from the idea of a stack of trays, which serves as a metaphor for data retrieval. Each tray represents a data element. The last data saved is like a tray that is added to the stack at the top. Because it is added at the top, it will be the first tray taken off the stack when the time comes. Likewise, the last piece of data **pushed** onto the stack will be the first data returned (or **popped**) when the computer retrieves information from the stack. Stacks are known as "last in, first out" (**LIFO**) structures. Stack abstract data types perform two primary operations:

- **Push**: occurs when a new data element is added to the stack
- **Pop**: occurs when the computer retrieves the data that was saved most recently

Stacks can include any data type, including strings, integers, real numbers, pointers, and even other stacks. Because the operations of a stack are the same regardless of the programming language being used, it is considered an abstract data type.

In many cases, stacks provide the underlying structure for backtracking programs, which retrieve instructions in an order that is the reverse of the order in which they were entered. An example of backtracking is recursion. Recursion has many uses, but in one example, it could provide an "undo" operation, using a stack of executed commands, with the most recently executed instruction at the top. With this stack and a recursive algorithm, the commands could be undone in reverse order.

Queues

A **queue** is one of the most common abstract data types. It functions like a checkout line: The first person in the line will be the first person to leave the line. Likewise, in a queue retrieval system, the computer returns the first data element that was entered into the system. Consequently, a queue is known as a "first in, first out" (**FIFO**) structure. A queue performs the same two operations (push and pop) as a stack abstract data type (only with the pop function taking from the other end of the stack).The verb associated with entering data into a queue is "to enqueue." Similarly, that which pertains to the process of taking data out of the queue is "to dequeue." In many cases, queues provide the underlying structures for buffers, which store data temporarily for transfer between two locations.

ARRAYS

An **array** is a type of data structure. It contains elements that are identified using two features: the name of the array and the element's location within the array. Arrays can have any number of dimensions. The following is an example of an array with a single dimension:

```
int[] numberList ← {3,7,5,1}
```

The elements contained within this array are 3, 7, 5, and 1. If the system were asked to access one of them, it would identify both the name of the array, `numberList`, and the single integer that corresponds to the element's location. The location is identified with an index value, which in most cases starts with 0 and counts up for each member. By this system, the first member of the array `numberList` would be referred to as `numberList[0]`. As you can see, the other values are `numberList[1]`, which contains the value 7, `numberlist[2]`, which contains the value 5, and `numberList[3]`, which contains the value 1.

ARRAY ELEMENTS

All **elements** inside an array should be of the same data type due to the way that the computer stores an array in memory. Elements of the same data type each require the same amount of memory for storage, and this is critical to the storage and indexing of the array as a whole. When an array is stored in memory, the thing that is actually stored to represent the array is the memory address of the first item in the array. The system then allocates a specified amount of memory based on the size of the array and the data type of its members. For instance, consider an array of five integers, with each integer requiring four bytes of storage. The first item (element 0) in the array may be stored at memory address 2000, and the system would automatically place elements 1 through 4 in addresses 2004, 2008, 2012, and 2016. With each element requiring the same amount of memory, the computer can determine exactly where in memory any item in the array is located. If the members have different data types, therefore, the process is more complicated, as it cannot be assumed that the space allocated for each member will be equal, and the memory address for any given element would be unpredictable.

ONE-DIMENSIONAL ARRAYS VS. MULTIDIMENSIONAL ARRAYS

A **one-dimensional** array is essentially a list in that it is just a series of similar data items constituting an array structure. **Multidimensional arrays**, however, are more like a list of lists; they have what can be thought of as rows and columns—two "dimensions." An array of this type may be referred to as a "table" or a "matrix." In order to reference a datapoint in a multidimensional array, the programmer needs an index value for each dimension—not just the one index value needed when dealing with a one-dimensional array. Consider the examples below.

2	4	6	8	10	12	14

If the above array were an int array called `list`, we could refer to the first number in the array with the term `list[0]`. The value stored in `list[0]` is the integer 2. We need only one index value because this array is one-dimensional.

A multidimensional array is a similar structure. However, for each additional dimension, another index value is needed to reference a specific datapoint. In the example below, two index values would be needed, because there are two dimensions:

2	4	6	8	10	12	14
4	6	8	10	12	14	16
6	8	10	12	14	16	18

If the above array were an int array called `table`, and if we are using a programming language in which the row index is written first, we could refer to the last value in the second row with the term `table[1][6]`. The value stored in `table[1][6]` is the integer 16.

For more dimensions, we would need more index values. In many programming languages it is possible to have a large number of dimensions in an array, but one-, two-, and three-dimensional arrays are most common.

Row-Major Order vs. Column-Major Order

Remember that a two-dimensional array looks like a matrix or a table. It has rows and columns. **Row-major order** and **column-major order** are two different techniques for storing the values of the array in memory. Programming languages handle this differently. If a language uses row-major order, the items in each row are stored consecutively, beginning at the first row. When the end of the first row is reached, the elements in the next row would then be stored, and so on. On the other hand, in column-major order, the contents of the first column are stored first, beginning from the top of the initial column. When the bottom of the first column is reached, the next column would then be stored, and so on. See the examples below for what the memory space may look like based on different ordering systems.

Sample array:

1	2	3	4
5	6	7	8
9	10	11	12

The series of memory addresses where the array is stored, if row-major order is used:

1	2	3	4	5	6	7	8	9	10	11	12

The series of memory addresses where the array is stored, if column-major order is used:

1	5	9	2	6	10	3	7	11	4	8	12

Multidimensional Arrays

A **multidimensional array** is a data structure that is also considered an array but is more complex than an array that has only one dimension, or one index counter. When a system accesses elements in a multidimensional array, it identifies them using the array name and an index for each dimension. Consider the following multidimensional array:

```
int[][] numberTable ← {
    {1, 4, 8}
    {3, 7, 5}
    {2, 9, 0}
}
```

The elements contained within the array are 1, 4, 8, 3, 7, 5, 2, 9, and 0. If the system were asked to access one of them, it would identify both the array name, `numberTable`, and the two indices that correspond to the element's location. The first index is the row of the data element, and the second index is the column of data element. (In real life, we would need to know that the programming language we were working in followed this common convention.) Both indices count the members upward from 0. For instance, `numberTable[1][0]` identifies the 3 data element. Other elements include `numberTable[0][1]`, which is 4, and `numberTable[2][1]`, which is 9.

Homogenous Arrays

A **homogenous array** is a common type of abstract data structure in which all data must be the same data type (int, float, char, etc.). It can store a block of variables in either a one-dimensional list or a multidimensional array consisting of rows and columns. The program must declare the dimensions of the array. Consider the following example:

```
char Letters[][]
```

The above array is identified by the variable `Letters`. It will have four rows and five columns, and contain values of the char data type. Any time during the program's execution, code can refer to the array using its name or to a specific data element using the array's name along with an index or indices. An **index** is an integer value that identifies the position of a single element in the array. For instance, in FORTRAN language, the reference `Letter[1][1]` would identify the entry corresponding to the first row and first column. A programming language using the integer 1 to refer to the first element in an array is known as one-based indexing. In C, the same entry would be identified as `Letter[0][0]` because, in C, indices start at 0 rather than 1—zero-based indexing.

Heterogeneous Arrays

A **heterogeneous array** is a common type of abstract data structure capable of storing different data types. Consider, for instance, a set of information containing the name of a product, its price, and the number of product units sold. This information could be stored in the following array:

```
String ProductName ← "Book IV"
float Price ← 29.95
int UnitsSold ← 2318
Object[] Params
Params[0] ← ProductName
Params[1] ← Price
Params[2] ← UnitsSold
```

`Object[]` declares a dynamic array named `Params`. In this case, it consists of three components: `ProductName`, which is a char data type; `Price`, which is a float data type; and `UnitsSold`, which is an int data type. The program can refer to the entire array using its name or to parts of the array using the array name, a period, and the component's name. An example of such a reference is `Product.UnitsSold`, which would evaluate to 2318.

Storing Data in Arrays vs. Variables

Using an array for data storage and manipulation has many advantages over using simple variables. First, the programmer can create many variables with one declaration statement instead of painstakingly declaring each variable individually. Second, passing data to methods is much easier when you must pass only one array of values rather than many individual values in separate variables. In this case, the array could also have any amount of data, and this amount would not have to be specified in the method header. Lastly, using a loop and an array is an easy and efficient way to move through data values, because it requires only a small amount of code. If the same data were contained in simple variables, loops could not be used as simply as with arrays, where the index value will change from one data item to the next.

Data Structures

A **data structure** contains a number of related variables. Using data structures, systems can process multiple variables at once. This ability is very useful when handling large amounts of data, such as customer lists, inventory lists, etc. A data structure would allow all this data to be grouped so that they can be processed efficiently. Procedural programming languages can handle a limited number of advanced data structures. Database systems can support the most advanced data structures.

One type of data structure is an array. It stores data in a list, where it can be accessed easily. Generally, an array contains values of only one data type. Procedural languages (such as C, FORTRAN, and COBOL) and object-oriented programming languages (such as C++ and Java) both make extensive use of arrays.

A data structure stores multiple related variables using a conceptual arrangement. Consider, for example, a day planner, which arranges information in a conceptual way. It consists of tables with rows and columns. Each page has a column to represent the day, and each row may represent an hour of the day. The entries in each table would list the activities planned for the corresponding day and time. Another example of a conceptual arrangement of data is a technical manual, which is divided into chapters, headings, subheadings, paragraphs, and sentences. Using data structures, systems can group variables together in a structure that corresponds to a real-life entity—a useful ability when a system must keep track of large amounts of data, such every loyal shopper at a large retail store chain, every subject in a global study, or every item in a national system of warehouses and shipping vehicles. Types of data structures include lists, stacks, queues, trees, and arrays. Procedural languages such as FORTRAN and COBOL support a limited number of advanced data structures. Object-oriented languages such as C++ can handle a vast assortment of data structures, including custom classes and objects that reflect a specific real-life object or system of objects.

Records

A **record** is one of the simplest data structures. It contains one or more data elements and stores them in sequential positions in the computer's memory. In many cases, these elements are of completely different data types (i.e., integers, real numbers, strings, or any other type of value). A record consists of a name and different fields. Each field holds a data element. For example, a record might store information on a house. Each field within the record would contain a different characteristic of the house—square footage, dimensions, lot size, cost, street address, construction, names of owners, and any other pertinent information. Expressing these elements requires different data types, both numeric and textual. While records are a data structure in programming, they are also the building blocks of databases.

Integer Data Types

An integer data types, or **int**, contains a whole number. Using ints, programs can perform traditional arithmetic operations, such as addition and subtraction, and comparisons, such as less than, greater than, or equal to. In most cases, integer data is stored in **two's complement notation**, which allows efficient math on signed values (that is, values that are either positive or negative). Consider the following example:

```
int MaxOccupancy ← 300
```

This statement declares and initializes the variable: `int` specified a new variable of the integer data type, `MaxOccupancy` specifies the name of the variable, and `← 300` assigns the integer 300 as the value contained in the variable.

Real Data Types

Real data types are more often known simply as **floats** (short for "floating-point numbers") or **doubles** (referring to double-precision—the ability to store a wider range of floating-point numbers). These may contain numeric data other than whole numbers. They are stored in a floating-point notation. Real data types can be used in the same operations as integer data types, even though the actual methods of performing these operations will be different. Consider the following example:

```
float Length, Width, SquareFeet
Length ← 27.5
Width ← 18.4
SquareFeet ← Length * Width
```

In the above code, `float` declares a floating-point number variable, or real number variable. `Length`, `Width`, and `SquareFeet` are the names of the variables being declared. Often, multiple variables of the same data type can be declared in one statement. Two floating-point values are assigned to these variables, 27.5 to `Length`, and 18.4 to `Width`. `SquareFeet` is then assigned the value that the `*` operator will return when it multiplies the floats `Length` and `Width`. Even though the value will be a whole number, 506, it will actually be stored in memory as a float, because at least one of the two operands (`Length` and `Width`) was a float. It may not be obvious, but the operation called by the `*` operator in this case is different from the operation that the same operator would call if `Length` and `Width` were integers.

CHARACTER AND BOOLEAN DATA TYPES

Character data types, often call **chars**, store combinations of numbers that map to actual characters (pieces of text). The system by which a program determines which character matches which numeric code is called **character encoding**. The most common encoding standard today is **Unicode**, while **ASCII** (American Standard Code for Information Interchange) remains familiar despite its limitation to Latin characters.

Chars can be used in the following operations, among others: comparing symbols to determine their correct alphabetical sequence; creating one long string of symbols by combining multiple, shorter strings of symbols; and determining the presence of one string of symbols inside another string. Below is a simple example of char declarations and assignments:

```
char Vowel, Consonant
Vowel ← 'a'
Consonant ← 't'
```

In the above example, `char` declares the variables, which are named `Vowel` and `Consonsant`. Note that single quotes are used for the single characters assigned to the variables. In programming, often single quotation marks set off single characters, while double quotation marks set off strings—a different data type.

Boolean data types take their name from Boolean algebra, a system of logic defined by logician George Boole. Often referred to simply as **bools**, these data types can store only two values: true, represented in binary by a 1, or false, represented in binary by a 0. Therefore these data types require only one bit of storage. Many control structures and decision statements make use of bools, such as loops and if statements. Consider the following example:

```
bool hungry ← true
if( hungry )
   eat()
end if
```

In the above example, `bool` declares a Boolean variable named `hungry`, which is initialized with a value of `true`, or `1`. While if statements often use relational expressions that return a bool (for example, `x < 10`, which will return `true` or `1` when `x` is less than 10), they can also have a simple Boolean variable as their condition. In this case, `hungry` holds the value `true`, so the code block containing `eat()` will be executed.

Trees

A tree is a hierarchical abstract data structure that consists of **nodes**. The top node is known as the root node, while bottom nodes are known as terminal nodes, or leaf nodes. Consider the following example:

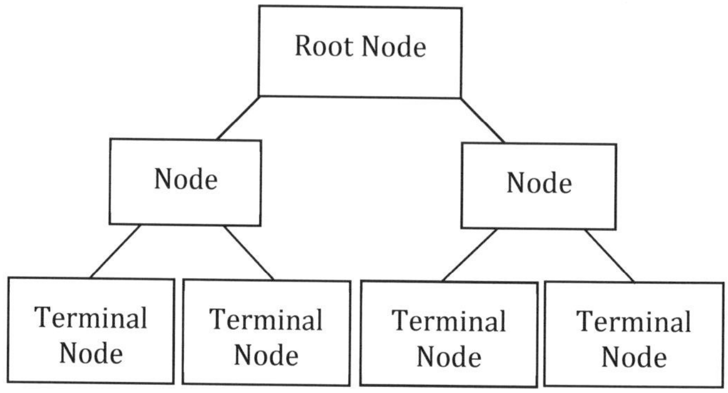

Nodes cannot be connected to more than one higher-level node. The depth of a **tree** is its total number of horizontal layers. In a binary tree, no node will have more than two descendants. A node's descendents are known as its "children." A node's ancestors nodes are known as its "parents." If we isolate one parent and its children, we have a subtree from the main tree.

Static vs. Dynamic Abstract Data Structures

Abstract data structures fall under two main categories:

- **Static structures** do not change in size or shape over time. Consider, for instance, a list of people born in a specific year. If the list is complete, it will neither increase nor decrease. The number will remain the same. Static structures are easier to maintain than dynamic structures because they only require a method of accessing data and changing data at a set location in memory, because no members need to be moved, removed, or added.
- **Dynamic structures** can change in size and shape over time. Consider a list of names of people who belong to a certain organization. As the organizaiton's membership increases or decreases, the list must change in size. Dynamic structures can be difficult to maintain because they require a method of adding or removing entries and acquiring more memory space if the structure grows.

Implementation Strategies

For One-Dimensional Homogenous Arrays

One-dimensional homogenous arrays are ideal for storing sequences of data because they store data elements in consecutive memory cells. Consider the following example, which stores weekly weight measurements:

```
int[] Weight
```

The above declaration statement establishes a one-dimensional homogenous array referred to as `Weight`. It contains integer data types and consists of consecutive memory cells. If the address of the first entry in the array is `x`, the address of the other entries in the array can found easily because their position is sequential starting with `x`. For instance, the fifth entry in `Weight` would be located at the following address:

```
x + (5 - 1)
```

In other words, assuming that each member of the array occupies one memory address, a person could find the location of any array element by adding its zero-based index (hence the subtraction of 1) to the address of the beginning of the array.

FOR TWO-DIMENSIONAL HOMOGENOUS ARRAYS

Two-dimensional homogenous arrays are ideal for tables of information. They come in two varieties: **row-major order**, which stores data row by row in the computer's memory, and **column-major order**, which stores data column by column in the computer's memory. Consider the following example—a two-dimensional array that contains the weekly weight measurements of multiple people:

```
int[][] Weight
```

The above declaration statement establishes a two-dimensional homogenous array referred to as `Weight`. It contains int data types and consists of rows and columns. The entry in which the first row intersects the first column has the address of `x`. Assuming row-major order, a specific entry in the array could be located using the following formula:

```
x  +  (c * ( i - 1 ))  +  (j - 1)
```

In the above formula, `x` represents the address of the first element in the first column, `c` is the number of columns in the array, `i` is the row containing the desired entry, and `j` is the column containing the desired entry. The expression `(c * ( i - 1 ))`, by multiplying the row index and the number of columns, "skips" the memory addresses for all the rows before the desired row. Then the expression `(j - 1)`, which will evaluate to the row index, adds the appropriate number of addresses.

FOR HETEROGENEOUS ARRAYS

Consider the following fixed heterogeneous array, which contains the name of each product, its price, and the number sold:

```
struct Product {
char[] ProductName
float Price
   int UnitsSold
}
product[5]
```

The array consists of five sets of ten contiguous memory spaces. In each set, the first eight spaces contain character data types that identify the product's name. The ninth cell contains a float data type identifying the product's price. Finally, the tenth cell contains an integer data type identifying the number sold. Counting memory addresses here is more difficult than in homogeneous arrays, as each data type will occupy a different amount of memory. The char data type usually uses one byte, the float data type usually uses four, and the int data type usually uses four as well. Thus, each element of `Product` will use (8 * 1) + 4 + 4 = 16 bytes, and the entire array will therefore use 16 * 5 = 80 bytes.

To change the entry in `Price`, we would input the following statement:

```
product.Price ← 5.50
```

Note that we use a lowercase *p*, indicating that we are referring to the object `product`, which is an instance of the struct Product. In this example, the code is case-sensitive, and it is important to remember to use the instance of a class or type and not the class itself, unless it is defined as static. Using a lowercase first letter to indicate an instance of a class with the same name is a feature of the very common object-oriented programming language C++.

In non-managed languages, dynamic heterogeneous arrays are best created using pointers, which allow for memory management methods to be performed.

For Lists

A **contiguous list** is the best technique for storing static lists of names. It consists of a large block of memory cells, which are divided into groups to form subblocks. Each subblock stores a name on the list. For instance, 200 consecutive memory cells would be allocated for a contiguous list to accommodate 20 subblocks of 10 cells apiece. If a name on this list does not use the entire allotment of 10 cells, the empty cells are typically still filled, but not with spaces or nonprintable characters.

A **linked list** is the best technique for storing dynamic lists. It relies on pointers, which enable each item on the list to point to the location of another item on the list, though the two items could be in very different locations in memory. This allows the data to be stored in various locations and linked together, instead of being stored on a large block of consecutive memory addresses. A program can therefore add information to the list without the risk of exceeding the capacity of a single, large block. Different languages handle the structure of linked lists differently, but a common set of characteristics includes each element in the list containing both a data field and a pointer field, where the pointer fields include pointers to the next (and sometimes also the previous) element. Linked lists may contain sentinel nodes, which demarcate the first and last elements in a list, or they could include null pointers to indicate that no node succeeds or precedes the current one.

For Stacks

When creating a stack, a programmer must allocate a memory block with sufficient space to hold the stack at its largest size. The first entry in the stack will form the base end. Additional entries are inserted by being stacked on top of the base entry. The top of the stack will change locations as the program pushes and pops entries; consequently, the address of the top must be marked by a **stack pointer**, which is stored in an additional memory cell. When a new entry is pushed onto the stack, the pointer will be pointing to the vacant location immediately above the most recently added entry. The new entry will be placed at this location. When an entry is popped out of the stack, the pointer will be pointing to the location immediately above the removed entry that is to be removed.

For Queues

When creating a queue, a programmer must allocate a memory block with sufficient space to hold the queue at its largest size. Information is pushed into the queue at the tail and popped out at the head. Consequently, there must be two pointers—a head pointer and a tail pointer—to track activity at both ends. The **tail pointer** always points to the first vacant location at the tail, and the **head pointer** always points to the first filled entry at the head. When the head and tail pointers are pointing at the same location, the queue is empty. In order to prevent the queue from crawling through the computer's memory, the programmer may implement a **circular queue**, which uses the vacated spaces at the head when adding an entry to the tail, thereby allowing the queue to loop through the same locations in memory.

For Binary Trees

In a binary tree, a parent node cannot have more than two child nodes. When stored in the computer's memory, binary trees usually rely on a linked structure with pointers. Each node counts as a single entry, and consists of three parts:

- Data contained in the node
- A **left child pointer** that points to the node's first child
- A **right child pointer** that points to the node's second child

The nodes at the bottom of the tree must use null pointers to indicate there are no additional nodes, and the node at the very top of the tree must be identified by **a root pointer**.

Binary trees are sometimes stored as a single block of contiguous memory cells in an ahnentafel list—a method borrowed from genealogy—rather than a linked structure. In such a list, the root node is followed by both its children—left then right—after which are the left child's two children and then the right child's two children. This pattern continues until the tree is finished. As one might notice, this is most efficient for complete trees.

Literals

A **literal** is a preset, unchanging value used by programs. Literals are set to a value directly instead of being assigned a variable. Consider, for instance, writing an error message in an application. The error message is triggered when a user attempts to enter text in a locked field. The developer might write a method for this error message as follows:

```
MessageBox("Entry is not allowed in field " + field1)
```

In this example, the literal is enclosed in quotation marks (the common method for denoting a string literal), and a variable is appended to the end. There would be no reason to assign the literal value to a variable, as the message will never need to be different, while the information that changes is derived from the value of `field1`.

Literals are problematic in programming for two reasons:

- They can be difficult to interpret and troubleshoot at a later date. This especially true of numeric values.
- They can be difficult to locate and alter in the program.

Constants

A **constant** is a name that describes an unchanging value. While variables provide a way to assign human-readable names to values that can be changed during the program, constants provide a way to assign human-readable names to values that will not change during the program. Constants remedy problems associated with literals, especially the difficulties of locating and changing literals. Consider the following declarative statements that establishes a constant:

```
const String c_companyName ← "Davis Company"
```

This statement assigns the name `c_companyName` to the value "Davis Company." Since the name of this company is not going to change while the program is running, to is helpful to have it readily accessible as a constant. In any place where the company name is needed, it is easy to include in a string of text:

```
String sGreeting ← "Welcome to " + c_companyName + " !"
```

As the company's name is a constant value that is not expected to change at runtime, and it is likely to be referenced in many places, it makes sense to store it as a constant and place it in a global utility namespace for easy use throughout the program. This way, if the company were to change its name, a developer would only need to change the value of the constant `c_companyName`. Note that the main difference between a constant and a variable is that the constant, once initialized and assigned a value, cannot be changed by the program.

Type Conversion

Type conversion is the process of converting one data type to another. This is important mainly because of how computers store data. When a user enters information, it is common for programs to take it in as a string. However, if the information the user is entering is numerical data, there may be some need to do some calculations using this data, depending on the purpose of the program. Strings cannot be used in calculations the same way that integers and floats can. For example, if the string "6" is added to the string "4" using a plus sign, in most languages, the result will not be 10 but instead "64" because the plus operator will concatenate the two strings. If we want to add 6 and 4 mathematically, we must be working with values that are stored as numbers, not as text numerals. Since many inputs will be as text, but many calculations will need to be done using numbers, it is very helpful to have a built-in way to convert text to numbers and numbers to text. The same goes for conversion from an integer to a real number. If we try dividing 10 by 4 in code, since both numbers are integers, we will get 2 instead of 2.5. Dividing 10.0 by 4.0, on the other hand, will yield the answer that we understand as correct, 2.5. Because many built-in operations work differently when they are given different data types, the ability to convert one data type into another is an integral part of performing calculations correctly in programming.

CASTING BETWEEN DATA TYPES

Casting between data types is used when a programmer needs to either increase or decrease the functionality of an object. For example, in many programming languages, when you divide an integer value by another integer value, the answer will be returned as an integer. This often results in a loss of precision because a calculation such as 5 divided by 2 would yield a 2 rather than a 2.5 due to integer division. By casting one of the values, either the 5 or the 2, to a decimal before the calculation, we increase the functionality of the variable, allowing decimal division to be completed.

CODE EXAMPLES

EXAMPLE 1

Trace the following code and give the answer:

```
float ans ← ( 7 / 3 ) + ( 6 / 12.0 ) - ( 6 % 4 )
```

This code will follow the rules of order of operations. First, `7 / 3` will occur. Because these numbers are both integers, integer division will occur, truncating any decimal values, leaving us with 2. Next, `6 / 12.0` will be performed, but as floating-point division, because at least one of the values is a floating-point number. This results in a value of 0.5. Lastly, `6 % 4` returns the remainder after dividing 6 by 4, which is 2. Therefore, we have 2 + 0.5 − 2, giving us 0.5 as the value of `ans`, which is a float data type, capable of storing a floating-point number.

EXAMPLE 2

What numerical input for the integer variable x will result in the capital letter C being printed on the screen, assuming ASCII character codes?

```
char MyChar ← x
print x
```

When you declare and initialize a character variable, the data stored is a numerical code for a character, not the character itself. Characters are often declared using the character in single quotes, because the single quotes signal to the computer that the character should be stored as the corresponding numeric code. For example, the capital letter A would be represented as `'A'`. The most basic system for encoding characters is ASCII (American Standard Code for Information Interchange). In ASCII, each character of the Roman alphabet, each numeral, and several other characters each have a numeric code.

Therefore, when you declare a char variable and initialize it with a number value, like `x` in the above code, and notably not a letter in single quotes, the computer will interpret this number as a character code. Because the data type is char, the computer will simply represent the value as the corresponding letter, even though the value in memory is really a number. In ASCII, the capital letter *A* is 65. The other capital letters follow in alphabetical order; *B* is 66, *C* is 67, *D* is 68, and so on. Knowing this about ASCII, we will also know that "C" will be printed if the value of `x` is 67.

EXAMPLE 3

Write code to divide 13 by 5 and give the answer as a whole number and a remainder.

In order to get the whole number portion of a number as well as the remainder, we will need to perform two calculations on these numbers. First, we must use integer division to get the whole number. If you use the division operator with two variables of int data type, it will return only the whole number result and ignore any remainder. Next, we need to get the remainder that was ignored during the integer division. To do so, we must use the modulo operator. Rather than returning the whole number and ignoring the remainder, this operator returns the remainder and ignores the whole number. Once we have both these values, we can display each number individually.

```
int whole ← 13 / 5                //integer division
int remainder ← 13 % 5            //modulo division
print "The answer is " + whole + " with a remainder of " + remainder
```

This will result in the following text being printed (assuming the `print` function or the plus operator will convert the integer values to text):

```
The answer is 2 with a remainder of 3
```

EXAMPLE 4

What is wrong with the statement below, and how could it be fixed?

```
int total ← 4.7 * 2
```

In this example, `4.7 * 2` will give the answer 9.2. Since this is a floating-point number, we are unable to store it directly in the `total` variable, because it is defined as an integer. In many languages, this statement would not compile, because compilers themselves are written to assume we want an integer to be stored in variables of the integer data type. The only way we can store this value is by adding some type of operation to convert the result of the multiplication into an integer. We can do this in a few ways. We could simply truncate the number by removing the decimal point and the digit after it. We could also use a math function to round down to 9. Still another option would be to use a type conversion function to convert the answer to an integer before storing it in the variable `total`. Programming languages and development environments will vary in how they interpret a statement like the one above, how they alert the developer to this issue, and what built-in functions they provide to allow the developer to fix the problem.

EXAMPLE 5

Write an equivalent statement using a loop to simulate the modulo operator.

In module division, we can forget entirely about the actual quotient—or number of times that the divisor "goes into" the dividend. We only need to find the remainder, and it is not overly complicated to develop a loop that does this. One possibility is the following:

```
int modulo(int dividend, int divisor)
   while( dividend > divisor )
      dividend ← dividend - divisor
   end while
   return dividend
end modulo
```

This code uses repeated subtraction to continually reduce the dividend by the divisor. Once `dividend` is no longer greater than `divisor`, we know that the divisor cannot "go into" `dividend` one whole time, so the new value of `dividend` must be the remainder. This is the value that the function returns.

Integer vs. Floating-Point Data Types

An integer is a data type that can only store a number that does not contain a decimal point. The number can be negative or zero, but it cannot contain a fraction, a decimal point, or any digits to the right of the decimal point. Examples of integers are −45, 0, and 32. You might use an integer to give someone's age in years, or to count how many items you have purchased from a store. A floating-point number, or float, is a data type that stores numbers with a decimal point and up to a certain number of significant digits. Examples of floating-point numbers are −20.45, 4.0, 0.0, and 3.14159. You might use a floating-point number to calculate a grade point average or doing calculations with numbers that contain fractional values, such as pi. Many students ask why we can't just use a floating-point number for everything, since it can store whole numbers as well as numbers with fractions. The answer is that floating-point numbers usually take up more space in memory and are harder for the computer to calculate with. In fact, when you store a whole number as a float, the number that is stored is of the same precision as any other float; in other words, the whole number 3 would be stored not as 3 but as 3.000000. Therefore, when possible, we use the integer data type when we do not need the precision of a float.

Efficiency of Using Boolean Data Type vs. Using a String

The first advantage of using a Boolean data type instead of a string data type for a value that can be "yes" or "no" is that Booleans take up minimal space in memory. Because a Boolean variable can contain only two possible values, it needs only one bit of memory—though in many languages, the minimum allocation for any variable is one byte. A string can be much larger, and storing the actual text "yes", "no", "true", or "false" would certainly take more than one byte. The exact difference between the space used by the two types will depend on the programming language being used, but generally, a Boolean takes up less space.

The second advantage of using a Boolean data type is that, when they are used in if statements, since there are only two possibilities, an else statement can be readily used, rather than testing for other cases. For example:

```
if( raining == true )
   print "Bring an umbrella."
else
   print "Don't bring an umbrella."
end if
```

Because the above Boolean `raining` has only two possible values, we only have to check if it is true, and we can use an else statement to handle the only other case—that `raining` is false. If we had instead used a string in this situation, we would have to check if `raining` contained "yes", then check if `raining` contained "no", and finally add an else statement to check for any other possibility that wasn't expected.

Code Example

Imagine a program to run a vending machine that only accepts bills (no coins), contains items that can be any price, and gives the appropriate amount of change for each transaction. This particular vending machine contains only peanuts and cashews. Identify the variable types that would be best to use for the number of bills, the item price, the type of item, and the change.

The variable for the number of bills should be an integer because the machine only accepts bills and no decimal point is needed when counting whole bills. The variable for the prices of the items should be a floating-point number, because the prices could be any dollar amount, not only whole dollars. A variable for item type could be a string for a typical vending machine. But in this case, it would be more efficient to use a Boolean, as there are only two items available. If the vending machine had the ability to hold more than two items, a data type with more than two possible values would be necessary. Lastly, the change that is given should be a floating-point number, because, like the prices of the items, the change for a transaction may not be a whole dollar amount.

Concatenation

Concatenation is the process of combining two strings together to form a new string. The most common concatenation operator is the plus symbol, but it can vary from one programming language to another.

Code Example

A program stores the first name "John" in `fName`*, the last name "Kennedy" in* `lName`*, and the middle initial "F" in* `mInitial`*. Write code to concatenate these variables so that a string named* `fullName` *contains the string "Kennedy, John F."*

The solution to this question lies in ordering our variables correctly (so that the last name is first), along with adding the necessary spaces, the comma after the last name, and the period after the middle initial.

```
String fullName ← lName + ", " + fName + " " + mInitial + "."
```

This code would result in the correct concatenation being stored in `fullName`. Notice the use of the literal space and comma characters. Without including those, the pieces of the text would be mashed together, resulting in an incorrect format. These characters must also be enclosed in double quotes to denote that they are literal strings. The variable names must not have quotes around them, because the values of the variables are needed. If they had quotes around them, the concatenation operators would interpret them as literal strings, so the names of the variables would be the text used. The result would be "lName, fName mInitial."

Writing and Calling Procedures

Procedures

A **procedure** is a set of instructions that carry out a certain function. By including all the steps of a function in a single procedure, developers are able repeat common tasks with a single call of this procedure, rather than needing to enter the steps again and again. Furthermore, if a task needs to be done differently, and that task has an associated procedure, the change need only be made in one place, rather than in every part of the code that performs the task. For instance, if a program needed to set a piece of data in a database, the developer could write code that connects to the database each time the data is to be set, sets the data, and closes the connection. What if the databases's name or connection information changed? Without a procedure, the developer would have to find all the places where the program code accesses the database—which could be hundreds or thousands of places. Because this would be impracticable, a procedure that sets the data would likely be made, and this procedure could be called whenever a piece of data is to be set. Then the developer would be able to make any necessary changes only once, in this procedure, saving countless hours of time and potentially many errors.

A procedure always has a name, which is written in the code when the procedure is called. This name is set when the procedure is defined. A procedure can be written to accept certain data that it will need to perform its function; these are called **parameters**. The actual values that are passed to the procedure through these parameters are called **arguments**. Procedures give control back to the main part of the program when they return a value.

If data is needed from the procedure, the type of data is often used to define the procedure. For example, a procedure that finds the lowest integer in a list would likely return the integer, so it might be defined `int GetLowest( list[] )`. This data is returned to the main part of the program when the procedure ends.

On the other hand, if (as in our original database example), no data is needed from the procedure, it can be written to return a value such as zero to signifying that it ran successfully. The declaring statement for such a procedure might be `void SetData( FieldName, FieldData )`, with "void" meaning that no value will be returned.

See the following pseudocode of our database example:

```
/* open() and close() are procedures that connect to and disconnect
from (respectively) a given database */

void SetData( FieldName, FieldData)
   open( database1 )
   FieldName ← FieldData
   close( database1 )
end SetData
```

In this example, `SetData` is the procedure's name, and `DBName`, `FieldName`, and `FieldData` are parameters, which allowing any data to be passed to the procedure. Anywhere in the code, a developer could set the CustomerCount field in the database to the integer 15,000 by writing the following:

```
SetData( CustomerCount, 15000 )
```

If the information needed to connect to the database should ever change, now only `SetData` needs to be modified.

Code Example

A method named `getLowest` *accepts a list of integers as well as the number of integers in that list and returns the lowest number in the list. Write the method, and then code to use this method to find the lowest number in each of the three lists below. Display the sum of those numbers and store it in a variable named* `sum`*.*
List 1: 3, 6, 5
List 2: 4, 1
List 3: 5, 4, 9, 6

The method can use a variable called `lowest` to hold the lowest value in the list. First, the method sets the first value in the list as `lowest`. Then, a for loop will step through each value of the list. Finally, an if statement inside the for loop can reassign the current value as `lowest` if it is less than the value already contained in `lowest`. This method could be written as follows:

```
int getLowest(int[] list, int size)
   int lowest ← list[0]
   for( int i ← 0; i < size; i ← i + 1 )
      if( list[i] < lowest )
         lowest ← list[i]
      end if
   end for
end getLowest
```

Once the method is written, calling the method for each of the three lists and storing the summed result in an int variable is straightforward:

```
int sum ← getLowest( list1, 3 ) + getLowest( list2, 2 ) +
    getLowest( list3, 4 )
```

Creating User-Defined Functions

The exact process and syntax for creating a user-defined function varies among programming languages. However, the high-level process is generally the same. First, the developer must create a name for the function. Keywords of the language cannot be used, nor can the names of any predefined functions. In most cases, the name must start with a letter and can only contain letters and numbers. In most languages, the developer will also need to determine what the data type of the output will be, because this information will be part of the function declaration statement. Next, the developer must specify the number and types of inputs that need to be provided to the function. For example, does the function need a single string as an input, or does it require four integers? After the inputs have been specified, the developer will write the function code. This is where the work is performed and the inputs are used to produce an output. The final step is generally return the output to the main function. Some languages include a "success" value that can be returned by functions that do not have an output, while others may allow functions to simply end, and still others may specify that an otherwise normal value will signify success when it is returned by a function.

Reasons for Creating User-Defined Functions

Typically, a developer creates a user-defined function because the functionality that is needed is not included in a predefined function of the language. In many cases, a developer does this when they also see a need to reuse the custom functionality over and over again. It is generally not worth the extra effort to create a user-defined function if the functionality is only needed once. In that case, the developer only needs to create the functionality once in the main program. However, it is more often the case that a program needs some procedure to before performed multiple times. It is these cases where user-defined functions are very useful. The developer also has strict control over the inputs and outputs of any user-defined functions they create.

Using and Calling User-Defined Functions

User-defined functions are generally called in the same way that predefined functions are called. The specific syntax required varies from language to language, but the calling of the function is done using the name of the function along with the inputs. The function itself specifies the number and types of inputs that should be provided. Once the function is called, then control over the processing is passed from the main program to the function. The function performs its specified action, and then passes the result and processing control back over to the main program. The same function may be called multiple times in the same main program.

Return

The term "return" refers to the manner in which outputs are provided from a function back to the main program. The word "return" is used because the function takes an input from the main program, performs work on the input, and then gives data back the main program. With user-defined functions, the developer has complete control over the number and types of outputs that are returned. In addition to user-defined functions, predefined functions also return outputs to the main program. However, in these cases, the developer does not have control over the number or types of outputs that are returned. The predefined function must be used as is, and the returned outputs should be handled appropriately.

Arguments

An argument is a value that is passed between programs, routines, or functions. In many cases, this argument is a variable that is used to store a value. When a user-defined function is created, the developer specifies the types and number of inputs that will be provided to the function. These inputs are called "parameters." Upon calling the function in the main program, the developer must specify the values that will be passed to the function in these parameters. These values are the arguments. As an example, consider a function `mult(a,` `b)` that requires parameters `a` and `b` to be numbers. When the function is called in code using the numbers 3 and 4 as inputs, the statement will be written `mult(3, 4)`. In this scenario, 3 and 4 are the arguments. Interestingly, not all functions require arguments to be passed to them. A function can be written to operate without any inputs, and such a function can still return an output value.

PARAMETERS

The terms "parameter" and "argument" are sometimes used interchangeably, although there is a distinct difference between the two. Remember that an argument is an actual value passed to a function or subroutine. A parameter, however, is the item that specifies what type of value needs to be passed. A parameter is used in the definition and creation of the function to specify what type of input the function requires. For example, if a function is defined as `mult(a, b)`, then `a` and `b` are the parameters of the function. When the function is called in the main program as `mult(1, 2)`, then 1 and 2 are the arguments being passed.

PASSING AN ARGUMENT BY VALUE VS. PASSING BY REFERENCE

When parameters are passed to a function, they can be passed either by value or by reference. Passing by value is straightforward. The value itself is passed to the function. This could be an integer value, like 2, or a character, like "a." Passing by reference is more complicated. When a reference is passed to a function, instead of passing the value itself to the function, the value's location in memory is passed. This may be done using a pointer or using a variable that is of a reference data type, such as a string. When the function needs to manipulate that value, it uses the reference to find the value located at that memory address. Remember the difference between primitive and reference data types. Reference data types are automatically passed by reference when they are used as an input to a function. This can be useful when the developer needs to make changes to a value that is passed in as an argument, but for one reason or another cannot easily return the value at the end of the function.

PROPAGATED ARGUMENTS PASSED BY REFERENCE

In some cases, it may be necessary for changes made to inputs of a function to be propagated throughout the entire program, even though those changes may not necessarily be considered formal outputs. In this case, it is necessary to pass these inputs into the function by reference. When arguments are passed by reference, the address of the value in memory is passed instead of the value itself. When the value of the argument is changed, the value stored at that memory location gets updated to reflect the new value. Later in the program, when that memory address is accessed, the new value will used because that is the value currently stored at that location. This is how a developer can propagate changes to an argument throughout an entire program. It should be noted that some modern programming languages do not support true passing by reference, but in such languages there is generally a way of accomplishing the same result.

DECIDING TO PASS A PARAMETER BY VALUE OR BY REFERENCE

The main factor that will affect this decision is whether the function or subroutine should be able to make changes to the inputs that will be visible throughout the rest of the program. If not, then the arguments should be passed by value. In effect, this creates a duplicate, independent variable within the function that is only editable within the function, and indeed only exists while the function is running. Whatever variable was passed to the function from the main program does not undergo any changes. If these variables need to be changed in the main program, then they should be passed to the function by reference. This way, the main program and the function are both effectively using the same variable. Inside the function, the variable is handled like any other variable would be, but the changes made to it are being automatically applied to the value that the main-program variable is assigned to.

PARAMETERS THAT ARE AUTOMATICALLY PASSED BY REFERENCE

Some data types are automatically passed by reference due to the way they are stored in memory. Remember that primitive data types are small pieces of data that can generally be stored completely within the register of the CPU. These types of parameters can be passed by value. However, some data types are stored in other areas of memory and are referred to with a memory address. Some examples of these data types include lists, strings, and arrays. Since these are referenced by a call to a memory location, these types of parameters are automatically passed by reference and not by value.

Passing Arrays to Functions

Arrays are passed to functions by reference. This means that the array in the main program that is passed to the function is effectively being used inside the function as well—any changes made to it are going to be made to the location in memory that the entire program is referencing. The actual data that is passed from the main program into the function is the memory address of the first item in the array. This is often called the **first address** or **foundation address**. With the first address as a point of reference, the function can access the space in memory where the array is stored. In accordance with how arrays are stored in memory, since all the items in the array are the same type and size, the function can access any element in the array.

Efficiency in Storing Arrays

It is generally a good idea to store all arrays in a program using the same method. This makes things less confusing because a consistent method is followed. If some arrays are stored in row-major order while others are in column-major order, a developer may be more likely to inadvertently access an incorrect array element. However, in some cases, it can be more efficient to store some arrays in row-major order and others in column-major order. This typically occurs when operations are being performed that require specific handling of both arrays at once. Matrix multiplication is a great example of this. When matrix multiplication is performed, the program can step through each row of one matrix while stepping through each column of the other. This makes matrix multiplication much more efficient than having both arrays stored in the same manner.

Common Input Methods

There are many ways that inputs are taken into a system. The most rudimentary is for input values to be hard coded into the program itself. Such a program is not scalable, as there is no way to for someone using the program to change the inputs. This is typically only done by those who are learning to program or developers trying to make an algorithm.

A far more common way to provide input is with prompts or fields that accept inputs typed on a keyboard. Another common form of input is through buttons or other controls that can be clicked on using a mouse or touchscreen. In addition to keyboards and mice, Existing files may also be used as input to a program. A user can put all necessary data in the file with a certain format that the program is designed to read, and the program can then read the file and use or manipulate the information contained in the file.

Common Ways to Handle Output

At some point, the output from most programs needs to be in a format that is consumable by a human being. There are several ways of accomplishing this. The most common way to handle output in the early days of personal computers was through text displayed on a screen. Since then, **graphical user interfaces** (GUIs) have become virtually ubiquitous. In these cases, outputs may be given to the user through anything that can be put on a screen, including not only text in a console but also images, videos, and digital visualizations of documents. Another way to handle output is through printed materials. The program may print items onto a physical media like paper so that a human is able to read the output.

Functions

In some programming languages, a **function** and a **procedure** are the same thing, and they may also be called routines, subroutines, or methods. However, in some programming languages, a function is different from a procedure. In these cases, a procedure is a set of steps that perform some kind of task. A function, on the other hand, is a procedure that returns a value to the calling code. Consider the following example:

```
float SquareFootage ( float Length, float Width )
   float SquareFeet
   SquareFeet ← Length * Width
   return SquareFeet
end SquareFootage
```

The first line is the function's header, which declares the data type that will be returned (in this case a float), the name of the function (`SquareFootage`), and the formal parameters. Inside the function, a local variable named `SquareFeet` is declared, `SquareFeet` is given the value of the `Length` and `Width` variables multiplied, and finally `SquareFeet` is returned to the calling code. This function could be called in the main program or parent function as follows:

```
float Price ← 100 * SquareFootage ( 100, 200 )
```

The above statement calls the `SquareFootage` function and assigns actual parameters 100 and 200 to the formal parameters. The returned float is multiplied by 100, and the result becomes the value of the float variable `Price`.

METHODS

While the term "method" can be used broadly to refer to a set of steps (i.e., a procedure) or a particular process for solving a problem (i.e., an algorithm), it has a more specific meaning in object-oriented programming. In object-oriented languages, a **method** is a procedure or function that is a member of an object. Methods help to determine how their parent object will respond to a wide range of events. In the object-oriented paradigm, every system consists of objects. Each object performs a specific set of functions and interacts with other objects to solve problems. Consider, for instance, an object-oriented program that makes uses of spreadsheets. A particular spreadsheet might be an object, and it may have a method to open it, one to save it, one to insert rows, one to insert columns, and so on. In the common programming language C++, methods are often known as **member functions**.

IDEs and Programming Language Paradigms

VISUAL DEVELOPMENT ENVIRONMENTS

A **visual development environment** (**VDE**) enables a computer programmer to use the shortcut of point-and-click technology instead of laboriously typing out all the code. Sometimes, computer programs contain repetitions of vast code strings which can be extremely tedious to retype; a VDE eliminates that tedium. Often, a VDE also contains a form design grid with which the programmer can design the user interface. Most VDEs also allow customization by the user. For instance, a programmer may be able to choose from a background color for a program.

INTEGRATED DEVELOPMENT ENVIRONMENTS (IDES)

CHARACTERISTICS OF AN IDE

An **integrated development environment** (**IDE**) is a single environment available to a programmer that has many development tools integrated into one. The use of an IDE means the developer does not need to have a separate tool for each of the many common tasks associated with developing a program, including coding, compiling, debugging, and testing. It also helps to cut down on development time because, again, the developer does not have to perform these tasks separately. They can all be performed inside of the IDE as development occurs. Visual Studio is a very common and widely used IDE. Most all developers are familiar with this IDE, even if they do not use it on an everyday basis.

Components Included in an IDE

Different integrated development environments (IDEs) contain different components. However, there are some components that are generally common to all IDEs. These components include **source code editors** and **debuggers**. Many IDEs also contain a **compiler**. Some other components that might be offered in an IDE include an interpreter, an auto-complete editor, and version control. More recent IDEs usually contain tools for use in object-oriented programming, such as class browsers and object browsers. An IDE may be built with a certain language in mind, and which IDE is most commonly used by developers varies from language to language. Individual developers may also have their own preferences regarding which IDE to use or whether to use an IDE at all. The best-known IDE today is Visual Studio.

Effect on Development Times

An IDE can shorten development times primarily due their integration of the various tools that are needed and their user-friendliness. An IDE contains the main tools that a developer needs, and these tools are already integrated. There is no need for the developer to use separate compilers, debuggers, or other tools to complete the development work. Not having to integrate these separate tools can save a great deal of time. Modern IDEs are also relatively user friendly. They often have features that save typing time and help to avoid simple mistakes. For example, an IDE might feature automatically completed typing of commands, functions, or variables. It may also color-code items so that the developer not only knows that they have typed the item correctly, but they also know how the compiler will interpret that item. For example, built-in functions may be in blue text, while user-defined functions are in green text, and variables are in orange text. The IDE might also have a variable viewer, which will allow the developer to step through lines of code and see how the values of individual variables change with the execution of each line. Compared to typing raw code into a text file, coding with these user-friendly features takes far less time and effort.

Advantages

There are several advantages to using an IDE. The most obvious is that it makes development work easier for the developer. Many IDEs include features like intuitive code editors and visual tools, which make coding faster and more convenient. Furthermore, IDEs reduce development times because separate tools are not necessary, which makes the process of coding, compiling, and debugging less complex and time-consuming. Finally, IDEs are very helpful for debugging, because they generally include debugging tools that show the developer what happens for each line of code.

Programming Paradigms

Object-Oriented Paradigm

The object-oriented paradigm views software systems as collections of objects. It led to the emergence of object-oriented programming, or OOP. Each object in a program consists of data and a set of procedures (known as methods) for interacting with that data. Objects can work with other objects in order to solve problems and generate certain outcomes. Consider, for instance, a text document that contains sales data. Under the **object-oriented paradigm**, the document is created as an object containing information (i.e., sales data) and methods for changing that data (i.e., adding data, deleting data, sorting, etc.). Assume the program wants to extrapolate sales projections. By having the sales data object interact with an object containing mathematical functions, the program could generate the desired projections. There are a few key terms associated with the object-oriented paradigm:

- An object is a programming unit consisting of data and methods for interacting with that data.
- A class acts like a template for objects. Multiple objects may be based on the same lines of written code. All objects based on this code are the same class.
- An instance is an "instance of a class"—or in other words, a specific object.

Imperative Paradigm

The **imperative paradigm**, or **procedural paradigm**, views programs as sequences of commands that control data and perform calculations in order to solve a particular program. This paradigm aligns well with what people generally view computer programming to be. It serves as the basis for machine language and pseudocode. The programmer develops an algorithm that tells the computer what to do, and this sequence of commands carries out the algorithm, performing an operation or generating an output.

Declarative Paradigm

The **declarative paradigm** views programs as descriptions of data and the logical relationshps governing it. The programmer provides a description of the problem to the programming system, and the system solves the problem using a series of general-purpose, problem-solving algorithms. Consequently, the focus is on creating the logical relationships that represent the system or problem rather than on writing algorithms. Logical programming languages are a very common type of declarative language. Declarative programming finds more uses in artificial intelligence, natural language processing, and higher-level mathematics than it does in traditional development of information systems.

Functional Paradigm

The **functional paradigm** views programming in terms of a mathematical function with an input-to-output relationship. In essence, the program is series of functions that accept input and generate output. The output of one function becomes input for another function, and so on. In this way, predefined functions (also known as predefined programming units) can be nested inside one another with simpler functions going inside the more complex functions.

Basic Steps Associated with Software Development

There are some basic steps that are common to computer program design, regardless of which design methodology a developer or team may be following. The first step is to determine the requirements for the software. The developer must know, in relatively exact terms, what the software needs to do. The next basic step is to design the solution, typically through the creation of an algorithm. After this, the actual coding can be done. After coding is completed, then testing must be performed to ensure that the software functions as anticipated. The type and length of testing is often determined by the specific model being followed. After testing is completed, the software can be released, and it then enters the maintenance phase. It can remain in the maintenance phase for years in some cases.

Categories of Program Statements

Statements that make up a procedural or object-oriented program generally fall under three categories:

- **Declarative statements** define the terminology that is unique to the program so that the terms may be used later in the program. Common examples of items that are declared in statements are variables, functions, constants, and classes.
- **Imperative statements**, also called **expressions**, are the instructions that tell the computer which operations or computations to do for each step of an algorithm.
- **Control flow statements** dictate which statements will be executed. Some control flow statements, such as if statements, may specify that a statement or block of statements will only execute if a given condition is true. Other control flow statements, such as for loops, may specify that a statement or block of statements be executed a given number of times.

Most programs follow the same basic structure, which starts with declarative statements and then has a main body of control flow statements and imperative statements. Other functions may be declared in the initial portion, but they are normally written after or below the main function.

Name Binding

Name binding is the process of associating a programming object, such as data or code, with an identifier. Programming languages perform name binding as an aid to programmers. Once an identifier is associated with an object, the identifier is described as "referencing" that object. Binding is related to scope, because scope dictates which objects are referenced by which identifiers, both in the human-readable code and when the code is executed. If binding occurs before the program runs, it is described as **static name binding**. If binding occurs while the program is running, it is described as **dynamic name binding**. In dynamic binding, the program receives both the request for the object and the object itself at runtime. Dynamic dispatch is a type of dynamic name binding used by several languages, including C++.

Concurrent Processing

Concurrent processing is the ability of a program or operating system to keep a number of processes logically active concurrently even though only one operation can take place at a time. The operating system creates this illusion of **concurrently active processes** by interleaving the execution order of their commands, thus juggling the execution of many processes at once. Problems may arise when the processes must communicate between themselves or access the same resources.

Issue of Communication

In concurrent processing, a main program simultaneously opens and operates multiple other programs. In many cases, one program may need to reach a certain point before another can continue running; consequently, they must communicate between themselves as they execute. Consider, for instance, two programs that must update a list. If they access the list at the same time, it may result in only one update being applied and the other update being lost. To avoid this problem, programmers must design the system such that certain data items are given **mutually exclusive access**, meaning only one application can access them at any given time. There are two methods for achieving mutually exclusive access:

- Program each application so that it can identify all the other applications and block their access when it is accessing the data. This method can be problematic because the whole system can crash from an error in one segment.
- Program the data item itself with a **monitor**, which prevents other applications from accessing it when it is already being accessed.

Event-Driven Programming

Event-driven programming allows the tasks in a program to vary based on some input provided to the system. This input could come from the system itself, another system, or a human user. Event-driven programming uses **event handlers**. The program "listens" for events and stores information about each event as it happens. When there is an event, and event handler determines what action needs to be taken based on the specifics of the event. Event-driven programming can become very complex, as some systems have a very large number of events that could occur. It is necessary to account for all these events so that the program knows how to react when any one of them occurs.

Synchronous and Asynchronous Sequential Systems

Synchronous sequential systems use digital circuits that are synchronized by clock signals, which are governed by a specific timing margin. When a clock signal is sent, the entire system changes state. A sequential system consists of a combinational logic device and a state register. When the state changes, the state register sends the previous combinational logic state as an input through the combinational logic device. The clock should only move as quickly as required to calculate the most time-intensive calculation.

Asynchronous sequential systems are not governed by clocks; rather, they have modular designs consisting of numerous concurrent hardware devices that achieve synchronization through communication interfaces. Asynchronous systems are typically more difficult to design because they must account for all possible states in all possible timings. If they fail to do so, the logic will be unstable. However, stable asynchronous systems are considered superior to synchronous systems because they run as fast as their gates allow.

Parallel Processing

Parallel processing occurs when a computer performs several tasks or actions simultaneously. It requires multiple processing units and has given rise to multiprocessor machines. There are two common number of architectures for parallel processing:

- **MIMD**, or **multiple instruction, multiple data**, involves connecting multiple processing units (i.e., CPUs) to the same main memory. This way, each processor can function independently while synchronizing its work with other processors by leaving messages in common memory cells. This architecture allows different instruction sets to be performed on different data sets.
- **SIMD**, or **single instruction, multiple data**, involves linking several processors together so they can simultaneously execute the same instruction on different sets of data. This architecture is best suited for situations where the same tasks must be performed on a large block of data.

Accessibility Features

Although people generally use mice, keyboards, monitors, and headphones or speakers to interact with computers, there are also many people with disabilities that restrict or prevent their use of one or more of these devices. is difficult or impossible to use. Such people make up one of the major groups affected by the digital divide—the gap between people who use computers and the internet and people who do not. Bringing accessibility features to these people helps to bridge the digital divide.

Some examples of accessibility features are text-to-speech, speech-to-text, high-contrast display modes, head/mouth stick keyboards, increased font size, increased window size, keyboard access to all features, and tooltips or alt text. When writing programs, these accessibility options should be incorporated into the user interface, so that the effect of disabilities on user experience is minimized.

Periodically Updating Software

There are several reasons why software must be periodically updated. One of the most obvious reasons is to correct bugs or defects. The longer a piece of software is used and the more people it is used by, the more likely it is that bugs or other issues will be found that were not noticed before the initial release of the software. Updates are needed to correct such issues. Another reason for periodic updates is to handle new user requirements. As technologies advance, users generally expect their software to advance as well. Fulfilling new user requirements usually involves adding new features and functionality. One more major reason why software may need to be updated is to maintain compatibility with operating systems or other platforms. Operating systems themselves often undergo updates, and some updates may cause support for older pieces of software to cease. Therefore, these older pieces of software require updates in order to remain available to users.

Negative Impacts of Not Updating

A lack of updates to a piece of software can have many negative consequences. One of the most catastrophic consequences could be that the software ceases to function. Other challenging but less devastating effects include the necessity to implement workarounds. This occurs when a defect is discovered, but no fix is implemented. Users must find a way to work around the defect. This is not ideal because it typically leads to increased work effort. Lastly, a lack of updates leads to an increased cost of ownership for a piece of software.

Increased Cost of Ownership Due to Lack of Updates

Software that is not updated on a regular basis becomes more and more costly to own. One reason for this is because defects are not corrected. As defects arise, users must find other ways to work around these defects. This leads to the process taking more time to complete, which results in lost productivity. Additionally, when there are no updates to software, features that become necessary are never added to the software. Thus the needed functionality must be obtained elsewhere, often through the purchase of an additional piece of software. Furthermore, as a given copy of software gets older, it may become less efficient and require more hardware or system resources, it may become susceptible to costly malware or other attacks as vulnerabilities are found, and it may become incompatible with operating systems or other software that is integrated with it, requiring the use of virtual machines or other workarounds. At some point in time, the software becomes so costly that continuing to use the software is not feasible.

Debugging and Testing

Exception Handling

Exception handling is the process by which a program manages special conditions (known as exceptions) that change the normal function of a program. Put simply, **exception handling** signals that a program could not execute properly. It can be carried out by a computer language construct or a hardware device. When the program recognizes an exception, it will save the current state of execution in a certain location, and then transfer program execution to an **exception handler**, which is a specially designed subroutine. In some situations, such as a page fault, a program will use the saved data to resume normal execution. In other situations, the exception cannot be handled in way that allows the program to continue running. Runtime environments use automated exception handlers, which attach to the engine and identify the root cause of the exception by recording all debugging information that was in the computer's memory when the exception was thrown. Exception handling is often difficult to carry out in modern enterprise-level applications.

Exception Handling Syntax

Most programming languages use the same basic types of exception handling syntax. For instance, the most popular syntax initiates an exception program using a special statement such as "throw" or "raise" followed by an object or a special type. When defining their scope, exception handlers begin with a marker clause such as "try" or "begin" and conclude with a first handler clause such as "catch," "except," or "rescue." After the scope has been defined, the exception often includes several handler clauses that identify the types of exceptions it handles as well as the name of the exception object. In some programming languages, exceptions can use an else statement to account for the event that an exception is not found by the time the handler's scope is finished. The end of the exception uses clauses such as "finally" or "ensure" to allow code to execute at the end of an exception-handling routine and free computer resources used by the exception.

Test Case Example

Which test cases would be most useful for the following decision statement:

```
int x ← getNum()        //gets user-input integer, returns it
if( x < 5 )
   print "low"
else if ( x < 10 )
   print "medium"
else
   print "high"
end if
```

When writing test cases for decision statements, it is important to always run tests that test the boundaries of the conditions. In testing, finding these boundaries is done in a process known as **boundary value analysis**. When we use this type of analysis, we make test cases that use the maximum or minimum values for the conditions that the decision statements check for. When a condition does not have an upper or lower boundary, we also test for extreme values, since we cannot test for boundaries. In this case, the following values should be tested:

A value of 0 would test a relatively extreme value that should compute as less than 5 and result in "low" being printed.

A value of 4 would test the highest integer that is less than 5. This would be the upper boundary for getting a "low" result, so "low" should be printed.

A value of 5 would test the lower boundary of the range that should result in "medium" being printed, since it is not less than 5, but it is less than 10. We would want to see that the program correctly prints "medium" in this case.

A value of 9 would test the upper boundary of the "medium" range, since it is less than 10 but not less than 5. We would expect "medium" to be printed in this test.

A value of 10 would test the lower boundary of the else statement. Because 10 is not less than 10, execution should pass over the else if statement to the else statement and print "high."

Lastly, a value of 15 would test a relatively high extreme. It should also cause the program to execute only the else statement and therefore print "high."

Error Types

A **syntax error** is an error in the format of written code wherein some rule of the programming language is not being followed. This results in the compiler or interpreter not being able to covert the code, as compilers and interpreters follow the rules of their programming languages. For example, if a language requires a semicolon at the end of each statement and you forget to write one, this will cause a syntax error.

A **round-off error** results when decimal values are rounded, resulting in an answer that is incorrect. For example, dividing 7 by 2 in general mathematics would yield 3.5. However, in many programming languages, since 7 and 2 are both integers, integer division would be performed, resulting in the truncation of 3.5 to 3 and in the answer being 3, which isn't correct.

An **overflow error** occurs when an attempt is made to store a value that is outside of the bounds of a data type in a variable of that data type. For example, in C++, a signed integer cannot hold a number larger than 2,147,483,647. This is due to the number of bytes allocated for each signed integer data type. Code could conceivably be written that allows situations where the program tries to store a larger number than 2,147,483,647 as an integer. The result would be an overflow error.

A **runtime error** is an error that occurs during program execution. For example, trying to open a file that does not exist will not show up as an error during compilation. Only when the program attempts to access that file while executing will it become apparent that the file is missing, and the result will be a runtime error.

A **compile-time error** is the counterpart to the runtime error. The problem is found by the compiler, before the program ever runs. Syntax errors are an example of this. When program code is compiled, the compiler will generate errors for any code that it does not understand. These are compile-time errors.

A **logic error** is an error in an algorithm that does not cause any problem with execution but still results in an erroneous, inaccurate, or unexpected output. For example, imagine we tried to average three numbers using the following code:

```
double ans ← 2 + 4 + 6 / 3
```

The answer, stored in `ans`, would be 8. Because `2 + 4 + 6` is not in parenthesis, `6 / 3` would occur first, and then 2 + 4 + 2 would be computed from left to right. The correct algorithm for computing an average is to add the numbers up first and then to divide by the number of numbers (in this case, 3). If this algorithm were coded correctly, the desired answer, 4, would be stored in `ans`. This situation is an example of a logic error.

The computer would not inform the user that anything is wrong; it would just display the answer it calculated. As one might imagine, logic errors can be difficult to find, because the results are not always obviously wrong and because the computer cannot assist in finding them. They are also difficult to correct because the problem is due to the writing of the algorithm, not to a simple typing mistake, a missing file, or the like.

Importance of Displaying Descriptive Error Messages to Users

Even when a program runs as intended, there is still the possibility that users will attempt to do something that program cannot do. In other cases, there are instances where files don't exist where they should, users enter invalid information, or servers are down. It is for all these reasons that error messages must be used to tell users what is happening. Descriptive error messages enable the user to understand the reason why a program does not seem to be working correctly or cannot perform a specific action. If a programmer uses generic error messages for every error they account for, such as displaying the word "Error" when there is a problem, the error message is of little help to the user. More descriptive error messages, such as "Unable to locate file" or "Server connection not found," help users know where to begin troubleshooting for themselves, and they allow users to pass on more specific information to those they contact for support.

Importance of Testing Programs with Valid and Invalid Data

When writing software, it is important to make it fault tolerant. Fault-tolerant software is software that is resistant to errors and will not crash when given data that it doesn't know how to process. It is for this reason that software must be tested with a wide range of data. For example, let's say we design a program that computes the average of all of the numbers that a user enters. The simple algorithm applied would be to add up all of the numbers and divide by the total. However, if the user enters in 0 numbers, the total numbers is equal to 0, and the program may attempt to divide by 0. Alternatively, the user might enter a letter where the computer is expecting a number. In each of these examples, it is up to programmers to think of situations that are outside of the norm and make sure that the program handles both valid and invalid data. Once these situations are identified, error messages and directions to the user can be created so that the program can continue running under these conditions.

Importance of Testing Classes, Methods, and Libraries in Isolation

Testing classes, methods, and libraries in isolation is also known as unit testing. Unit testing allows external variables to be minimized and makes sure that the item being tested performs as intended without any external interference. There are many benefits to unit testing. First, bugs are more easily found because there is no interaction with outside elements. Next, it will save time debugging, because you will know that any part of your program that has been thoroughly unit tested will most likely not be the cause of any future problems. Lastly, the unit tests can be used by other developers as examples of how the code is supposed to perform. In this way, it almost acts as another set of documentation.

Example

In order to completely test the following code:

```
if(x>=2 AND x<=10)
```

what values must be tested?

When testing decision statements, it is important to test one data point of each span of the if statement, including endpoints. For this example, testing a value less than 2 and a value greater than 10 tests the values outside of the if statement on both sides. Then, testing the endpoints x=2 and x=10 is also necessary. Finally, testing a value within the boundaries such as 5 would be the final piece to test all possibilities. So, a test set such as 0, 2, 5, 10, and 12 would be sufficient to test all possibilities properly.

Short Circuit Evaluation

Short circuit evaluation happens when a logical operator stops computing because the result has already been determined after only checking one of the two Boolean values. For example, in an AND logical operation, both Boolean operators must be true for the entire Boolean expression to be true. Therefore, if the first item is false there is no need to check the second item. We know that logically the second item does not matter, and we "short-circuit" to the conclusion that the entire expression is false. Similarly, in an OR logical operation, only one Boolean operator must be true for the entire Boolean expression to be true. Therefore, if the first item is true, there again is no need to check the second item. We again know through logic that the second item does not matter, and we "short-circuit" to the conclusion that the entire expression is therefore true. When a computer uses lazy evaluation, the second Boolean expression would still be checked during each of these example operations, wasting precious calculation time.

Unit Testing

Unit testing is the process of testing the smallest possible section of code to ensure that it is working correctly. This section of code is the "unit" referred to in the term "unit testing." In some cases, the unit may be as small as a single function. In other cases, the unit may be an entire module or interface. Unit testing allows developers to ensure that all code sections are functioning properly before attempting to put them all together and test interactions between the units. Today, most unit testing is automated. There are technologies available that will allow the developer to run hundreds or thousands of test cases very quickly and observe the results. In some cases, however, unit testing is still performed manually. The developer must be careful to ensure that he is performing true unit testing and not **integration testing**, which is testing to ensure that components are working together as intended. Ideally, no component should have communication with any other components during the unit test.

User Acceptance Testing (UAT)

User acceptance testing, often referred to as "UAT," is software testing that is done by actual end users or client personnel who represent the end users. Informal testing is often done throughout development by the developers to ensure that everything is working as expected. Depending on the development methodology being used, teams of developers or testers may be required to do more formal testing at certain stages of development. However, UAT is the final and most formal step in testing. Because the developers and testers are generally not the ones who will be using the software on a daily basis, most commercially produced software goes through very thorough UAT before being accepted as production ready. Before UAT begins, the team will usually decide on the details of the testing, such as how long the testing will run and who will do the testing. At the end of UAT, the users may request additional changes, or they may certify that the software meets all the performance and functional requirements. Generally, upon signoff that UAT is complete, the software is considered ready for a production deployment.

Black Box Testing

A **black box system** is a system that is described purely in terms of its inputs and outputs, with no visibility into the inner workings of the system. Imagine a black box with buttons on it, and when a button is pushed, some output, such as a sound, occurs. Using this box, you would not be able to see how it works. Some process is performed inside the box, but all you as the user know it what input you gave the box, and what output the box gave you. Computer programs are generally black box systems. The term "black box" is particularly common in software testing, where black box tests consist of feeding the software inputs and then analyzing the outputs. By contrast, white box tests involve analyzing the program code.

Bugs

A **bug** is an error or defect in a piece of software that prevents the software from performing as expected. Bugs can be identified by the developer during testing. They can also be identified by user testers during UAT. Finally, a bug may be identified by a user after the software is in use in production. If an issue is raised with the software company when the software is live, and if a bug is then identified, it is often necessary to perform an emergency update to the software to correct the problem. Occasionally, developers and users may disagree on whether an issue is being caused by a bug. A user may report receiving incorrect output, while a developer may state that the software is performing as designed. The developer could argue that incorrect requirements were given to the team for development or that the user is not following the correct procedures for using the software. Nevertheless, if a bug is found, a modification is normally required.

Debugging

Debugging is the process of working through a piece of code to uncover errors, generally known as bugs, and correcting them. Debugging can become quite difficult as the code grows. Some applications consist of thousands or even millions of lines of code, so it can become very tedious to determine exactly where an error is occurring. One way of debugging involves stepping through sections of code one line at a time to ensure that each statement runs as expected. Tracking of variables can also be incorporated into this activity to ensure that the values inside the variables at each step are in line with expectations. Another rudimentary way of debugging is to include message boxes at certain steps within the code. This way, a developer can tell when the code reaches a certain point because the message box they put at that point in the code will appear. The developer will usually include pertinent details inside the message box, like the values of variables or which specific line the code has successfully run through.

Program Testing

Before they can be released to the public or even tested by client users, computer programs have to be tested. Programmers may test software informally during the development process. Such testing may involve disk-checking, which is a process of checking the program for textual or logical errors, debugging code as soon as it is written, or simply performing a few test cases to help in development of an algorithm. There are also various diagnostic programs available to help programmers locate problems, measure performance, or perform automated tests with large datasets.

Larger software projects will involve thorough testing processes, which generally involve the following steps:

- **Gathering requirements**: making sure the team knows everything the software must do and what standards it must meet
- **Analysis**: looking at the requirements and the code to determine how to test for all the requirements
- **Design**: writing necessary test cases and setting up testing tools
- **Execution**: performing the test cases and using the testing tools
- **Reporting**: reporting any bugs that were found as well as the results from testing tools, such as performance metrics
- **Fixing**: adjusting the program code to remove known bugs or improve performance

Different development methodologies, regulatory bodies, and clients may define their own testing processes as well, usually with minor variations to these steps. For example, a certain methodology may involve a "planning" step or require testing at specific stages of development, or a client may require a process step dedicated to documentation.

Code Documentation

Characteristics of Good Documentation

Documentation of code is often overlooked by programmers. When a program is working, many programmers think that this is good enough, and move on to their next project. However, the lifecycle of a program dictates that clear and thorough documentation be written, as anyone who works on the program after the initial release will need this guidance. One important trait of good documentation is that it is up to date, reflecting any changes made to the code. Another trait of good documentation is that it points out preconditions and potential problems. If a programmer tries to use methods written by someone else, without documentation, they will not be able to easily figure out what exactly the method does, how it works, what its limitations are, or how it can be used effectively. Good documentation should also be clear and provide examples of the correct way to use the provided code. With good documentation, programmers who use another person's code will be able to use it in the way it was intended. Furthermore, good documentation is helpful even for the person who writes the code, as it helps them keep the code organized and will be useful reminder if they need to come back to the code after any period of time.

Documenting Libraries of Functions

A **function library** is a group of functions that are grouped together because they serve some common function. A common function library in Java would be the Math library, which contains several mathematical functions such as taking the square root, rounding, and generating random numbers. These functions are basically "black boxes", where the person using them must know what needs to be inputted and what will be outputted, but they do not need to know how the function actually works. However, if the function is not documented correctly, the user will not know what the valid inputs and outputs are. Therefore, documentation allows programmers to utilize library functions the way that the person who wrote them intended.

Support Documentation

One of the main purposes of **support documentation** is to help the users of software when things go wrong. A common inclusion in support documentation is the list of possible error codes and what caused them. Good documentation will contain error codes as well as the reasons they are showing up. This bit of information will be helpful in troubleshooting the software issue when similar problems and solutions are given within the documentation.

Modular Code

Modular code is code that is separated into small pieces, which themselves can be called modules. Each piece of code performs a particular action or function on its own. It could potentially be used as a standalone piece of code, but most often it is put together with other pieces to create a larger application. The same concept is used in construction today. Modular buildings are created by manufacturing smaller pieces of standalone items such as walls or roofs and assembling the final product onsite. This typically allows for quicker construction, and it also allows faulty pieces to be easily swapped out with identical pieces. Modular coding allows the programmer to create and test small pieces of functionality and then put them all together to create the final product. Similarly, if one piece of module fails, then it is easy to isolate the error and correct it.

Importance of Generating Modular Code

Modular programming is important for many different reasons. First, it typically allows for faster development times because modules from other applications or other parts of the application can be reused, often with only minimal reworking. If programs are written in a modular fashion, then pieces of functionality can be easily transferred to new programs. Programming in a modular fashion can also reduce the amount of time necessary to track down errors. Modules can be written and tested individually to ensure that they are functioning correctly before being placed into the larger program. This allows the programmer to test much smaller sections of code, and errors can be found and fixed more quickly in these smaller sections. Finally, modular programming allows multiple programmers to work together on a single application. Each programmer can be assigned a module or set of modules to develop, and the members of the team can work in parallel instead of having a single programmer write all the code.

Difficulties Caused by Not Using Modular Programming

There are several difficulties that may be encountered due to not using modular programming.

- First, it is much more difficult to correct defects in the code. If pieces of functionality are broken down into separate modules, then finding and correcting defects is easier because the programmer can easily identify which module is not working. Otherwise, the programmer may have to spend time stepping through every line of code in the program to locate the error.

- Another difficulty is longer development time. By using modular programming, multiple programmers can create separate modules at the same time and then join them all together. When not using this method, it is very difficult for more than one programmer to work on development at any given time. This slows down development time and causes the product to take longer to be finished.
- Finally, adding new functionality to the code will be more difficult as well. If the modular technique is used, it is generally easy to add additional modules for increased functionality. On the other hand, without modules, adding new functionality may require large sections of code to be rewritten.

Comments

Comments are explanatory statements inserted in the program code. Their main function is to aid the understanding of anyone reading the source code. Comments are set off with particular characters that signal to the interpreter or compiler to ignore the comment. Therefore the comments are not interpreted or compiled; they are simply skipped over. While the characters that set off comments and the method for writing comments may vary from language to language, some major languages use the two methods below:

```
// Two slashes set off a one-line comment.

/* A slash followed by an asterisk signals the beginning of a comment
that is on multiple lines. An asterisk followed by a slash signals the
end of the comment. */
```

In the first method, "`//`" marks everything following on that line as a comment. The compiler will simply move to the next line of code. This method can be used to set off a whole line or to set off the end of a line after a statement. In the second method, the comment is inserted between "`/*`" and "`*/`" and can span multiple lines. Both these methods are used in Java, C++, and C#. Comments should provide insight rather than redundancy. Consider, for instance, the following program statements:

```
counter++   // increments counter
```

Rather than stating "increments counter," which is obvious, the programmer could add just a little bit more detail to explain the purpose that `counter` serves in this particular situation. If `counter` were being used to count recursions of a specific function called `findNum()`, for example, the programmer could write:

```
counter++   // increments counter of findNum recursions
```

Comments for every statement can make code more confusing, as comments are difficult to read. Consequently, many developers include an explanation of the function using the multiple-line method at the beginning of a function.

Importance of Adding Appropriate Comments

Adding appropriate comments to computer code is a very important, yet often overlooked, task. There are many reasons why comments should be added to code.

- First, it helps the programmer to remember what is being done in the code and why things have been done a certain way. A programmer may write a piece of code today and then need to come back to it after some time—possibly many months. If appropriate comments are included, then the programmer will be able to pick up the code and quickly tell what is being done and why. This will allow for much faster updates.
- Comments can also help with troubleshooting by allowing the programmer to quickly identify what is happening in each section of code. This way, the programmer can focus on areas of the code where the errors are occurring.

- Another great reason to add comments to code is because the person who writes the code may not be the same person who edits or maintains the code in the future. Without clear comments, it could be very difficult for another programmer to edit a piece of code that they did not write.

Spacing and Indentation

When writing computer code, as long as the programmer follows the syntax of the language, the program will compile and run. The computer does not care about spacing and indentation if it does not violate the rules of the language. So, many times code is written in a format that is very difficult for a human to read. In fact, there are some languages in which an entire program could technically be written on one line. It is because of this that spacing and indentation are crucial for code readability. By following standard spacing and indentation rules for a language, code can be represented in a more organized and readable manner. For example, when writing nested decision statements, it is important to indent each nested decision so that they are visually grouped together. Methods within a class should be separated by spaces and comments so that programmers can easily identify the end of one method and the beginning of the next. When coding individually this does not represent as much of a problem, but since many programmers work in teams, it is important to follow indentation and spacing rules so that others on the team can easily read your code.

Using Descriptive Identifiers When Writing Code

Descriptive identifiers help programmers better understand the algorithms that are contained within a program. For example, if a program were to be written to determine the total cost of shirts ($20.00 each) and hats ($15.00 each) while applying a 7% tax, a programmer could write the following:

```
a=(b*c+e*f)*g
```

Although this equation may be correct, using more descriptive identifiers like this example below is a better idea:

```
totalCost=(shirtCost*numShirts+hatCost*numHats)*taxRate
```

While the algorithm has not changed, the descriptive identifiers are much easier to read and understand so that the programmer will know the purpose of this code just by reading the variables. In this way, using descriptive identifiers is also in some ways another way of providing implicit comments within your code.

Flow Diagrams

A **flow diagram** is an algorithm represented visually using shapes. It allows programmers to display all parts of a program in a way that is easily understood by other programmers. It is an essential part of planning complex computer programs. As shown in the diagrams, flow diagrams use symbols to represent different parts of the program. For example, a program begins at the top of the diagram. The program could then ask for input from the user using a parallelogram. Next, the program decides based on the user input represented by a diamond, and then both pathways are processed using a rectangle. Lastly, the output is displayed using a parallelogram, and the program completes with an oval.

Class Relationship Diagrams

Class relationship diagrams are designed to show which classes inherit from each other, which classes are composed of each other, and which classes are unrelated. When one class is contained within another class, this is known as a "has-a" relationship. For example, a library has a book. This type of relationship is more formally called a composition relationship because a library is composed of books. In order to display this relationship in a class relationship diagram, use a line with a diamond attached to the class that is the container for the other class. When one class inherits form another class, this is known as an "is-a" relationship. For example, a bank account is a type of fixed account, and therefore they inherit from one another. The fixed account would be known as the super class and the bank account would be known as the subclass. This is more formally known as class inheritance because bank account inherits the properties of a fixed account. In order to display this relationship in a class relationship diagram, use a line with an arrow pointing from the subclass to the super class. Lastly, if a class does not have any direct relationship with any other class, just draw it by itself. Printer does not relate to any of the other classes in any way, so it is drawn on its own with no use of arrows.

Programming Style Standards

Programming style standards are important not only for the functionality of the program, but for the readability of the program. Therefore, these standards are for the programmers who are using and sharing the code, and not the computer itself. Standards such as declaring constants in all capital letters, declaring classes with capital letters at the start of each word, and indenting decision statements and loops all help the readability of the code for the people who are reading it. Without these conventions, extra time will be needed to determine the variable types and the overall functionality of the program.

Stages of the Software Lifecycle

The five stages of the staged model of the software lifecycle are as follows:

- **Initial development**: The initial development stage is when the first live or production version of the product is developed and released.
- **Evolution**: During the evolution phase, improvements and enhancements are made to the software. Users may request new features or functionality, and new versions are released to accommodate these requests.
- **Servicing**: The servicing phase is when the software starts becoming expensive to maintain. Bugs may start being uncovered, and the team may no longer have the technical expertise required to maintain the system as it becomes older.
- **Phase Out**: The phase-out stage is when servicing stops and users begin migrating off the software.
- **Close Down:** The close-down stage is when the software is retired.

Feedback and Data Validation

End-User Feedback

Programs that have many daily active users tend to be never totally complete. They go through the software development process again and again. One major part of this process is the consideration of user feedback. When end users begin using software, programmers will get an honest evaluation of what works and what needs improvement. This feedback is useful in all parts of the development process, from predevelopment, to the beta release, to the live release to the public. The feedback continues to be useful as the program is updated. At each of these stages, programmers have an opportunity to develop software that is exactly what the end users say they desire. If software were released directly to the public without any end-user testing or feedback, the software would involve a greater risk of failing.

Peer Reviews

Peer reviews are a way for other developers on the team to review each other's code to ensure that the team's standard practices are being followed. Most development teams adopt standards that include industry best practices and that are to be followed in all code the team produces. Peer reviews are used as means of ensuring that the standards are followed. Most teams require that a developer's code pass through a peer review. Some may require this before user acceptance testing begins, while others may only require the peer review before the code is promoted into the production environment. Peer reviews may only ensure adherence to coding standards, or they may be used to confirm the code meets requirements, as would be the purpose of a code review during a project.

Data Validation Strategy

Data validation is the process of checking both the accuracy and the quality of data before using it in calculations. The simplest data validation strategy for user input is to make sure of two things: the data type must be correct, and the data must be within the predetermined bounds.

First, let's discuss data type. It is very important that the data type that is expected is received, because if data of some other type is entered, the code will not work properly or at all. For example, when a person is asked by a program how many items they would like to purchase, if the person enters "hi" or "3.45," the code will not work because statements that use this input will be working with variables of the integer data type. We can handle this with data validation—by checking whether the value entered is an integer. If it isn't, we can ask the user to enter an integer.

Next, we must take a look at the part of the strategy that requires values to be within acceptable bounds. If a program is calculating a student's grade based on a value from 0 to 100, the grade cannot be a negative number or a number greater than 100. If such a number were entered, we would need to have written the code with data validation in mind, so that the program would present an error message asking that a value between 0 and 100 be entered.

Data Validation vs. Data Verification

Data validation is used to make sure that inputted data is in an expected format and within an expected range. For example, if a user enters a string when the program is expecting an integer, there should be code that checks for and handles that. Similarly, code should also check for and handle situations where a user enters a value that is out of an expected range. For example, a user might enter the date of a transaction as during another year when only the current year is possible. Data validation involves checking whether data satisfies preconditions, not whether data is correct. The correctness of data is the domain of **data verification**. A common example of data verification is the checking of passwords. Whenever a password is entered, the software needs to check if the entered password matches the password on record. As one might infer from this example, data verification is important in authentication (i.e., comparing a live user's entered account credentials with the system's own information).

Low- and High-Level Programming Languages

The difference between **low-level languages** and **high-level languages** is, broadly speaking, how far removed the language is from machine language—the lowest-level language. Low-level languages are those languages that can be directly understood by the CPU or need very little transformation in order to be understood by the CPU. For example, machine language and assembly language are low-level languages. Machine language is of course directly understood by the computer. Assembly language translates readily into machine language. Essentially it just saves a programmer from needing to type everything in binary. High-level languages, on the other hand, are relatively easy for people to read, but require a lot of transformation to be made into machine language. Python, Ruby, and SQL are some of the highest-level languages. In these languages, the developer has very little control over specific actions the processor takes. In SQL, for example, the developer can tell the computer that they would like all of the rows in a specific table that contain the name "John." This request gets translated into a lower-level language by a process that is built into SQL interpreters or compilers, to save programmers a large amount of time and effort.

Machine Language

Machine language is the type of computer code that can be directly understood and executed by the computer (i.e., the processor). It consists entirely of binary—ones and zeros. The binary code translates into instructions that the processor can follow. Since it is nearly impossible for a human to program directly in machine language, people program in languages that are in more readable forms. Languages that require only a small amount of translation to become machine language are said to be low-level languages. An example of a low-level language would be any architectures **assembly language**. Languages that are more readable to humans tend to require a lot of translation to become machine code. These are known as high-level languages. All languages must be converted into machine language eventually, so that they can be understood by the computer. This process is known as **compiling**, and the tool that converts human-readable code into machine language is called a **compiler**. The specific machine language that will be the target language of the compiler depends on the operating system and system architecture of the machine.

Difference in Operation Time

Low-level languages operate faster than high-level languages there is little to no conversion required for low-level languages to be understood by the computer. The code needs to go through no compiling process, or perhaps a minimal compiling process, in order to run. Low-level languages provide specific and direct instructions for how the processor should operate. These instructions are very simple, so the code runs faster. High-level languages have layers of **abstraction**, which means that the developer who is typing code in that language cannot see or control many of the processes that will take place as part of that code executing. The language will have rules for how to break statements down into commands that are simple enough to be understood by the processor. Furthermore, a high-level language will have built-in rules for managing memory allocation, control flow, decision-making, and so on. This additional abstraction means that a simple statement in a high-level language equates to many lines of low-level code, so, for the same amounts of high-level code and low-level code, the high-level code will take more time to run.

Usage to Develop an Operating System

First, we should consider the function of an **operating system** so that we have an idea of the types of actions that may need to be performed. An operating system is responsible for managing memory, devices, and processes; it controls the hardware in a way that allows a person to make use of the hardware using computer programs. Because control of hardware is a key element in an operating system, hardware-level instructions will be necessary. Therefore, a low-level programming language must be used. Remember that low-level languages can control actions to the smallest level of detail, as they either are directly understood by the machine or require very little transformation to be converted into machine language.

Means of Classifying Languages

There is no objective standard used to classify a language as either low level or high level because the difference between the two is based the level of abstraction used by the language, which has several different dimensions, or layers. The single biggest abstraction is the ability of the language to control actions of the CPU. Low-level languages can directly control specific CPU actions, while high-level languages contain a layer of abstraction wherein they have their own processes for controlling the CPU that are not visible to the developer. Instead of thinking of languages as either low level or high level, it is more helpful to think languages on a spectrum. With machine language at the lowest point on the scale, some languages, such as assembly, would fall close to it. Higher up on the scale would be C and C++, because they manage CPU instructions without the developer needing to. Some languages would be even higher, such as Python and C#, because these have even more built-in functionality and are even farther removed from machine language. Coding in these languages may be slightly easier and the code may be more readable, but these languages use more processes that the developer cannot see or manage.

Ease of Learning

Most humans are not able to understand computer code in machine language. Programming in low-level languages usually requires a strong grasp of the binary and hexadecimal number systems. In addition, low-level languages require the developer to understand and account for things like memory usage and resource allocation. High-level languages are much easier to read and understand. Most high-level languages also do not require the developer to manually control memory usage or resource allocation. The compiler or the machine itself decides on the best and most efficient ways to handle these. Thus, although we cannot say that the higher level a language is, the easier it should be to learn, we can say that a person will have a much easier time learning to code in a high-level language than learning to code in assembly or machine language.

Ordering Languages from Low to High Level Example

Place the following languages in order from lowest to highest level, and explain the reasoning behind the ranking:

- *C*
- *Assembly*
- *Python*

Remember that low-level languages have the ability to directly control specific actions of the processor, while high-level languages keep most of this control—and its associated processes—in abstraction (i.e., hidden from the developer). Given this fact, the ordering of these languages from lowest to highest would be assembly, C, and then Python. Assembly language can be understood by the computer or easily translated into machine language, so the processor can execute specific instructions written in assembly language. Python is at the other end of the spectrum. It uses much higher-level commands and leaves the details of the commands to be determined by the compiler, which will translate them in executable code. C falls somewhere in the middle, with some high-level commands, but also commands that give the developer the ability to directly control some elements of CPU operation.

Types of Programming Languages

Machine language is the native language of a particular processor architecture. Writing directly in machine language is difficult and unommon, as it requires extensive knowledge of internal processor directives, and the ability to memorize commands in their binary form.

Symbolic language is the alternative to writing in machine code. All languages which replace the sequences of zeros and ones with symbols and acronyms are technically symbolic languages. That is, they use words or other symbols that translate into sets of CPU instructions. These words and symbols allow the programmer to write commands to control the computer without needing to write everything in binary.

Assembly language was the first type of symbolic language, named such because it "assembled" commands and values into sequences of binary code. When writing in an assembly language, the programmer must code every line of CPU instruction, meaning the ratio between a line of code in assembly language and a line of code in machine language is still one to one. Today, assembly language is still sometimes written by people, primarily for special-purpose computer applications.

High-Level Language

High-level language has long replaced assembly language as the predominant type of programming language. High-level languages possess a number of advantages over their forerunners:

- They do not require a one-to-one ratio between lines of programming code and lines of machine code.
- Their code is separate from the instruction set of the CPU; consequently, they can be used on multiple types and models of CPU.
- They are similar to natural language, allowing the programmer to write code in a more intuitive way.

Once a program is coded in a high-level language, it must be compiled into machine language so that the CPU can execute it. There are five categories of high-level language: procedural, object-oriented, functional, declarative, and special.

Procedural Category

The "procedural" category of high-level programming languages encompasses languages that were designed with the **procedural paradigm** of programming in mind. In the procedural paradigm, a program is a set of sequential instructions that must be executed in order. Several very common languages are considered procedural languages:

- FORTRAN (from "formula translation") It was prominent in the late 1950s, and it is still well-suited for science and engineering.
- BASIC, or Beginner's All-Purpose Symbolic Instruction Code, was available by 1964. It was used mostly as a teaching tool. BASIC does not require a compiler; as a result, it saw a revival in the 1990s as a means of programming personal computers.
- COBOL, (from "common business-oriented language") has been used since the 1960s for business applications.
- Pascal appeared in the 1970s and was commonly used for teaching programming.
- C, perhaps the best-known language of these, created specifically for programming UNIX operating systems. It was developed in the early 1970s, and it is still common as a general-purpose language.

OBJECT-ORIENTED CATEGORY

The "object-oriented" category of high-level programming languages comprises languages that lend themselves to the **object-oriented paradigm** of programming. Under this paradigm, developers define objects and assigns operations to them. Two of the best-known and most common programming languages are object-oriented languages:

- C++, or "C with Classes," is derived from C. Developed in the 1980s, C++ has come to be used for wide variety of applications. There are three principles in C++ language:
  - Encapsulation, the process of hiding information inside an object
  - Inheritance, the process of transferring properties between related objects
  - Polymorphism, the process of giving the same name to different processes
- Java was developed in the 1990s and took a lot of influence from C++. Broadly speaking, there are two types of Java programs:
  - Applications, which are compiled and run as executable files
  - Applets, which don't run as executable files but rather as embedded interactive elements on web pages or other documents

SPECIAL CATEGORY

The "special" category of high-level programming languages includes any languages that cannot be classified under the other categories, such as the following:

- Perl is capable of scanning text files, extracting information from text files, creating reports, and performing many of the same functions as the C language. Like JavaScript, PERL is known as a scripting language because it is written not in programs per se but in scripts. Scripts are read by an **interpreter** (rather than a compiler), which translates the code into excecutable code and then executes it right away.
- SQL (Structured Query Language) is used for managing relational databases and querying data in them.
- HTML (HyperText Markup Language) is the least like a true programming language of these three examples. It allows users to write richly formatted documents in plain text. The plain text is interpreted by web browsers, email applications, and other programs. With HTML, there is a universal way to encode a formatted page along with embedded media or interactive elements all into plain text so that it is easy to store and transmit.

FUNCTIONAL CATEGORY

The "functional" category of high-level programming languages includes languages that define new functions by identifying and combining more basic functions. Functional languages are not suited for designing information systems. However, they are useful in the academic sphere, particularly in high-level mathematics and artificial intelligence. An example of a functional language is Lisp (or LISP, from "list processor"), which was developed in the late 1950s., around the same time as FORTRAN.

Declarative Category

The "declarative" category of high-level programming languages includes many languages that are also considered functional languages. In the **declarative paradigm** of programming, langagues are meant to express the structure and logic of data rather than provide processes for handling data. This is in contrast with the **imperative paradigm** (which include procedural programming and object-oriented programming), where languages describe explicitly how to solve a problem. Declarative languages are useful in artificial intelligence and natural language processing. An example of a declarative language is Prolog, which was made available in the early 1970s. Intended for use in natural language processing, Prolog features the ability to define and query a system of logical relationships.

Object-Oriented Programming Concepts

Concepts in the Object-Oriented Programming Paradigm

There are many concepts that are specific to the object-oriented programming paradigm, but the following ten concepts are perhaps most important to understand:

- Class – a template for an object, which describes the characteristics of an object
- Object – an instance of a class, which carries specific values and methods that were identified as part of its structure in the definition of the class
- Instance – the specific copy of an object that exists during runtime
- Method – a function that belongs to an object or class.
- Message passing – the activity of objects communicating with each other
- Inheritance –the process by which classes impart their attributes to subclasses
- Abstraction – the process of simplifying and modeling programming problems
- Encapsulation – the process by which details of functions and values inside a class are hidden from other code, which can use the object but not change the data in it, except in a controlled way
- Polymorphism – a feature of classes wherein a given class and its subclasses can execute different functions when prompted by the same function call
- Decoupling – the separation of object interaction from its class

Classes

A **class** is essentially a way that a developer can create custom data types. Classes are quite prevalent in modern-day programming, and the majority of modern languages allow for the creation of classes in some form. By creating a class, a developer is able to specify the properties and behaviors of the objects inside that class and which operations may be performed on those objects. A class can be thought of as a blueprint for a data object. This blueprint lays out the structure by which the objects inside of that class must be built. Without classes, developers would be limited to using only the built-in data types of the programming language they were using. This would make it very difficult to create modern-day applications.

Defined Classes vs. Abstract Classes

The difference between a **defined class** and an **abstract class** can be somewhat confusing because the concept of abstract classes is a slippery one. A defined class is also referred to as a concrete class. Normally, a defined class is what the word "class" refers to. For a defined class, an instance can actually be created. An abstract class, however, contains at least one abstract method. This means that there is some functionality in the abstract class that is not totally defined. For this reason, instances of abstract classes cannot be created. It is not necessary at this point to understand the reasoning behind the creation of abstract classes. The key takeaway is that a defined class can be instantiated, while an abstract class cannot.

Instances of a Class

Remember that a class is essentially a blueprint for creating an object. An instance of a class is a created object. This concept is best explained by using an example. Imagine a new class called House. This class specifies that a House object must contain values for the number of bedrooms, the number of bathrooms, and the square footage, and a Boolean value for whether the house includes a basement. Now imagine this class being used to create three new house objects called house1, house2, and house3. Each of these three objects is an instance of the House class. An instance occurs when an actual object is created using a class.

Subclasses

A **subclass** is a class that define as child of another class and inherits the properties of that class. The parent class is also sometimes referred to as a **superclass**. A subclass can be created through single inheritance or multiple inheritance. In single inheritance, the subclass inherits properties from only one superclass. However, in multiple inheritance, the subclass inherits properties from more than one superclass. For example, Class C contains the properties of both Class A and Class B. It is also possible to have multiple levels of subclasses. For example, Class C inherits all properties from Class B, and Class B inherits all properties from Class A. Because classes that inherit properties can have additional properties, Class C may have some properties that are inherited from Class B only.

Relation of Classes, Instance Variables, and Methods

A class is a user-defined blueprint for objects; it defines the characteristics and functions of the objects that will be created based on it. Instance variables are variables that are defined in a class. These can be thought of as the class's attributes. Every specific case of an instance variable will be contained in an object. Since objects are instances of classes, the term "instance variable" reflects that the variable is one that will exist as part of an instance. Methods are functions that are defined in a class. These will be the member functions of objects created under the class.

As an illustration, imagine a class that defines car objects. Some characteristics of the class would be the type of car, its color, and its horsepower. These characteristics would be defined as instance variables. Each object that is created under the car class could have a different value for these instance variables. In other words, one object, Car1, could have the value "blue" for the color instance variable, while another object, Car2, could have the value "white" for the color instance variable. Functions of the car object would be, for example, move forward, stop, turn left, and turn right. Methods would be defined in the class, so that objects based on the class would have these functions.

Importance of Inheritance When Designing Classes

Inheritance is a term used in object-oriented programming which describes the ability of one class to inherit the attributes and methods from another class. This is an important part of programming when using classes because it limits redundancy and allows one very similar or related class to be based on another one. For example, we might have a class called Dog. This class defines that a dog has four legs, can bark, and can run. We might then make a class called Bulldog. A bulldog is still a dog, so the Bulldog class should inherit the attribute of four legs and the functionality of barking and running. In addition to these inherited attributes and methods, we can add attributes that are specific to a bulldog, like short legs and a large head. This allows us to focus only on the unique requirements of each child class and not have to worry about copying all the similarities from one class to the other.

Types of Methods Within a Class

There are a few generalized classifications of methods that are common within a class. First is an accessor method. This type of method is used to access the attributes of a class. Since it is standard to make all attributes of a class private, the only way to access the values contained within them is through the use of a method. These methods usually start their name with "get", often have no parameters, and return the value of the attribute. Here is an example in Java:

```
public static int getAge()
//This method returns the age attribute
```

Conversely, classes can also contain mutator methods. This type of method is used to change the attributes of a class. These methods usually start their name with "set", often have no return value, and pass in a value that is meant to replace the current value of an attribute. Here is an example in Java:

```
public static void setAge(int age)
```

Next, we have helper methods. These methods are often hidden from the outside and are only called from other methods within a class. They help to break larger tasks down into smaller ones, or are repeatedly called and used in order to prevent redundant code.

Lastly, we have the publicly available methods. These are the actions of the class that are used by other classes. For example, if we had a class called Math, we might have methods for adding, subtracting, multiplying, and dividing.

Use of Variables Within a Class

Variables in a class are also known as the **attributes** of the class. These attributes define the current state of the class. For example, to create a shape object one must know the attributes of that shape, such as its color, type, and its location in space. Without these variables, instances of a class would have no definite attributes and would not be able to be unique. Creating an object of that class allows one to define the attributes for that particular object.

Public vs. Private Access Specifiers in a Class

A **private access** specifier defines a variable or a method that can only be accessed by other parts of the current class. This may be used on a class in order to hide information that should not be accessed by outside sources. Certain helper methods, as well as most attributes, are marked as private in order to further restrict and control their use. A **public access** specifier defines a variable or a method that can be accessed by the current class as well as any other outside class. The public access specifier is used in most cases where the variable or method can be accessed without restriction.

Constructors in a Class

A **constructor** is a special method in a class that is called whenever an object of that class is first created. A constructor's purpose is to set aside memory for the object as well as initialize any attributes within the class. These attributes may be initialized to default values, or parameters may be passed to the constructor when it is created in order to alter these attributes so that they are set upon instantiation. Multiple constructors can be created for a class by overloading the constructor, which means having different constructors with either a different number of parameters, or parameters with different data types.

Multiple Constructors in a Class

A class may contain more than one constructor because it may have different ways that it should be initialized. The class may allow some flexibility to initialize all or only some of the attributes. For example, let's say we had a class called "pizza" that contained the pizza's size, cost, and topping type. By default, the size could be "medium", cost could be "$9.99", and the topping type could be "cheese". The class could have one constructor that allowed the object to be created with a user defined size, cost, and topping type, overwriting all of those default values with user supplied ones. Then, we may have another constructor that only allows for the pizza's size to be supplied as a parameter for the constructor. This may be used when the user wants to create a pizza with the default cost and topping type, but be able to start the object's size with a different value than the default.

CLASS DIAGRAMS

Class diagrams are one tool of the **Unified Modeling Language** (**UML**). They illustrate the relationships between classes in object-oriented systems. Each class is illustrated by a rectangular box, and lines are drawn connecting the boxes in order to show the relationships (known as **associations**) between classes. Class diagrams are capable of showing three types of associations:

- One-to-one relationship – established when two classes associate with each other
- One-to-many relationship – established when a single class associates with multiple classes
- Many-to-many relationship – established when a group of classes associates with another group of classes

BENEFITS OF IMPLEMENTING INTERFACES

The main benefit of implementing an interface into a design is that an interface allows the developer to maintain control over the minimum functionality required for certain classes. It is not necessary for the interface to be written with the specific details of the functionality in mind, but the interface enforces the rule that a particular function must exist in the class. Consider an example: an interface is created called `Boat`. `Boat` is defined so that `start_engine()` is a required function. Multiple subclasses of `Boat` may exist, such as `SkiBoat`, `SpeedBoat`, `TugBoat`, and `FishingBoat`. The interface doesn't need to incorporate the specific of how `start_engine()` will work, but it does ensure that anything under the class `Boat` must have `start_engine()`.

INHERITANCE

Inheritance is a functionality in object-oriented programming. It is important in object-oriented programming because it is a key to writing classes efficiently. As the name implies, inheritance allows a developer to create a new class that inherits the properties of another class. A parent-child relationship then exists between the two classes. This can create many coding efficiencies because it allows for modular design of the code, and it allows for code from the parent class to be reused in child classes without having to duplicate the code.

GENERALIZATION

In object-oriented programming, **generalization** applies to a class of objects whose features are the same as another class's but less specific. The generalized class will be identical to the other class except in that it will have fewer properties. Generalization is useful for identifying what classes would be able to use inheritance.

RELATION OF OVERRIDING AND INHERITANCE

Inheritance is key to being able to override a function or method. Subclasses inherit the properties of their parent classes, or superclasses. In a subclass with inherited methods, these methods can be overridden. In order to override the function, the function contained in the subclass must have the same name, the same number of parameters, the same parameter data types, and the same return type. When the method is called for the subclass, the functionality of the subclass method will be used, overriding the functionality that was inherited from the superclass. **Overriding** is commonly used when the methods in a superclass are close to what is needed for its subclasses, but slightly different. The developer may choose to allow the subclass to inherit from the superclass and then override some methods to make the sure the functionality is written exactly as needed.

INHERITING OVERLOADED METHODS

Overloaded methods can be inherited from a superclass. Remember that in inheritance, the subclass receives all the methods and properties of the superclass. If the superclass contains overloaded methods, then the subclass will also have those overloaded methods. Remember that overloading occurs when a class contains multiple methods with the same name but different quantities or types of parameters. Imagine a class with a method sum( ). The function sum( ) may be defined as sum(int a, int b), sum (int a, int b, int c), and sum(int a, int b, int c, int d)—three separate functions all named "sum." Now the method can be called using the name "sum," and depending on the number of arguments passed, the method could provide the sum of two numbers (a and b), three numbers (a, b, and c), or four numbers (a, b, c, and d). If a subclass is created to inherit from the class that sum() is in, then the overloaded sum( ) method will be passed down to this subclass.

Using Inheritance for Classes with Private Data

Using inheritance for classes that have private data is not advised because in many languages these two concepts work in ways that contradict each other. Data encapsulation is an attempt to protect the class from being changed by anything that is outside the class and that isn't changing the class in a controlled way through a public method. Inheritance shares all of the properties of the class with another class. When inheritance is used, the protection gained from data encapsulation is lost. For this reason, it is not recommended to allow any class using data encapsulation to be used in a parent-child class relationship.

Abstraction

Abstraction filters out the details and only reveals the necessary parts of a system. Doing this obscures details that are not necessary and allows the engineer to focus on the details that are important at the time. As a real-world example, when you drive a car you understand that pressing the gas pedal makes the car move and pressing the brake pedal makes the car slow down and stop. In reality, when you press these pedals, lots of things are occurring. When you press the gas pedal, it turns a pivot that pulls the throttle wire, which connects to many other mechanisms that finally open a valve to deliver gas to the car. All of this information is not necessary to correctly drive the car. Having to do all of these things manually would interfere with the point of having one pedal that obscures the details and allows the driver to concentrate on driving the car.

Data Encapsulation

Data encapsulation is a method by which a developer can protect the integrity of data by putting it inside an object. Through data encapsulation, the developer can make specific values and functionality within a class inaccessible to the rest of the program. Using data encapsulation gives the developer confidence that a class's values and functions that should not be changed from outside the class will indeed not be affected by operations outside the class. Such protected members of objects are considered private. When using data encapsulation, the developer will likely also need to create some public methods inside the class. These public methods will allow other objects to access the encapsulated data in a very controlled manner.

Availability of Data Encapsulation

Data encapsulation is possible in some form in nearly all object-oriented programming languages. Any language that provides the ability for a developer to create custom data objects needs to also provide the ability to protect those objects. This protection is provided by data encapsulation. While the syntax and specific method of encapsulation vary from language to language, the functionality exists. In functional programming languages, on the other hand, true encapsulation does not exist, but the same purpose (i.e., data hiding) can be achieved through other means.

Reasons to Encapsulate Data Within a Class

The most common reason a developer will encapsulate data within a class is to protect the class from being altered in an unintended manner. Often, developers create public classes that are available for use by other developers. Without data encapsulation, these other developers would have full access to the original class, and they could intentionally or unintentionally alter the functionality of the class. On the other hand, with data encapsulation, other routines can interact with the class only in ways that are controlled and intended by the writer of the class. Direct access to the values and methods in the class is not provided, and access is tightly controlled through the use of public methods in the class.

Accessing Values Inside an Encapsulated Class

By using data encapsulation, a developer sets values and functions inside the class as private. These values and functions can then only be accessed by other functionality that is internal to the class. So, how do encapsulated classes interact with any other objects? The answer is by using methods called **getters** and **setters**. Getters and setters are public methods created within a class for the specific function of either getting or setting certain values inside the class. Since the getter and setter functions are internal to the class, they have full access to the values in the class. Because these functions are public, code outside the class can access them, so the code can also indirectly access the values in the class, albeit in a manner that is controlled by the public functions of the class. This allows other objects to interact with the class, yet it maintains the integrity of the encapsulated data by keeping the interactions very controlled.

Importance of Data Encapsulation in Object-Oriented Development

Data encapsulation is one of the fundamental premises relied upon in object-oriented programming. Since developers are given the ability to create custom data structures or objects, they need some way to control how much interaction other functions have with these objects. In most cases, there is no need for outside functions to have unlimited access to object members. Data encapsulation allows the object to be treated as a black box by the rest of the program. It can "see" inputs and outputs of public functions, it cannot "see" anything else inside the object. This prevents the inadvertent changing of values inside the object.

Polymorphism

The word "**polymorphism**" suggests the ability of one entity to change into various forms. In programming, the term relates to functions and objects. It may refer to the ability of functions to operate on different data types. What appears to be a single function is actually a set of similar functions that share the same name but accept different data types. When this function name is used in a function call, the data type of the input is used to determine which of the functions to execute. Also known as **function overloading**, this capability is built into some languages, and in some languages the same effect can be achieved with user-defined functions. The term may also refer to using the same name for different functions, variables, or data types that are in different classes.

Importance of Polymorphism in Object-Oriented Programming

Polymorphism is very important in object-oriented programming because it allows functions to be flexible. It is difficult to program many different scenarios using a very rigid set of rules. If that were the case, then separate functions would need to exist to handle every possible input. Polymorphism allows the same function name to be used for a variety of inputs. It also allows different classes to have functions with the same name that perform different operations—ones that are necessary give the object's intended properties and behaviors. This not only allows for more modular code design, easier debugging, and shorter development cycles, but helps developers maintain an overarching logic in their definitions of classes and systems of classes.

Overloading vs. Overriding a Method

There is often confusion regarding the terms "overload" and "override" when it comes to methods. Overloading a method is the practice of giving two or more functions the same name, but defining each one to accept different data types as arguments or to accept a different number of arguments. For example, we could have two methods named `findAverage`. One of these might find the average of two integers, and the other might find the average of three integers. This would be an example of having two methods with the same name but a different number of arguments. We could also make another method called `findAverage` that accepts two doubles. Even though there is an existing method that has the same number of parameters, because the parameters are a different data type, this is third `findAverage` function will be considered a valid and separate function by the compiler.

The term "overriding" also refers to functions having the same name. However, in the case of overriding, one of the functions belongs to a class, and the other belongs to a subclass. In this case, when an instance of the subclass is created, the default call to that method would be the one that exists in the subclass. There are often ways to access the parent class's method instead, but whether this is possible and how it is done will vary from one language to another.

Overloading and overriding methods in a class are similar techniques, but they have some key differences. The practice of overloading a function means that multiple methods with the same name are created in the same class. Each of these methods uses different input parameters. The method by that name is then said to be "overloaded." Overriding a method relies on inheritance from a superclass. When a subclass inherits a method, the method will have the same name as the method in the parent class. However, the subclass method "overrides" the parent class method, meaning that if the function name is used, the subclass method will be the function that is called. In summary, overloading and overriding are both performed on methods within a class. However, overloading means methods have the same name but different parameters, while overriding means methods have the same name and same parameters, but can have different levels of precedence depending on which class they are in.

Reasons to Overload a Function in a Class

A developer may want to overload a method in a class when there is some functionality that needs to be provided in the class but that may need to be written differently depending on what type of input it received. Overloading allows inputs to be different in number or in data type. If the number of parameters or the data types of the parameters are the same in two different function declarations, this is not overloading.

Program Compilation and Interpretation

Source Code vs. Object Code

The computer instructions of a program that are written in a programming language and are comprehensible to humans are known collectively as **source code**. In order to be readable to a computer processor, source code must be converted into digital data. Source code is often quite similar to human language, which makes it easier for programmers to write, edit, and understand. There are two devices that translate source code into executable code (i.e., **object code**): an interpreter and a compiler. An interpreter translates one statement at a time while a program is operating, whereas a compiler translates a group of program statements and creates an executable file from it. In either case, the process of converting source code to machine-readable code must occur for a program to run. Machine code is the name for the set of instructions used by the microprocessor. It is composed of operation codes, which themselves are composed of command words indicating operations and operands indicating locations of the data used in each operation.

Compilers

A **compiler** translates code from a programming language into machine-readable language. At its lowest level, machine language is made up of digital bits of information, ones and zeros. Humans are not able to read code that is written in machine language in any useful way. They need some form of symbolism that at least minimally resembles natural language. Therefore, most programming languages utilize keywords (i.e., names of built-in items such as data types and control flow statements) that are based on actual words in human language. This allows humans to read code written in programming languages with some level of ease. In order for that code to become something that the computer can execute, it needs to be converted into machine language (ones and zeros) by a program called a compiler. Modern-day compilers are very complicated and advanced. They are generally specific to one programming language, and for any given language, there may be many compilers available from different vendors. In summary, a compiler is a program that translates high-level programming language code into low-level machine language so that it can be executed by the processor.

Software Interpreters

A **software interpreter** functions in much the same way as a human interpreter. Just as a human interpreter converts one language to another so that people who speak different languages can communicate with each other, a software interpreter converts a piece of code in one language into code in a language that is "understood" by the CPU. An interpreter functions in real time, converting each line of code as the program runs. Interpreters may convert the code into machine or assembly language, or they may convert it into some intermediate step. In short, the interpreter acts as the middle man; it takes code that has been entered, converts it, and passes it on, and it does this one line of code at a time.

Classification of Languages as Compiled or Interpreted

The classification of a language as either **compiled** or **interpreted** is technically dependent upon the specific use case and not the language itself. It would be more appropriate to classify a piece of code or an application—rather than a whole language—as either compiled or interpreted. It is entirely possible to use the same language to create both compiled code and interpreted code. In one instance, the code may be compiled and converted to machine language before runtime. In another instance, the code may use an interpreter that converts it to machine instructions one line at a time during runtime. Therefore, the implementation of the code—not the programming language—is the real difference.

Compiled vs. Interpreted Code Operation Speeds

A piece of compiled code operates faster than interpreted code. Remember that when code is compiled, it is converted into a machine-readable format. When running compiled code, the CPU can perform the actions specified in the code directly. There is no additional conversion step required (or rather, the conversion has already been done), so the performance is quick. Interpreted code, on the other hand, requires the code to be interpreted line by line in real time as it runs. This adds extra processing time that causes the code to run more slowly. Think of it this way: compiled code means the CPU is running an application directly, while interpreted code means the CPU is running an application (the interpreter) that in turn is running the application that was developed.

Software Development

Software Development Life Cycle

The problem definition is the stage where the purpose of the program is stated, as well as any issues that must be overcome. The analysis stage represents the time period in which materials are gathered, information about the details of the system are compiled, and prototypes are created. During the design stage, developers outline the details for the overall application. The development stage comes next, and is when the code is actually written. Once the software is built, it must be tested. Even after release, the cycle is not complete because continued maintenance will occur, which may consist of more development and testing based on new requirements.

Design Specification

A **design specification** (also known as a design document) is a document that specifies what a product or process should do. Often, clients can verbally specify what they want, but this can be misconstrued. By the time the next meeting occurs, the client may be explaining the product in a completely different way. By having a design specification, it is detailed in writing exactly what is expected of the programmers, and any changes to this document must be communicated and approved. By having this sort of document available, the clients will know exactly what they will be getting, and the programmers will be working towards a well-established goal with no confusion as to what needs to be done.

Decomposition

Decomposition involves taking a very large and often complicated problem and reducing it to smaller more manageable "modules". In software engineering, the ideal way to do this is through the use of modular programming with functions. Functions accept inputs and give outputs without the programmer necessarily understanding or knowing what goes on within it. This is beneficial in many ways for large-scale projects, as these projects are more easily distributed among team members, each completing functional tasks and then bringing them back together for testing purposes. For example, creating a video game from scratch without functions would be a daunting task. However, breaking individual components of the game into functions, such as a scoring system, a collision system, and a control system, makes programming the game a lot easier and more organized.

Top-down Design vs. Bottom-Up Design

A **top-down design** is the decomposition of a system into smaller parts in order to understand the smaller, modular parts. In top-down design (also known as stepwise design), all of the top-level systems are defined, and as more details about how they work are needed, they are built. Breaking problems into parts like this allows multiple programmers to work on a problem simultaneously. The details are understood as the problem is broken down into its smallest parts.

In **bottom-up design**, the smaller parts of the system are defined first. These parts are then combined to form the larger components. Eventually, enough parts are linked, and the system's purpose is achieved. Seeing all of the smaller pieces at a low level allows programmers to better understand how these parts can be reused.

Stepwise Refinement

Stepwise refinement is used in top-down design. Using this technique, we first define a large problem that needs to be solved. We then break that problem down into smaller tasks until a simpler algorithm is able to solve each of those smaller tasks. By working this way, it is easier to get a better understanding of the scale and the scope of the project, and you are able to take a large daunting task and dissect it into smaller, solvable pieces. It is also helpful to note that these smaller pieces can be delegated to different programmers in order to work together more efficiently.

Black Box Program

A **black box program** is one where the user does not know or need to know the inner workings, only the inputs and outputs. The programmer knows what is going on inside the box, but these details are hidden from the user. When creating a black box program, it is important that the programmer conveys the pre-conditions and post-conditions to the user so that they can use the program appropriately. For example, if a program is able to calculate the area of a rectangle but only allows integers for the length and width, the user should understand these requirements so that they do not supply a decimal value. They should also understand that the output of the program will be a number that represents the area of that rectangle.

Object-Oriented Programming

Object Oriented Programming (OOP) is a programming style that focuses on the creation of objects that have attributes and methods instead of using only functions and logic. The four main building blocks of OOP are classes, objects, methods, and attributes. Classes are the blueprints for creating new objects. They are user-defined data types that state the attributes and methods of an object. An object is an instance of a class. These can correspond to a real-world object or an abstract entity. Methods are the functions that are defined within a class that describe the behavior of the object. For example, if we create a class to describe a bank account, there will most likely be methods included for depositing and withdrawing funds. Attributes describe the current state of the object. For the previous example using bank accounts, there may be an attribute that holds the current amount of money in that bank account.

Functional Programming

Functional programming is the term denoted to any programming approach that utilizes function call instead of creating objects. Each task is broken down into one or more smaller tasks, which eventually combine to solve the problem. Some benefits of functional programming include avoiding confusing problems and errors in the code because of its simplistic style and flow, and better modularity because pieces can be easily examined and modified.

Importance of Design Risk Assessment

A **design risk** is the potential for a design to fail to satisfy the requirements of the project. Design risk assessment attempts to identify possible areas where a project may fail. By completing this process as software is developed, possible software failures can be identified early. By being proactive in the process of identifying risks of failure, less time will be spent on software that has to be reworked because of some unforeseen circumstance.

Chapter Quiz

Ready to see how well you retained what you just read? Scan the QR code to go directly to the chapter quiz interface for this study guide. If you're using a computer, simply visit the online resources page at **mometrix.com/resources719/oaecompsci** and click the Chapter Quizzes link.

Computing Systems, Networks, and the Internet

Transform passive reading into active learning! After immersing yourself in this chapter, put your comprehension to the test by taking a quiz. The insights you gained will stay with you longer this way. Scan the QR code to go directly to the chapter quiz interface for this study guide. If you're using a computer, simply visit the online resources page at **mometrix.com/resources719/oaecompsci** and click the Chapter Quizzes link.

Operating Systems

Basic Functions of an Operating System

An **operating system (OS)** is a piece of software that manages a piece of hardware. Generally, it offers an interface so that the hardware can be controlled, and it provides a platform for computer programs to be run using the hardware. Examples of common consumer OSs for personal computers are Microsoft Windows and Apple macOS. An OS can roughly be thought of as the manager of a computer. It controls the hardware of the device and how the applications on the device interact with the hardware. If the device is connected to any other devices, the OS manages those connections as well. The OS distributes the available resources of a machine among the programs that are running. Commonly, programs run as **processes**, and each process is given a priority so that sufficient resources can always be given to applications and services that are critical. Resources and activities that an OS manages include processor time, main memory (or RAM) space, storage (or hard disk) space, permissions, connected devices, and display. In the event that the computer or device has a problem, such as insufficient memory, the OS can generally notify the user and provide options for resolving the problem.

Components of an Operating System

An operating system, or OS, manages and controls computer functions through the use of several components with dedicated purposes. These components include the following:

- A **memory manager** allocates random access memory, or RAM, to applications and system processes. It can allow for monoprogramming, in which only one program executes at a time, or multiprogramming, in which multiple programs execute at one time techniques such as partitioning and paging.
- A **process manager** controls programs and services, which run inside the OS as their own named processes. The process manager typically plays a significant role in resource allocation because many OSs assign priority levels to processes and allocate resources based on these priority levels.
- A **spooler** is dedicated to sending outputs to devices that process data slowly (such as printers). The spooler forms a queue of tasks and sends each tasks only when the device is ready. This way, the device does not need to be capable of storing the tasks, and the system is always ready to send a waiting task without dedicating resources that could be used for something else.
- An **interrupt handler** examines and categorizes interrupt commands, which are signals that alert the CPU to stop a process. Such signals may come from input/output (I/O) devices, from the OS itself, or from applications running on the OS.

Security Controls Used by Operating Systems

Operating systems include a range of features and measures to ensure that the system and the data it contains remain secure. Among the most common are the following:

- **User authentication** requires users of the operating system to log in to the system with **credentials** (i.e., usernames and passwords). The purpose of user authentication is to limit access to data or functionality based on permissions. An OS can also log the actions of each user to provide an audit trail.
- **Antivirus and antimalware** can be installed as applications in their own right, but they are increasingly included as OS components. These types of software access a database of viruses and malware and regularly search the computer for files that match ones in the database. They generally also include virtual firewalls, which monitor network traffic and control which applications can use network connections. Antivirus and antimalware may include a variety of other features, including detecting changes to the OS's **registry** and warning the user when the user allows an application such as an intaller to make administrator-level changes.
- **Privilege levels** are used by many OSs to determine what types of changes a user or another application should be allowed to make. The two most basic and common privilege levels are "administrator" and "user." With aministrator privileges, a user or application can make changes to the system itself, such as registry edits. With user priveleges, a user or application can access applications and files that are owned by them or are allowed for all users.

Functions of the Operating System

The operating system (OS) manages the computer itself and allows applications to run using the computer's resources, so that users can simply use the applications without needing to know about or manage any technical settings or processes. The OS is responsible for processing and storing data, communicating with peripheral devices (e.g., printers or scanners), keeping track of files and their permissions, keeping track of applications, and allocating system resources. Generally, OSs allow for multithreading, or the running of multiple processes at the same time. Not all system and CPU architectures are compatible will all OSs. Furthermore, an OS may be able to run with a certain CPU but still not take full advantage of the efficiencies the CPU offers. For example, an OS that does not support multicore processing may be able to run on a multicore CPU, but it will not function any more efficiently than it would on a single core.

Different Operating Systems

There are different operating systems (OSs) for different computing tasks. For instance, single-user operating systems (e.g., DOS) can receive input from only one user at a time. Modern operating systems tend to be multi-user, meaning that they can be accessed and used by several different people or programs at the same time. Multi-user operating systems (like IBM's OS/390) are used in mainframe computers. Network OSs, which have been largely replaced by client-user network stacks, allow multiple users to share information, programs, and peripheral device access.

Semaphores

A **semaphore** is a technique by which a program manages access to a resource that only one process can use at the same time. Operating systems use semaphores to manage processes' access to system resources. Using a flag system, a semaphore prevents two processes from accessing the same resource simultaneously. A set flag, which has a value of one, specifies the resource is being used. A clear flag, which has a value of zero, specifies the resource is available. However, if the flag process is interrupted during execution, it can still result in two processes accessing the same resource. To avoid interruption, a semaphore either temporarily disables the system's use of interrupt commands or uses a test-and-set instruction, which executes the entire flag sequence in one instruction, or executes none of it. Semaphores execute sets of instructions that establish critical regions in the computer system. Only one process can access these regions at a time—a requirement known as mutual exclusion.

Deadlock

Deadlock occurs when multiple processes are blocking each other from using resources, or when multiple processes must create new processes to complete their function but the schedule table is full. Three conditions must be present for **deadlock** to occur:

1. Processes are competing for nonshareable resources.
2. Processes are requesting only part of a resource. As a result, the processes are using some of the resource and then returning to use more at a later time.
3. Processes cannot forcibly retrieve the resources they have been allocated.

Operating systems use a variety of techniques to overcome deadlock:

- A **kill** command forcibly removes one or more processes that are filling the schedule table. This technique only treats the third condition; thus, it can only affect the system after the deadlock has occurred.
- **Spooling** prevents deadlock from occurring. The process executes as if it has access to the resource, but in reality, its data is being stored for execution at a later, more convenient time.
- An algorithm may require each process to request all the resources it will need before it needs them, or before it starts. Like spooling, this technique prevents deadlock from occurring.

Interacting with Operating Systems

A person using a desktop, notebook, tablet, or smartphone is in contact with the operating system (OS) as soon as the OS boots. Most OSs present a desktop-style interface, where shortcuts to applications may be placed, and in some cases, small data displays that update themselves periodically may be placed as well. This desktop forms the main backdrop of a user's experience on a computer or mobile device, but its use is limited to only those activities which are accessible through shortcuts. By and large, OSs offer a variety of other functions available in various menus, as well as complete list of applications, and one or many control panels where utility programs can be run and system-wide settings changed. The user's control over look and feel varies from one OS to another, but for the most part the user has a great deal of control, from display settings (such as resolution, zoom, and brightness), to fonts and font sizes, to aesthetic features like wallpapers and color themes.

Improving Computer Security with an Operating System

Operating systems primarily mediate communication between the user and the computer, but it is also essential that they have a method for guaranteeing the security of the information that is stored on the computer. For instance, most operating systems have a credentialing system in which each user of the computer has a username and a password. Contemporary operating systems can also detect changes to system settings, such as the registry, and can warn the user before the user allows a program to make changes at the system level. Finally, operating systems generally have reliable systems of protecting files using permissions. Every file on a computer with a standard operating system like this has a set of permissions that determine which users can read or modify files. Likewise, folders have permissions that control which users are allowed to move files into the folder, take files out of the folder, or modify files in the folder.

Computing Systems and Communication Between Devices

Important Components of a Computer System

The two fundamental componononents of a computer system are the **system unit**, or processing unit, and **memory**, or storage. The system unit of a computer contains the **central processing unit** (CPU), also known as the microprocessor. The memory component includes the **random access memory** (RAM) and **secondary storage**, such as a hard disk. Alongside these two basic components, a computer also needs inputs and outputs in order to be used. These functions typically served by peripherals, such as keyboards, mice, speakers, monitors, and printers. The system unit communicates with these peripheral devices.

CPU

The abbreviation "CPU" stands for "central processing unit." The CPU is like the brain of the computer; it is where most processing in the computer takes place. The CPU carries out instructions from running applications and the operating system. These operations could be input or output functions, basic arithmetic, or logical comparisons. The CPU receives instructions that have been converted into machine language from programming code. Instructions in machine language direct the CPU to carry out very specific operations, such as loading a piece of information into a specific slot in memory or capturing a piece of information from an input location. Importantly, CPUs read and execute these instructions extremely quickly—more than 100,000 basic instructions per second in the first commercially available CPUs, and generally at least 1 billion per second in modern CPUs.

Parts of a CPU

The **central processing unit**, or **CPU**, is a microchip that carries out the instructions in computer programs. It generally includes three basic parts:

- An **arithmetic-logic unit** carries out operations (addition, subtraction, multiplication, etc.) on data.
- A **control unit** manages the activities of the CPU.
- A **memory unit** manages **registers**, which are data storage cells that provide temporary information storage within the CPU. There are two types of registers: special-purpose and general-purpose.

General-purpose registers provide temporary storage for data the CPU is using. Specifically, these contain the inputs to and outputs from the arithmetic-logic unit. Before the CPU can perform operations on data contained in main memory, the control unit must retrieve the data and send it to the general purpose registers. Then, the control unit informs and turns on the required circuitry within the arithmetic-logic unit and identifies the registers to which the output should be sent.

Multicore Processors, Hyper-Threading Technology, and Benchmarks

Multicore processors have become the modern standard for providing more processing power in less time without using multiple individual CPUs. Multicore processors are faster than single-core processors because they contain the circuitry of two microprocessors on a single CPU. The operating system and software of the computer must be configured for to make use of multicore processing; hence, older operating systems will not benefit from a multicore processor even if they are running on one. Another method of providing more processing power in less time using a single CPU is **hyper-threading** (sometimes called Hyper-Threading Technology, or HTT, which is a proprietary hyper-threading technology). In hyper-threading, a single processor core is divided into two or more virtual cores, known as **threads**. In this arrangement, the same effects and benefits of multicore processing can be achieved. Because CPUs were complicated to begin with, became a great deal more complicated over time, could be fine-tuned in different system builds, and had different architectures with different technologies integrated, the specifications of CPUs became less accurate indicators of real performance. Instead, the computer industry developed a way to measure the relative performance of any given CPU, known as benchmarking. A **benchmark** is a test or series of tests run on a CPU to compare its processing speed with known standards.

Handling Tasks

A computer's central processing unit (CPU) is managed by the kernel of the operating system. It receives tasks as streams of bits, which generally form simple instructions. These instructions typically consist of moving data from one address to another, storing data that is input by the user, and so on, and they may include the data or the address of the data on which these operations will be performed. Instructions may be stored briefly, but they are eventually performed by the arithmetic-logic unit of the CPU. A memory unit in the CPU keeps track of pieces of data and may store them in high-speed memory units inside the CPU, which are collectively called cache. Otherwise, the memory unit may store data in main memory, or RAM, which is a separate chip located elsewhere on the motherboard. A simple action on a computer may result in a large number of instructions for the CPU, but the CPU is capable of processing millions or billions of instructions each second, so the performing of individual instructions is not noticeable.

Ways a Processor Can Process Instructions

A processor is said to be serial processing when one instruction must be entirely completed before the processor can move on to the next instruction. Pipelining, on the other hand, is when a processor can begin working on the next instruction before it has finished the prior instruction. In parallel processing, the processor can work on several instructions simultaneously. Due to their design, parallel processing and pipelining are faster and more efficient than serial processing.

Word Size

In computing, **word size** is the number of bits that a processor core can process at one time. When a processor's word size is greater, the computer can process more bits at a time and therefore run faster. A 64-bit processor, for instance, is processing data eight bytes at a time (one byte being eight bits). The 64-bit word size has become the standard for modern computers. The word size of a processor is determined by the size and capacity of the processor's registers.

Circuits, Vacuum Tubes, and Transistors

A **circuit** is a pathway for the flow of electric current. In order for current to flow, a circuit has to be closed, or complete. A **vacuum tube** is a small, hollow cylinder containing a tiny wire circuit that enables the flow of electrons. There is no air in a vacuum tube, which allows the electrons to flow more freely. The original vacuum tubes used in computers functioned like switches; they could be given one of two values (i.e., "on" and "off," or one and zero). Thus they were used to store bits in processing. However, vacuum tubes are notoriously unreliable and energy-intensive, so they were eventually removed from computer manufacture altogether. They were replaced by **transistors**, which have the same ability to function as switches and be turned on and off millions of times every second. Transistors are very small and made of semiconductor material, so they are less expensive and more reliable than vacuum tubes.

Computer Power Supply

The **power supply unit** (**PSU**) for a computer converts alternating current (such as from a wall power outlet) into direct current, which is required by the internal components of the computer. A power supply is regulated by an on-off switch, and a network of wires carries power to the drives, motherboard, and other components. A sudden increase in power can endanger the components of the computer, so machines are often plugged into surge protectors or surge suppressors to prevent damage, and the PSU for the computer may have a surge-protecting function as well. In addition, computers often have a voltage regulator that maintains a sufficient level of current. Finally, many computers, particularly servers, are plugged into **uninterruptible power supplies** (**UPS**s), which, in the event of a power outage, provide a few moments of power to allow for a computer to be powered down appropriately or for a backup generator to come on.

System Clock

The **system clock** is a device that controls the speed of computing operations. It is located inside the CPU of a computer. The system clock is regulated by quartz crystal vibrations, which create digital pulsations. These pulsations, also known as ticks or cycles, set the speed at which data will be processed. When the microprocessor works quickly, computer applications work quickly. The speed of the system clock is measured in hertz.

Cache

Cache is a special type of memory that computers use for frequently required instructions. The presence of cache accelerates processing functions. Cache that is built directly into the CPU is referred to as **level 1 cache** (or **L1 cache**) or system cache. This cache holds information that the CPU needs very quick access to. It is limited in size. A larger cache that takes slightly longer for the CPU to access is **level 2 cache** (or **L2 cache**). Generally L2 cache is on a nearby chip, though it may also be built into the CPU. Finally, **level 3 cache** (or **L3 cache**) takes the longest of all to access, though it can still be accessed for quickly than main memory (or RAM). Cache types and sizes depend on the CPU and motherboard. Furthermore, certain CPU architectures may require more cache than others, because architectures determine how machine-language instructions need to be formatted.

Cache Memory

Cache memory is a special memory area that is inside the CPU. As high-speed memory, it provides ready access to information that is needed immediately. Cache memory saves the registers from constantly having to extract data from main memory, speeding up program execution because the machine cycle is not hampered by having to communicate with main memory. If information is changed within cache memory, it is later saved to main memory.

Computer memory can be categorized into the following three types based on when the data stored in the memory will be needed:

- Registers in the CPU contain information that is needed to perform the current operation.
- Main memory, or RAM, stores information that will be needed soon.
- Mass storage, including a hard disk or solid-state drive, stores information that will not be needed for some time.

Mass Storage

Mass storage, also known as secondary storage, includes any devices that provide additional memory storage, such as hard disks, solid-state drives, flash drives, compact discs, DVDs, magnetic tapes, etc. Storage devices can be divided into the following two types based on their connectivity:

- Online storage devices can operate without human intervention because they are attached to the machine.
- Offline devices only operate after some type of human intervention, such as turning on the power or plugging the device into the correct port.

Mass-storage devices offer advantages such as stability, low cost, high storage capacity, and archival storage functions. A disadvantage is that they require substantially more time than main memory to access. Importantly, mass storage disks are not accessed directly by the CPU, as registers and RAM are. Instead, they are organized by a filesystem. In a filesystem, the operating system uses a database of the physical disk locations for files. This allows the files to be organized in folders without being physically moved around the disk.

Virtual Memory

The hard disk of a computer contains **virtual memory** (sometimes called a **pagefile** or a **swap partition**), where files and program parts can be stored until they are needed. Virtual memory is like a backup or alternative to RAM; it is used to store information when the RAM is full. The operating system of a computer designates parts of the hard disk for use as virtual memory, and these sections of the hard disk are called **blocks** or **pages**. The main issue with virtual memory is that it is drastically slower to use than RAM (particularly when a hard disk and not a solid-state drive is being used). Some operating systems may use virtual memory regardless, but they may have little or no need to use it as RAM overflow if the computer has enough RAM for the user's purposes.

Main Memory

Main memory is the area in which a computer stores information. It consists of numerous circuits, each of which holds one **bit**. From an organizational standpoint, main memory is divided into units known as **cells**.

Each cell holds one **byte** (eight bits) of information. Programmers conceive of a cell as consisting of a row of bits. The leftmost bit is regarded as the high-order end because it contains the most significant bit. The rightmost bit is regarded as the low-order end because it contains the least significant bit. Cells are identified by an addressing system that starts with zero. Multiple cells can combine to store long strings of information that may exceed eight bits. In addition to storage circuitry, main memory also includes circuitry that enables other circuits to store and retrieve information. The process of retrieving data from main memory is known as a read operation, which requests the address of the desired data. The process of storing information to main memory is known as a write operation, which requests that information be placed at a specific address.

RAM

Random-access memory (**RAM**), or main memory, is the short-term storage location for data in a computer. It is typically used to hold machine-language instructions and data for open applications and the operating system. In programming, when memory locations are referred to using addresses, these locations are in RAM. Generally, RAM is in the form of long, narrow circuit boards with a series of chips of equal sizes. These "sticks" of RAM are connected to the motherboard by slots into which they are inserted. RAM is intended only for the immediate needs of the computer. As program instructions are processed, results are stored in RAM before they are applied. Data that is not readily required is stored in long-term memory on a computer's hard disk.

How RAM Functions

Random access memory (RAM) is composed of semiconductor memory cells placed inside an integrated circuit. Because the memory cells are made of semiconductor material, reading and writing in this memory can be done extremely quickly—on the same level of speed as the CPU itself operates. Most RAM is **volatile** memory, meaning that if power is lost, the data in the memory disappears. In contrast, hard-disk storage uses a magnetic disk to store bits, and a magnetic head inside the hard-disk drive reads and writes data from and to the disk. Hard disks, unlike RAM, are not accessed directly by programs. Instead, the operating system and applications access the hard disk through a **filesystem**. Hard disks provide **nonvolatile memory**, meaning that the data stored on the disk remains on the disk even when power to the system is shut off.

Dynamic Memory

Dynamic memory is one method of implementing RAM. Rather than using flip-flops to store bits of information as static RAM does, **dynamic RAM** (or **DRAM**) uses small electric charges that fade out very quickly. As a consequence, the computer must use refresh circuits that replenish the electric charges multiple times per second. This storage method allows for quicker response time and greater storage density. By using **synchronous dynamic RAM** (or **SDRAM**), a computer can achieve ever faster response and retrieval times.

Memory Chips and the Motherboard

Memory chips, also known as RAM, are critical storage components in computers. They are the storage location for data that is in use by the operating system and open applications. Like hard disk drives, CPUs, GPUs, and many other computer components, RAM memory chips have had to advance to keep up with contemporary performance standards. While an average desktop computer in 2005 may have had 512 MB of RAM, by 2015 many new computers came with 4 GB or 8 GB. These larger capacities are necessitated by concurrent advances in graphics and CPU computing power, along with the development of software that takes advantage of these advancements.

The motherboard is so called because it is the main circuit board in a computer. All the computer's various peripherals, like the keyboard, the mouse, etc., connect to the motherboard. Furthermore, the individual components of a computer, such as the hard drive, the CPU, and the RAM, either sit on the motherboard or connect to the motherboard through **bus** cables. A typical motherboard contains expansion slots, where the user can install additional components with inputs and outputs that are accessible from outside the computer's case.

ROM

Read-only memory (ROM) is where the initiating routines of a computer system are stored. ROM is permanently stored on an integrated circuit chip and is not dependent on the presence of electric currents; in other words, it does not disappear if the computer is unplugged. ROM is unchanging and cannot be altered by the addition or deletion of data. It is responsible for the display of characters on the computer screen. It also contains the ROM BIOS (basic input/output system), which directs the computer to the operating system and loads the needed data for the OS into RAM. The ROM BIOS is also responsible for accessing the hard drive.

EEPROM

Electrically erasable programmable read-only memory (**EEPROM**) is a chip or set of chips that store basic information like date and time, CPU type and speed, language, RAM capacity, and other configuration settings—generally referred to as a computer's ROM. This type of memory is classified as nonvolatile because stored data does not depend on electric current to exist. In a computer, much of the ROM needed for booting is stored on an EEPROM chip or chips. Whenever the configuration of the computer is changed (e.g., a new CPU has been installed), the information in ROM must be updated. Otherwise, the computer may be unable to boot properly. The user can update EEPROM using certain keys while the computer is booting. This technology came to be commonly used in computers in the 1990s, and it was an advancement over EPROM (erasable programmable read-only memory), which had to be physically removed from the computer in order for the ROM to be updated.

CMOS Chips and Flash Memory Chips

Complementary metal-oxide-semiconductor (**CMOS**) chips are used to store information like date and time. These chips are powered by batteries and therefore retain their contents even when power is lost. The CMOS chip is the reason why a computer is able to maintain an accurate date even if it has been off for a long time. CMOS chips can be reprogrammed, for instance to reflect daylight saving time. A flash memory chip, on the other hand, does not require a battery. This kind of memory chip can be reprogrammed many different times. Flash memory chips are used to store programs in mobile devices and computers.

Data Storage

When computer professionals talk about data storage, they often refer to the storage medium and the storage device. Storage media are pieces of physical material where data is stored, such as hard disks, magnetic tapes, or DVDs. Storage devices, on the other hand, are compononents that read data from the media and (with few exceptions) write data to the media. Such devices are broadly called drives, and they are managed by the operating system's device manager. For instance, a DVD is storage media, while a DVD drive is a storage device. The difference between media and devices may seem blurry in some cases, such as in the case of hard disk drives and USB flash drives. In these cases, the device and the media still exist separately, but they are in the same physical component.

Optical Drives

In the late 1990s and early 2000s, **optical drives** and discs gradually replaced floppy disks as a means of storing software packages and personal or business data. These drives use low-power lasers to "burn" data onto plastic discs. The data is in a binary format, where an indentation made by a laser represents a zero and no such indentation represents a one. Initially, the CD-ROM (compact disc read-only memory) was the most commonly used optical disc. Its 800 MB of storage offered far more capacity than the floppy disk, and soon most software was distributed on CD-ROMs rather than floppies. In the mid-2000s, the CD-R (compact disc recordable) became widely available, allowing people to store their own data on CDs, or make their own audio CDs. Because CD-Rs were inconvenient and time-consuming to write to, they became a common form of backup storage media, replacing the tape drive and the Zip drive (a proprietary high-capacity floppy). Desktop computers started to come with internally installed optical drives capable of writing to CD-Rs. Eventually CDs were largely replaced by network downloads for software distribution and by USB flash drives and cloud services for data storage.

DVD Drives and USB Flash Drives

In the late 1990s, the **DVD** (Digital Video Disc or Digital Versatile Disk) was developed, and it became increasingly common through the 2000s. Like CDs, DVDs use optical (i.e., laser) technology to read and write data on discs. Though DVDs look exactly like CDs, they store more data in a smaller space, and they may have more than one layer of data on a single disc surface. Thus, they have more storage capacity—a normal DVD-R can store 4.7 GB. Though DVDs have come to be replaced in most of their uses by Blu-ray Discs, downloads, streaming, or USB flash memory, they have gone through many developmental advances, and they remain commonly available.

Beginning in the early 2000s, USB flash drives have come into widespread use for storing and transporting data. Flash drives are called "drives" because they include the reading and writing capability with the media itself in one device. The operating system of a computer interfaces with a flash drive through a **Universal Serial Bus** (**USB**) connection. Flash drives store binary data using electricity to change the charges of semiconductor cells. A large number of these cells together form a single chip, and a USB connector is added to form the characteristic stick shape of a USB flash drive. The first flash drives available to consumers typically had an 8 MB capacity, but technological improvements have lead to capacities of 1 TB or more.

Hard Disk Drives vs. Solid-State Drives

Storage media has evolved over the years. Today, the two main types of storage are the **hard disk drive** (**HDD**) and the **solid-state drive** (**SSD**). Both of these types allow a large amount of data (in excess of one terabyte) to be stored. While both HDDs and SSDs store bits electronically and often serve as the local disk for a personal computer or mobile device, the way each one works is rather different from the other. An HDD is typically housed in a stainless-steel case. Inside this case, a magnetic disk spins while a magnetic head reads and writes data on it. The functioning of an HDD is audible, typically as a low-pitched, quiet, rhythmic whirring. In contrast, a solid-state drive has no moving parts, so it is effectively silent. Rather than reading and writing magnetic bits to a disk, a solid-state drive uses semiconductors (i.e., microchips) to store bits. Without the need to read and write bits magnetically, a solid-state drive works very quickly—about as fast as the rest of the computer is already running. Solid-state drives are newer than hard disk drives, so they tend to cost more per byte of storage.

Cloud-Based Storage

Cloud-based storage has become a very popular storage solution for businesses. This is because cloud storage offers many benefits over local storage, including lower cost, higher storage capacity, and better data availability. Cloud-based storage is relatively inexpensive when compared with local storage devices. Cloud storage customers pay a predictable monthly rate, whereas a company that uses local storage will need pay for the devices themselves, the space the devices are in, and the expertise to set up and maintain the devices. As a result, the total cost of ownership for cloud-based storage is nearly always lower than the cost of ownership for local storage. Cloud-based storage also offers practically unlimited storage space. Many cloud-based storage providers charge their customers based on how much data they store or how much data they retrieve. If a customer needs more data to be stored or retrieved, they can simply upgrade their plan and have immediate access to even more storage space. Cloud providers may even provide different tiers of storage that vary based on need to access the data. So a business can, at a very low cost, store huge amounts of data that it is unlikely to access. Also, cloud storage providers generally have large data centers that are physically secure and have data redundantly stored within the center itself and usually across multiple regions. Therefore, users of cloud-based storage can access their data with minimal latency even in quite different locations. They also do not need to worry about servers losing power or being damaged, or data that is not backed up being lost or corrupted.

Universal Serial Bus (USB)

The **Universal Serial Bus** (**USB**) standard was developed to offer an easy way of connecting peripherals to computers. The standard itself provides specifications for cables, plugs, and ports (or connectors). It creates a universal way for motherboards to not only communicate with devices but also provide power to them. One of the many conveniences brought to users by USB is the ability to "hot-swap," or plug in and unplug devices as needed without having to restart the computer. Like many computer-related technologies, the USB standard has made steady advances, with USB 2.0 being superseded by USB 2.0 Hi-Speed, which was superseded by USB 3.0, which was superseded by USB 3.1, and so on. The USB standard supports many different connector types, a few of which are a familiar sight. Type A ports are widespread; they are the port that is most commonly available on desktops and notebooks. Micro-B as well as newer type C connectors are common for mobile device charging. A USB cable may have a different plug on each end, so that a printer with a type B port can be connected to the type A port on a computer. Type A and B ports for USB 3.0 and above may be made with blue inserts instead of white or black for ease of differentiation from USB 2.0 ports.

Peripheral Devices

Peripheral devices, generally known as peripherals, are devices that are designed to connect to a computer and perform some function that the actual computer cannot do by itself (such as printing). They are used for input, output, or both, but they will normally be viewed by the operating system as **input/output devices (I/O devices)**. Some common peripherals used for input are keyboards, mice, scanners, webcams, and microphones. Less common peripherals used for input are biometric authentication devices, such as fingerprint scanners and retinal scanners. Some common peripherals used for output are monitors, printers, and speakers. Computers and peripherals must be compatible in order to work together. For example, if a computer only has VGA video output, a monitor that has only HDMI inputs cannot be used with that computer without an adapter.

Common Communication Methods Between PCs and Peripherals

Peripheral devices, or peripherals, can be connected to a computer through several different methods. A couple of the most common connection methods used today are USB and Bluetooth. USB is a wired connection, while Bluetooth connects devices wirelessly. In order to connect to Bluetooth devices, a computer must be equipped with a Bluetooth adapter so that it can receive the signals that the device is sending. Many new computers, particularly **notebooks** (or laptops), have this capability built in. Though these types of data connections are nearly ubiquitous today, other types have been common in the past, such as PS/2 for mice and keyboards, and parallel ports for printers. Furthermore, a network connection, such as Ethernet or Wi-Fi, is often used with peripherals that may need to be shared, such as printers.

Bluetooth

Bluetooth is a short-range wireless technology. It allows for the exchange of data between mobile wireless devices. Information is transmitted via radio waves, and once devices are connected they can be remembered, letting devices reconnect automatically once they are within range. Some example uses of this technology include Bluetooth speakers, game controllers, and smart watches. Each of these devices can be used to connect wirelessly to a cell phone as long as the device is within a specified range. This range is usually less than 10 meters, but some more powerful devices can have effective ranges of up to 100 meters.

Mice

One common peripheral device is the **mouse**, which is used to move the cursor around the display screen. While mice come in many shapes, sizes, and styles and may have anywhere from one to more than ten buttons, an average modern mouse has two buttons (one on the left and one on the right) with a scroll wheel in between them. By rolling the scroll wheel, the user can scroll up or down inside documents or images with having to click on the scroll bar or scroll buttons. The scroll wheel may serve other purposes as well, such as cycling through the options in a drop-down list or zooming in and out of an image. Objects on the screen can be selected by moving the cursor onto the object and clicking the left button of the mouse. Objects can be opened or activated by double-clicking the left button. By placing the arrow on an object and clicking the right mouse button, the user can normally open a **context menu**. By placing the cursor over an object, holding down the left button, and moving the cursor, the user can "drag and drop" (i.e., move) the object. The functionality of a mouse can be greatly expanded through the use of certain keys on the keyboard and various clicking patterns.

Display Device Options

When personal computers first became common, the typical display was a **cathode ray tube** (**CRT**)—the same type of display used in older televisions. In a CRT display, electron beams interact with a display surface to produce dots of various colors that make up an image. The CRT display was made obsolete by the **LCD (liquid crystal display)**. These displays work through a series of light and liquid crystal networks. They offer a crisper image quality with none of the issues common to CRTs, such as distortion, inconsistent brightness, and flicker. Plasma displays, which made use of small cells of gas that respond to electric currents, were a competitor to LCDs for a time. However, they fell out of use as LCDs became less expensive. The LCD itself came to be rivaled by the **LED** display, which uses an array of LEDs (light-emitting diodes) to form images. Some displays may use both technologies.

Graphics Cards

A **graphics card** is responsible for receiving video output from the computer and sending it to the display device or devices as a video signal. Some computers, particularly laptops, have what are referred to as **integrated graphics** cards. In integrated graphics, there is no actual graphics card. Rather, the functions of a graphics card happen in the motherboard of the computer. Because the motherboard must perform many functions aside from graphics processing, integrated graphics quality and performance tend to be limited. The performance is easily enough for an operating system and various office applications, but it is unsuitable for demanding activities like video editing and gameplay.

A standalone graphics card (or **video card**) is like small motherboard in itself, with its own **graphics processing unit (GPU)**. Like other "cards" (such as sound cards and network cards), they are a rectangular shape. In a typical desktop computer, a graphics card attaches to a slot in the motherboard in such a fashion that its video outputs are accessible from outside the computer case. Standalone graphics cards categorically provide more speed, performance, and quality than integrated cards. Today's graphics cards have computing power on the level of a CPU, include their own video RAM, and have a cooling fan for the GPU. This arrangement not only provides better graphics (in the form of more advanced rendering and higher resolutions) but also prevents graphics functions from competing with other functions for system resources, such as RAM. Standalone graphics cards are considered a necessity for graphically demanding activities such as gaming, 3D modeling, and video editing.

Integrated Devices

An **integrated devices** describes when a hardware device is combined within another device. A simple example is a motherboard that has an integrated video card. This means that the motherboard itself has a video card as part of its hardware, and there is no need to purchase a standalone one. Integrated devices also exist in many types of mechanical hardware. For example, an elevator is an example of an integrated device. The elevator itself is a mechanical device, but is controlled by a computer panel that allows people to input which floor to which they would like to move. This electronic controller is also responsible for determining which floor to travel to next if many are inputted from within the elevator or on particular floors where people are waiting to board.

Hardware vs. Software

One of the most obvious differences between **hardware** and **software** is that hardware is something that you can physically touch, while software is not. Some examples of hardware include disk drives, CPUs, monitors, keyboards, and mice. Hardware may be used for input and output, storage, or processing. Software, on the other hand, is any program that can be run on a machine but that is not built into the machine as an unchangeable feature of the hardware. This includes operating systems, word processors, games, web browsers, and so on. While hardware and software are obviously different, one will not be useful without the other.

Components of System Software

The **system software** of a computer includes the operating system (OS), utility programs, and device drivers. The fundamental operations of a computer are controlled by the OS, which allows applications to run using system resources. Utility programs allow a user to access system tools provided by the OS, which may be used for peformance analysis, configuration, or other system management functions. Finally, device drivers allow the OS to use each component of the computer's hardware and manage how components interact with applications running on the OS.

Embedded Systems

An **embedded system** is a microprocessor-based system that performs a specific function in a real-time environment. An example of a machine with an embedded system would be a vending machine. A vending machine is a mechanical system that is controlled by a microprocessor. Sensors detect the bill or change that is inserted and then digitally display that value. The sensors will also detect which item is selected in the vending machine. If enough money has been inserted, the microprocessor will instruct the correct item to be vended. Because the vending machine is a mechanical system that contains a dedicated computer that controls it, this computer system is considered embedded, and it is an example of an embedded system.

Using Sensors in an Embedded System

An embedded system is a computer system that is part of a larger mechanical system. Sensors are an integral part of an embedded system, because they allow data that will affect the actions of the mechanical system to be brought into the embedded system. For example, sensors on an elevator can determine the car's position. When the elevator gets close to the floor on which it needs to stop, the microprocessor can tell the motor that turns the lift cable to slow down. When the car reaches the floor, the motor will stop and the doors will open. This communication between the real world, the microprocessor, and the mechanical portions of the system are only possible because of the sensors in this system. All these components work together to allow the system to function as it should with minimal manual control or intervention.

Types of Computers

A **cluster** computer is a group of computers that work together as one system. A cluster is used for computation-intense tasks for which a single computer would not be sufficient. In a cluster, each computer is called a **node**. The cluster contains a head node, which passes computation tasks to the other nodes in the cluster. Clusters are often used at research facilities or universities, where a large amount of processing power is required.

A desktop computer is what many people think of as a typical computer. At minimum, it includes a motherboard with a CPU and RAM, a hard drive, and power supply, all contained in a box, called a case. Peripherals, such as a mouse, a keyboard, and a monitor are connected to the case. The monitor, the keyboard, the mouse, and possibly the case are usually put on a desk, and thus the name "desktop computer." Many components of desktop computers can be cheaply and easily upgraded. Therefore, desktops are a popular choice for enthusiasts who build their own computers. Desktops are used in the home and workplace for authoring documents, browsing the Internet, editing photos, playing games, video calling, and much more.

A mobile computer is one that is designed to be portable. The components of mobile computers tend to be much smaller than those in desktops, and the necessary input-output devices are integrated into one case, making additional peripherals optional but upgrades difficult and expensive. The most basic example of a mobile computer is a notebook (often called a laptop). Other mobile devices, such as smartphones and tablets, are also technically mobile computers, though they generally are not thought of as computers, as they have noticeably different operating systems, user experiences, and means of adding applications—compared to traditional desktops and notebooks. Mobile computers can be used for most of the purposes that desktop computers can, albeit with some performance being sacrificed for portability.

Workstations, Microcomputers, and Microcontrollers

A **workstation** is a high-end, specialized computer built to allow a user to perform specific types of work, such as desktop publishing, software engineering, computer-aided design (CAD), and computer-aided manufacturing (CAM). In most cases, a workstation can only accommodate one user at a time. Workstations are more typically more powerful than **microcomputers**. Though the term "microcomputer" is no longer commonly used, the personal computers most people have at home or the office are technically microcomputers—small computers that use a microprocessor and are designed to be used by one person at a time. Microcomputers are generally outfitted with basic programs and utilities. Sometimes, a group of microcomputers is joined together to create a local area network (LAN). Desktop computers, notebooks (i.e., laptops), smartphones, tablets, and video game consoles are all classified as microcomputers. A **microcontroller**, meanwhile, is a miniature computer chip embedded into a machine, like a car or an oven, to provide special functions.

Distributed Systems

A **distributed system** is a group of software units that are processed on different computers via networking technology. Common types of distributed systems include global information retrieval systems, computer games, network infrastructure software, and company accounting systems. At one point, distributed systems were created from the ground up; however, by understanding the common systems (security, communication, etc.) that all distributed infrastructures share, developers have been able to create standardized infrastructures that can be installed on any network and that enable the creation of an **enterprise system** by developing a single, unique application to be run by that system. Two examples of these enterprise software frameworks are Jakarta Enterprise Beans, which facilitates the development of new distributed systems through units known as "beans," and the .NET framework, which uses units called "assemblies."

Network Servers

Network servers are centrally located computers that host basic programs and files for all the computers on a network. For instance, the network server for an office might contain a set of files that need to be available to all employees. Servers allow the computers on a network to share applications, utilities, and files. In addition to storing files and applications, servers can manage print functions, send and receive faxes, and manage web activities. The individual computers on a network are called clients. Clients are connected either through wireless connections or through a series of cables.

Computer Networks

Importance of Computer Networks

Computer networks are extremely important in today's society. Most people's day-to-day routine involves interacting with a computer network for at least some of the time, if not the whole time. Networks are what allow computers to communicate with each other. Computer networks form the entire basis of the Internet. Browsing the Internet, making purchases with a credit card, driving with navigation, using a smartphone, and streaming entertainment all require computer networking. Without computer networks, these activities wouldn't be possible. Computer networks have completely changed the way people live their daily lives.

Types of Networks

- **WAN** (wide area network): a network covering a large area; typically composed of several smaller networks
- **MAN** (metropolitan area network): a network extended across an entire metropolitan area; often made up of interconnect LANs
- **LAN** (local area network): a network restricted to a small area, such as a network for a single home or office

- **HAN** (home area network): a network restricted to a single home
- **PAN** (personal area network): a network devoted to interconnecting a single person's electronic devices, such as their computer, phone, printer, earphones, etc.

Cell Phone Networks

Cell phone networks work using normal radio waves, antennas, and automatic switching between antennas based on proximity. When you make a cell phone call, the cell phone communicates with a base station antenna using radio waves. Typical radio signals can reach cell towers up to 45 miles away. Once this connection is made, the information is then sent through a computer network. If the user moves away from a one cell phone tower and closer to another one, the phone call is automatically switched to the tower that has the stronger signal. On the other end of the call, the radio waves send signals out from the towers nearest the receiver of the call to make the connection to their phone. A wireless LAN works in a similar way, but it is limited to low-power transmission to prevent interference with other equipment.

Wi-Fi and Wi-Fi Hotspots

Wi-Fi, which takes its name from a shortening of "wireless fidelity," is a standard for broadcasting wireless networks. Network routers can send and receive Wi-Fi signals within a certain radius. These Wi-Fi broadcast points are called **Wi-Fi hotspots**. Most public buildings and businesses have Wi-Fi hotspots so that people can access the Internet on their mobile devices without needing to use mobile broadband. Many mobile devices with cellular broadband connections can broadcast Wi-Fi as well, so that a person can connect their notebook to the Internet using their cell phone's broadband service.

Cable Internet Connections vs. Fiberoptic Internet Connections

Cable Internet is typically provided by a cable TV provider. It is delivered on a separate channel from the TV signal but on the same coaxial cable. The signal that is delivered through the cable is electrical, so it can encode binary data. The user has a cable modem in their home which decodes the signal that is transmitted over the cable. A **fiberoptic network** works by sending photons (i.e., light) through a cable made up of many small fibers that can carry light. The photons are sent in pulses representing binary data. Because light travels much faster than the electromagnetic waves in coaxial cables, fiberoptic connection speed is extremely fast by comparison. As with a cable signal, a fiberoptic signal needs to be converted into network data once it reaches its destination. In both cases, once the signal is decoded, it can be sent through a router to give an entire home or office an Internet signal.

Portable and Mobile Internet Access

When a computer has **portable internet access**, it can get online from any number of different locations. Portable internet access can include wireless internet, Wi-Fi, or satellite access. A mobile internet connection is slightly different, in that the device remains connected even while moving, as long as it does not leave the mobile provider's coverage area, which is typically quite large. In other words, the user does not have to connect to a different port, hub, or hotspot in each location. **Mobile internet connections** can be through Wi-Fi, WiMAX, and cellular broadband. Speeds of these types of networks have gradually increased over the years. Many cell phone service providers now also offer cellular broadband, and providers are continuously upgrading infrastructure, such as satellites and broadcast towers, to accommodate the latest generation of cellular broadband networking.

LANs and WANs

The term "LAN" is an abbreviation of "local area network," while "WAN" is an abbreviation of "wide area network." Both these terms describe computer networks in which computers are connected to and communicate with one another. The connections between the computers can be wired or wireless. A LAN is typically contained within a smaller geographic area, such as a home or an office building. A Wi-Fi network within a home is an example of a LAN. A WAN, on the other hand, spans a much larger geographic area. Computers that are connected as part of a WAN can be across town, across the country, or even across the globe from each other. Think of a large corporation that has many office buildings throughout the country. It's likely that the corporation has a corporate network to which its employees' computers are connected. This corporate network that is spread across the country is an example of a WAN.

Wired Networks

A **wired network** is a system of computers and peripheral devices connected to each other by cables. Before the advent of wireless networking, all networks were wired. It is still common for local area networks to be wired. One of the benefits of a wired network is that it is easy to set up and take apart. Also, network cables do not have some of the issues that wireless networking has, such as signal fluctuation or interference. In many cases, wired networks transfer data faster than wireless networks, which are susceptible to interference. It is also impossible for an outside computer to steal the signal from a wired network. However, there are some obvious physical limitations associated with wired networks. The wires themselves can be cumbersome and are susceptible to physical damage. Moreover, the facility in which the networked devices are located must have adequate network ports and cables, and the devices themselves cannot be moved farther away from the network port than the cable will allow.

Function of Ethernet Networks

In an **Ethernet network**, data sent over the network is divided up into sections called **frames**. Each frame contains some sent data along with other information about the frame itself, such as the frame's origin, the frame's destination, and whether the frame has corrupted data. To prevent frames from interfering with each other, Ethernet systems once used carrier sense multiple access with collision detection (CSMA/CD). This technology allows devices to delay the sending of frames until the transmission lines are clear, and to sense when collisions happen by communicating with other transmitters. However, modern Ethernet systems use network switches to prevent frame collision and allow simultaneous two-way communication between devices.

Setting Up an Ethernet Connection

An Ethernet connection is a type of network connection used to connect computers to one another or to the internet. An Ethernet connection requires all participating computers to have Ethernet ports and cables. Ethernet cables consist of four pairs of twisted wires and two Ethernet-specific connectors, one on each end. In many cases, Ethernet systems revolve around a central router, known as a hub, to which each separate computer is connected. This cuts down on the number of connections that need to be made between individual computers.

IoT

The **IoT** (or **Internet of Things**) is all the appliances and other everyday devices that connect to the Internet. While people vary widely in how many Internet-connected appliances or machines they own, appliances and machines that in the past would not have connected to the Internet increasingly have this capability. Examples include washing machines, dryers, refrigerators, thermostats, alarm clocks, and cars. IoT devices are able to communicate with other devices and even be remotely controlled over the Internet. In addition, the IoT allows data about the use of everyday items to be collected so that it can be used to make more efficient items or adjust behaviors of the items. Devices that are part of the IoT offer some conveniences and can increase efficiency. For example, an IoT refrigerator order groceries automatically, an IoT thermostat can be set to the average temperature of homes in the area and be remotely controlled when users are on a trip, and IoT cars can connect seamlessly with roadside assistance services.

Client Server Architecture

Client-server architecture involves one central host computer that manages requests from many client computers. The centralized server is in charge of handling these requests and sends the information back to the correct client computer. An example of this would be if people wanted to play a video game together. All of the people who wanted to play would connect to a server that keeps the games in sync, allowing all the users to see each other's positions and play the game in sync. The benefits of this architecture are that all files are stored in a central location where all users can access shared and secured data. The disadvantages to this system are that the server is expensive, specialist staff needs to be on call to make sure the server is up and running correctly, and if any part of the network fails, a lot of services can be disrupted. The server itself is also susceptible to a "denial of service" attack.

Peer to Peer Networking

Peer to peer networking involves direct connections between individual computers, with no centralized computer directing the flow of traffic. One of the first and most famous examples of peer to peer networking was the invention of Napster. Napster was an application created in the 1990s that allowed users to share their music libraries with other users on the network. The benefit of a peer to peer system is that there is no single point of failure that can cause the whole system to go down because it is distributed. Therefore, the redundancy provided by this system makes it truly resilient to attack.

Cloud Computing

Cloud computing is the delivery of computing services over the internet. For example, instead of storing images on a local hard drive, the images could be saved on a server computer located somewhere else on the internet. The benefits of cloud computing include convenience, cost, and productivity. It is convenient and cost effective to have information readily available on any device that is connected to the internet. Productivity can increase because multiple people can all work on the same files at the same time, making changes in real time. Some disadvantages of cloud computing include risk of data confidentiality, speed, and cyber-attack vulnerability. Because the data is stored on the internet, it will have been sent and stored on multiple computers on its way to its final location. If any of these computers are not secured appropriately, there may be a chance that the data could be read by third parties. Cloud computing is only as fast as the network that it is connected to. If a person wants to work on a document in a remote area, the internet may not be available. Lastly, cyber-attacks are much more likely on a known cloud computing network than on your home network. These types of attacks, while rare, may prevent access to your files at any given time. Networks may also go down intermittently for other reasons such as software updates and other server issues.

Network Devices

The following devices are used when connecting multiple bus networks to create a single extended communication system:

- A **repeater** passes signals between two bus networks, it but has no ability to read the signals. This is the simplest method of connecting networks.
- A **bridge** first reads the destination address of a signal. It only forwards the signal to the other network if the signal is intended for a computer on the opposite side of the bridge. This is a more efficient method because two computers on the same side of the bridge can communicate without hampering communication on the other side.
- A **switch** is similar to a bridge, but it is capable of connecting more than two bus networks. It is also an intelligent device that only forwards traffic to its destination, instead of blindly passing it out to every computer on the network and relying on the machines to interpret whether the signal is for them or not.

Modems

A **modem** (or modulator-demodulator) is a device for converting digital signals into analog waves and sending these waves over telephone lines. In other words, a modem takes data from one computer and converts it into a sound which can be heard and translated by another computer. With the aid of modems, computers gained the capability of communicating over vast distances using traditional telephone lines. The creation of modems enabled such communication without requiring the invention and implementation of a new communications infrastructure. Today, most modems convert digital data into radio signals, and they are integrated into many devices. Fiberoptic networks use similar devices, called optical network terminals (ONTs), to convert fiberoptic signals into network data streams and vice versa.

Routers

Routers allow multiple networks to be linked, forming an internetwork (i.e., a network of networks). Routers are unique from other network devices because they enable each network to retain its own individual characteristics. Every device in an internetwork has two addresses. The first identifies its location in its network, and the second identifies its location in the internetwork. Assume, for instance, that a device in Network A wants to communicate with a device in Network B. The device in Network A sends the message to its access point, which then sends the message to the router for Network A. Each network's router has a forwarding table, which is used to send messages in the appropriate direction and to the appropriate address. Upon receiving this message, the router for Network A consults the forwarding table, and then forwards the message to the router for Network B. Finally, this router sends the message to its network access point, which contacts the appropriate device.

MAC Addresses

MAC address stands for Media Access Control address. Each MAC address is hard coded at the time of manufacturing to be a unique identifier for the individual device. MAC addresses are reused by manufacturers because there is an extremely low chance that any two devices with the same MAC address would exist on the same network. 281 trillion MAC addresses are possible, so the chances that two devices have the same MAC address on your local network is very close to zero.

Wireless Access Points

A **wireless access point** is any wireless connectivity device that enables other wireless devices to connect to a network, usually the internet. One example of a wireless network device is a wireless router. A router is usually connected to the internet via a physical cable. Wireless devices within range are able to connect to the router, sending data wirelessly. When the data reaches the router, it is sorted and sent over the internet via the physical medium. Other examples of wireless access points include mesh networks as well as "range extenders", which work in a similar fashion to a router but with multiple points that work together. With mesh networks and range extenders, your wireless device connects to the closest wireless access point. That point then "echoes" the data to the next access point, one that is closer to the main router. The echoing continues until the router receives the signal, at which point in time the information is sent via the physical medium once again.

Network Topology

"Network topology" refers to the arrangement of nodes within a network. A **network topology** can be either centralized or decentralized. There are three basic arrangements:

- **Bus network** – Each node in the network is linked sequentially along a single path.
- **Star network** – In this centralized topography, a central computer (also known as a switch or hub) connects all nodes and regulates network access.
- **Ring network** – In this decentralized network topography, each node links to two other nodes, and the final node connects to the first node, making a ring configuration. As long as the network incorporates two-way communication, a node failure or cable break will not bring down the entire system.

Bandwidth vs. Latency

Bandwidth is the amount of data that can be transferred during a period of time. **Latency** is the time it takes for a certain amount of information to get to its destination. Whereas bandwidth is typically measured as a rate (such as bits per second, kilobits per second, etc.), latency is expressed in units of time (typically milliseconds, or thousandths of a second). For example, if you are downloading a large file, bandwidth would be more important than latency because you want a lot of data to be transferred, but the time it takes for equally sized, tiny pieces of the data to transfer doesn't really matter, as long as many of them can be sent at the same time. On the other hand, if you are playing a multiplayer game where you need to know where other players are on the screen in almost real time, latency is more important. The higher your latency is, the greater the **lag** (or delay) will be, between when something happens on the server and when you see it happen on your screen. Think about bandwidth as being the size of a water pipe. A larger pipe will allow more water to come through at a time. In this analogy, latency would be the time it takes for a given unit of water to travel the length of the pipe. Though these two measures are related, they are not measuring the same thing. A smaller pipe means less water at a time, which in turn means that each unit of water will take longer to pass through.

EXAMPLES

EXAMPLE 1

A person wants to stream a 4-gigabyte movie that runs for 90 minutes. If the movie runs at 24 frames per second and each frame contains an equal percentage of the data, about how much data is contained in each frame, and about how many kilobytes of data must be transferred every second for the movie to play without buffering?

If the movie is 24 frames per second and it runs for 90 minutes, because there 60 seconds in a minute, we get 24 × 60 × 90 = 129,600 frames. We know that. 4 gigabytes is equal to $4 \times 1024^3 = 4{,}294{,}967{,}296$ bytes. We can divide this by 129,600 to get 33,140, which is about how many bytes per frame. Multiplying this again by 24 (because there are 24 frames in each second of the movie), we get 795,360 bytes. Thus, each second at least 777 kilobytes of data needs to be transferred in order to avoid buffering.

EXAMPLE 2

When streaming a multiplayer game, is it more important to send and receive information more slowly with higher quality graphics, or more quickly with lower quality graphics?

Multiplayer games are real-time applications. This means that the highest priority is to send and receive information as quickly as possible. If information travels too slowly in a real-time application, it may already be useless by the time it reaches its destination. For example, if you press a button to jump as an enemy character attacks you, if the information about your character jumping does not reach the server in time, your character will receive damage from the enemy character. Likewise, if you cannot see the enemy character or see the attack in time, no matter how fast your response time is, you will really be jumping after the attack has happened. Therefore, in multiplayer real-time gaming, sending and receiving information more quickly with lower quality graphics is usually ideal.

PACKET SWITCHING VS. CIRCUIT SWITCHING

Packet switching is when data is broken down into smaller groups of information called packets before being sent over a network. Data that is sent in one large chunk is prone to errors, and networks would be much more congested with this method. By breaking up data into packets, different items can be routed different ways through the network. Even if they arrive at different times, the pieces can be put back together based on the network protocol with which they were sent. **Circuit switching** creates one dedicated path of information for the duration of the connection. No other communication can be done on the same network channel while a connection is still ongoing. An example of this is the older landline telephone system. When a call is made, a circuit is reserved for that call and cannot be used until it is released.

TCP VS. UDP

TCP (Transmission Control Protocol) and **UDP** (User Datagram Protocol) are two different types of protocols found on the internet. A protocol is a set of rules that is decided upon so that communication can occur with minimal error. TCP is a connection-based protocol, so when using this type of message passing system, a connection must be made with the receiving computer before information can be sent. The benefit of this system is that because a connection has been made, there are several error checking algorithms available to make sure that the data is received and also correct. Although TCP is more reliable, these added checks result in a slower transmission rate. UDP does not require a connection, and therefore is described as connection-less. It is very simple in that it sends messages without any response from the receiving party. Because there are no data checks, UDP is very fast. However, the sender will not know if the message was received, and the receiver will not know if they got all of the messages.

Internet Architecture

Networks, the Internet, and Distributed Applications

A network is any system that links multiple computers either physically or wirelessly. It provides an effective means of sharing information and resources, such as data files, printers, and applications. When a computer connects to a network, it becomes a network **node**, and its resources can be shared. All **networks** have the following characteristics:

- Two or more computers are linked.
- A network operating system manages the sharing of peripheral devices.
- The connected devices, or nodes, each have their own unique address.

The **Internet** is a vast global system that connects computer networks. In essence, it is a network of networks linked through numerous electronic and optical devices. Built on the Internet protocol suite (TCP/IP), the Internet allows computer and smartphone users around the world to connect with each other, businesses, organizations, and governments.

Distributed applications are pieces of software that run on multiple computers, such as on a client-server network or a peer-to-peer network. There may be a client application with a user interface and a server application, or "back end." On the other hand, in a peer-to-peer architecture, each application on each computer can act as a client or a server.

Infrastructure of the Internet

The Internet arose as a series of smaller networks joined to a single spine, a T1 line created by the National Science Foundation in 1987 that linked 170 individual networks. The resulting NSFNET was the first main thoroughfare for data. Now, the Internet's backbone is composed of fiber-optic links connecting all of the routers on the network. The links between the routers are maintained by network service providers (NSPs) like SBC/AT&T. The networks administered by these companies are connected to one another by network access points (NAPs). The network service providers make it possible for Internet service providers (ISPs) like America Online and Comcast to deliver web access to the general public.

OSI Model

The **Open Systems Interconnection model**, commonly known as the OSI model, is a model that describes how computer systems communicate with each other over a network. It can be applied regardless of the specific technology being used. The OSI model is an attempts to standardize computer networking so that systems can be designed for better interoperability with other systems.

The OSI model includes layers of data flow. Each layer represents another level of abstraction. For example, the "top" layer, the application layer, is the one that an end user will see. The "bottom" layer consists of hardware the hard that sends, carries, and receives data. There are seven layers in all, and they are commonly known as the **OSI layers**.

The seven OSI layers are as follows:

7. **Application** – APIs (application programming interfaces) allow the use of data.
6. **Presentation** – Network data is translated so that applications can use it.
5. **Session** – Application sessions (periods of connection) are managed.
4. **Transport** – Data is transferred from one application to another using a protocol.
3. **Network** – A multi-node network is managed.
2. **Data Link** – Node-to-node communication is managed.
1. **Physical** – Raw data streams are transmitted over physical network lines.

Each layer relies on the layer below it to perform its function. Starting with the application layer, each layer below represents another level of abstraction and on step closer to machine level. The physical layer is the passing of data bits between two devices via a physical medium, such as an Ethernet cable. All the way at the top, in the application layer, APIs are set up to send and receive information at an application interface. In short, the OSI model uses layers to summarize the many levels on which pieces of software that use networking or are used in networking need to operate.

Downloading vs. Uploading

Both "**download**" and "**upload**" are terms used in networking. Downloading is the act or process of transferring data from a server or a group of peers to a client or an individual device. Uploading is the reverse—transferring data from a client computer to a server, or from an individal device to a group of peers. Both uploading and downloading can be done through file transfer protocol (FTP), but uploading to and downloading from ordinary webpages is far more familiar to most people. For example, one might download an application installer after purchasing a piece of software online, or perhaps download bank statements and tax forms from their bank's website. A common example of uploading is attaching files to emails. While a download can be started with a simple link to a file, uploading requires some web programming to allow users to select a file from their device. There are generally limitations on the types and sizes of files that can be uploaded in such an interface. While computers and smartphones are constantly sending and receiving data, uploading whole files manually is less commonly needed than downloading is. Therefore, many Internet service providers offer lower upload speeds than download speeds.

TCP/IP

Transmission Control Protocol and **Internet Protocol** together are commonly known as the Internet protocol suite, or more commonly TCP/IP. In short, TCP/IP is a set of rules by which computers send and receive packets of information over the Internet. Although there are additional protocols included in the TCP/IP suite, the two main ones are TCP (Transmission Control Protocol) and IP (Internet Protocol). TCP governs how applications establish a connection path, as well as how packets of information are divided before being sent. IP governs how Internet addressing functions, and it ensures that packets are routed to the correct destinations on a network. TCP/IP was intentionally developed with very little central management so that it would require little overhead and can easily recover from any errors encountered. For instance, if a packet of information is lost during transmission, computers use TCP to detect the loss and then retransmit, without guidance from a central piece of software. TCP/IP is central to transmitting information across the Internet, and thus it is one of the major topics in computer networking.

Application Layer

The **application layer** exists at the highest level of the TCP/IP structure. It allows users to directly connect to all of the other layers that are below it through the use of user interfaces. This layer provides users access to the network, as well as develops network-based applications. Some services it provides include e-mail, file transfer, and user login. This layer provides a number of protocols, including Hyper Text Transfer Protocol, TELNET, File Transfer Protocol, Simple Network Management Protocol, and Simple Mail Transfer Protocol.

TRANSPORT LAYER

The **transport layer** allows for data to be transferred between users and other network layers. This layer allows users to connect to the network on other levels, providing a reliable connection for secure and continued communication. This layer also supplies error checking, flow control, and verification of all data that passes through. Protocols included in this layer include User Datagram Protocol, Transmission Control Protocol, and Stream Control Transmission Protocol.

INTERNET LAYER

The **Internet layer** organizes the data into packets, addresses it, and routes it through the network. It is also known as the network layer. It is used to accept and deliver packets for the network, delivering them to the correct IP address and navigating the network to the packet's destination. Protocols of this layer include the Internet Protocol, the Internet Control Message Protocol, and the Address Resolution Protocol.

NETWORK INTERFACE LAYER

The **network interface layer** is also known as the data link layer. This layer gives the network the ability to communicate with the underlying hardware. It is also responsible for how data packets are initialized when they are sent out and routed over the network. The data link layer and the protocols associated with this layer determine the communication between the computer and the underlying hardware. This layer's main goal is to maintain continued communication between all computers on the network. Protocols located at this layer of the network include X.25 and IEEE 802.2. Some services provided by this layer include data framing, checksums, acknowledgement, and flow control.

PROTOCOLS, UDP, AND THE TCP/IP PROTOCOL SUITE

The set of rules followed by computers when transmitting data is known as a protocol. In 1978, the Advanced Research Projects Agency (ARPA) developed a foundational set of protocols required for networking; these protocols are known as the Transmission Control Protocol and the Internet Protocol Suite—better known as TCP/IP. This suite of protocols is the foundation on which the Internet was built. Some computers use the User Datagram Protocol (UDP), which is part of the Internet protocol suite as well. UDP is better-suited than TCP/IP for uses in which data needs to arrive in real time, such as videoconferencing. Both protocols break data down into packets, but UDP sacrifices reliability for speed, whereas TCP/IP uses various methods to guarantee delivery of every packet to the its destination.

IP ADDRESSES

Every device that is connected to the Internet has a unique **Internet protocol** (IP) **address**. In IPv4, an older version of the Internet Protocol (IP), an IP address consists of four numbers ranging from 0 to 255 separated by decimal points. An example would be "42.66.35.4". In the newer IPv6, IP addresses contain eight numbers, use hexadecimal numbers, and use colons as separators. An example of an IPv6 address would be "3005:ab3:5:4321:0:789:0:1". There are both static and dynamic IP addresses. A static IP address remains the same for a machine, while a dynamic IP address changes every time the machine connects to the Internet. The data a device receives over the Internet is sent to that computer's IP address. When device is no longer connected, the dynamic IP address may be assigned to another device. IP addresses are managed globally by the Internet Assignment Numbers Authority (IANA), which is run by the Internet Corporation for Assigned Names and Numbers (ICANN).

PURPOSE OF IP ADDRESSING AND HOW IP ADDRESSING WORKS

An IP address is a unique number that labels a device that is connected to the Internet. You can think of an IP address like a home address. If you know someone's home address, you can send them mail. Just as a home address is tied to a physical location that can be found by a postal service using the names and numbers it contains, an IP address is tied to a particular device that can be found by the Domain Name System using the Internet Protocol. These unique labels must exist because identification of each node in a network is essential to the network functioning properly.

Domain Names and Top-Level Domains

Because Internet Protocol (IP) addresses are difficult to remember, locations on the Internet are given a **domain name** that is generally more readable for humans. For a website, the domain name starts with the most specific identifier and gets broader. The "www" that you may see at the beginning of a web address is the **subdomain**. This is not part of the actual domain name, but it is useful for categorizing the information being access. For example, "www" is used for general Internet-based content. The subdomain "mail" would be used for a section of a website where email is accessed. After the subdomain are **labels**. There may be one or several labels, separated by periods. At the end of the domain name is the **top-level domain**. Consider an example address, "www.example.com". In this address, "www" is the subdomain, "com" is the top-level domain, and "example.com" is the domain name. Common top-level domains are "com," for businesses or other commercial ventures, "net" for Internet organizations, "org" for nonprofit organizations, and "edu" for education-related institutions. Countries and other political entities may have their own top-level domains, and a second-level domain may be included before this. For example, a web address that could be "com" could instead be specified as a United Kingdom commercial website with ".co.uk". Domain names are registered through organizations designated by the Internet Corporation for Assigned Names and Numbers (ICANN).

DNS

The **Domain Name System**, commonly referred to as the **DNS**, translates the readable Internet addresses into the IP addresses that are behind them. For example, if you enter "www.google.com" into your web browser, the DNS system looks up this address. Associated with this address will be all the IP addresses that your computer could actually connect to in order to access the web content at this address. A DNS server returns the IP address (or one of the addresses) to the user's web browser, which makes the connection to that computer. The web page is displayed when the content stored or generated at the address is received by the local computer. The IP address may be stored by the browse, along with content that was received. This way, the next time the browser is pointed to "www.google.com", the page will load faster, and it may not be necessary to access the DNS server. The part of the browser where this information is stored is called the browser's **cache**.

Common Web Browsers

There is a surprisingly large variety of **web browsers** available today, though perhaps the best-known among these are Google Chrome, Mozilla Firefox, Microsoft Internet Explorer, and Microsoft Edge (the successor to Internet Explorer). Because very many people use Microsoft Windows at work or in school, if not at home, the Microsoft browsers are widely used and familiar to many people. Browsers like Google Chrome and Mozilla Firefox became popular because, particularly in their early years, they were simpler and faster. Browsers are generally available to download and use for free.

A web browser functions by interpreting HTML code that is present on a static webpage or generated by a server hosting a dynamic webpage. Web design technology has evolved quickly since the Internet became widely available, and it continues to evolve today. Because of this, static HTML webpages have become rare, and browsers must be continually updated to accommodate various new types of dynamic webpages, to interpret new versions of HTML, and to maintain security standards.

Internet Publishing Works

There are countless of Internet publishing solutions today that allow a user to easily create and publish a website. In the past, people designed websites by creating HTML pages that contained links to each other, and then uploading this webwork of pages to a domain. They could use basic text editors or HTML editors to write the webpages in HTML code, or they could use a dedicated web design application (such as Adobe Dreamweaver), many of which offered templates, drag-and-drop editing, and so-called "what you see is what you get" interfaces.

Today, most nonprofessional web design is done through online website-building services. These services generally provide templates that can be adjusted or customized. The freedom that someone building a website has depends on the service. Though such services do a lot of the technical legwork that was once the main challenge of web design, they still require the creator to understand **search-engine optimization (SEO)**, webpage **metadata**, web design best practices, and content management. Designers who want more freedom may decide not to use a website builder. Instead, they may design a website theme or appearance and then implement a **content management system (CMS)**, such as the free and open-source WordPress. In a CMS, pages themselves and elements of pages become items in a database. When a user is on the live website, the CMS builds pages as users navigate to them, pulling the items that are meant to be on that page.

DEVELOPING A WEBSITE

Today's web publishing solutions make creating websites extremely easy. Years ago, a person needed to know how to write HTML. Later, web publishing software utilizing drag-and-drop technology allowed users to create elaborate websites without the need to learn virtually any HTML or JavaScript. Today, web design is quite high level. In other words, websites can be designed without knowing any code at all, and there are many layers of abstraction between the creator laying out a page and the actual code that the browser will interpret. The process of creating a website today is much the same as creating any other document or presentation. First, start with an idea of the finished product. Decide on the theme and layout and how the site should function. Ideally, a desktop version, a tablet version, and a mobile version will all be designed. Once these decisions are made, the components of the website can be created, such as an about page, a blog page, an FAQ page, and so on. The final step, which will likely continue long after the site goes live, is to create content, which will be populated into the pages from a database. Some people choose to create the content themselves, and others hire copywriters to write all the content. One of the last things to note is that the website needs to be tested on multiple devices to ensure that it displays appropriately. Since many visitors today use portable devices to access webpages, it is imperative the website be responsive and display correctly on phones and tablets.

WEBPAGE DESIGN SOFTWARE AND SERVICES

Webpage design software and services give non-experts the ability to develop their own websites. Many website-hosting companies offer subscribers templates for simple websites, such as blogs or professional portfolios. These templates are built using web programming languages. They limit creators to building pages out of predefined elements, adjusting page layouts by resizing the elements as desired, and filling the elements with content. Creators who want more freedom may opt to use a content management system (CMS). These systems also make use of web programming. They allow the creator to edit page layouts through a back end. A creator could code their own pages using HTML, **CSS (Cascading Style Sheets)**, JavaScript, etc., though many popular CMSs offer templates, which creators have a lot of freedom to adjust. Then, content can be entered into a database in the CMS, and the CMS will populate pages using this content. This way, a page's content can be changed without making any modifications to the code of the page itself.

HTML

The HyperText Markup Language, widely known as **HTML**, is a markup language that is used for making web pages. A markup language is different from a programming language. In markup languages, the code does not consist of sequentially executed statements. Instead, the code of a document is made up of elements (such as headings, paragraphs, and tables). An interpreter reads the whole page of code and generates a document based on the code. With HTML, programmers can put text in a document, add formatting to the text, position the text, and do much more. An HTML document consists mostly of elements, which are written in code using **tags**. Typically, a beginning tag and an ending tag go around the text or content that the element contains. For example, "<p>This is a paragraph.</p>" is a paragraph element. It is a way of presenting text. Formatting can be added to elements using **attributes**. For example, if we want the aforementioned paragraph to be in the font Arial, the code "<p style="font-family: Arial">This is a paragraph.</p>" would accomplish this. The fundamental parts of an HTML document are the head, enclosed in tags as "<head></head>" and the body, likewise enclosed in "<body></body>" tags. In the head, the title of the page is written and **styles** can be declared. We can use styles to make formatting rules that apply to all elements of a certain type. For example, we could leave the paragraph we made above without the attribute, but add a style in the head:

```
<style type="text/css">
   p {font-family:Arial;}
</style>
```

With this style for p elements in the head, all p elements on the page will take on the Arial font family attribute. In the past, creators would do much of their formatting using attributes inside tags. However, today, the use of styles is standard. Making a consist style for a whole website is made simple by Cascading Style Sheets, or CSS. Using CSS, we can make a **stylesheet**, which is a list of style statements, like "`p {font-family:Arial;}`". Then we can link each of our HTML pages to the stylesheet using a linking statement in the head.

XML

Extensible Markup Language, or **XML**, provides a set of rules and specifications for the electronic encoding of documents, using open standards produced by the World Wide Web Consortium (W3C). XML is designed to allow computers to generate and read documents that can also be read by humans. XML includes the following constructs:

- **Characters**: XML documents are made up entirely of characters. Most characters in an XML document are Unicode characters.
- **Processor and application**: The processor examines the markup, converts it into structured information, and then sends it to the applications. XML defines standards for the processor, but it does not have control over what the applications do with the data.
- **Markup, content, and tags**: Like HTML, XML uses markup tags enclosed in angle brackets ("<" and ">"). Text inside these angle brackets is considered markup, while any text not enclosed in angle brackets is usually content.

WEB DESIGN

Web design is the process planning, building, and maintaining a website. Initially, web design was less concerned with aesthetics, as simply putting content on the Internet and having it display quickly and correctly was a serious challenge. From this early stage, web design has evolved to include scripting languages, web programming languages, new versions of markup languages, networking technologies, web marketing techniques, and graphic design. A few broad principles have emerged from the development of web design as a field unto itself. These include the following:

- **User experience**: Websites should be easy and fun to navigate, and they should cause visitors no trouble in finding what they are looking for.
- **Responsivity**: Websites should be at least somewhat interactive, and these interactions should appear and function properly not just on computers but on mobile devices as well.
- **Visibility**: Websites should include content, metadata, and hyperlinks that will cause search engines to rank them appropriately.

HYPERTEXT

Hypertext is text, including tables, images, diagrams, etc., that is viewed on an electronic device and contains **hyperlinks**. Hypertext can be static, meaning it does not change, or dynamic, meaning it changes in response to the user. Dynamic hypertext usually includes user interfaces, such as drop-down menus. Generally, hypertext documents contain hyperlinks, which allow the user to access related information with a mouse click or a screen tap. Because hypertext is capable of interacting with and reading documents, it also provides a structure for extracting information from databases and presenting it. Webpages are generally written or generated in hypertext, and the Internet has a specific protocol, hypertext transfer protocol (HTTP), for communicating using hypertext.

Hypermedia

Hypermedia is an expansion of the concept of hypertext to include sound, video, and multimedia in general. It is interactive, and it uses hyperlinks so that the experience of hypermedia does not need to be sequential or linear. The Internet, taken as a whole, is an example of hypermedia. It includes a text as well as multimedia, and it can be navigated in any order. Like hypertext, hypermedia is by definition presented electronically, on a computer screen or the screen of a smart device. Creators can use various tools to create hypermedia.

Cyber Security Issues

Three-Pillar Approach to Cyber Security

Confidentiality

In cyber security, **confidentiality** means that data remains available only to authorized users. Keeping information confidential means that it has not been compromised by other parties and has not been disclosed to anyone who does not have access to it or should not have access to it. A great way to ensure confidentiality is by organizing information in terms of who needs access, such as different security clearances. Some extremely sensitive data should be only accessible by those with the highest clearance levels. A confidentiality breach can happen through hacking or even through social engineering.

Integrity

In cyber security, data that maintains its **integrity** is data that has not been altered or reduced in quality during its transmission over a network or while saved on any storage medium. Data that has kept its integrity can be said with certainty to not have been tampered with in an unauthorized way, whether that be on purpose through an attack or by accident through other means. Attacks during transmission occur during the course of the transfer of data from computer to computer, where a computer on the path to the destination could change the content of the files. Attacks during storage would have to be a more direct attack on the server housing the information.

Availability

In cyber security, **availability** means information is readily available for authorized users whenever they need it. Systems that are "available" to users are ones that are online and accepting communication requests in an acceptable amount of time. For some systems, this acceptable amount of time may not be extremely fast; however, certain systems have very short time constraints as to when information must be available, with any downtime having significant repercussions. For example, critical systems such as medical equipment, power generation systems, and safety systems have requirements that may be defined as "extreme", since most of these must be available 24/7 with very short delays on transmission times. These types of systems often have safeguards against situations that may cause them to go offline, such as redundancy and built-in batteries.

Threats to Security

Phishing

Phishing is an attempt to gain someone's personal information using a fraudulent request. In a phishing attempt, a scammer will use some "bait" to trick the victim into sharing personal information. An example is sending an email that appears to be from the victim's bank requesting personal information to verify the account. This tactic could be used for any account, such as PayPal or Facebook. Phishing is not limited to email; scammers attempt phishing over the phone, by text message, and even through calendar invitations. Phishing is a form of wire fraud and is thus generally illegal. Many countries now have laws that specifically address phishing.

Social Engineering

Social engineering does not involve any understanding of a computer system itself, but instead involves the ability to make people give up secure information because they believe they are talking to someone who is allowed to have it. For example, if a password was needed to get into an electronic lock, instead of hacking the lock an attacker could walk into the building and pretend that they're a new hire at the company and forgot the password. Someone may just give it to them because they believe the story.

Trojan Horses

The **Trojan horse** (or simply Trojan) is a type of malware. It takes its name from the story of the Trojan War. In this story, an invading force leaves a large wooden horse in front of the city of Troy as a gift, and then the attackers pretend to leave. The people of Troy believe the gift is genuine and take it into their city. However, some invading soldiers have remained behind, hidden inside the horse. At night, they exit the horse and open the gates of the city to a now-returned invading force. A Trojan horse in the computer world works by using this same tactic. A user is typically tricked into opening a file or clicking a link that is disguised as legitimate—a Trojan horse. Once the user clicks on the link or opens the file, the Trojan horse has worked. Whatever script or program runs can perform a variety of tasks. For example, it may spy on the user. A type of program called a **keylogger** can record the typing of usernames, passwords, credit card numbers, or other personal data, and send it to the scammer. The Trojan could be **ransomware**, which locks the functionality of a device until an amount is paid to a provided contact. Many Trojans are used to open a back door to a device, so that the scammer can gain unauthorized access to the device.

Computer Worms

A **computer worm** is type of malware program that can clone itself. In addition to being able to duplicate itself, it also has the ability to stay active on each of the computers in which it resides. A computer worm replicates itself by taking advantage of an operating system's automatic processes that usually run in the background. A user will most likely not notice a worm until it utilizes enough system resources to start slowing down or completely breaking the functionality of the computer. Once a computer worm is on a user's system, any number of malicious activities can occur, including encrypting files, opening specific websites, or logging key presses. The main difference between a worm and a computer virus is that a computer virus requires the user to complete some action in order to spread it, while a worm is completely autonomous in its duplication on other systems.

Key-Loggers

A **key-logger** is a type of malware that hides in an operating system's background processes, unknown to a user, and records all of their keystrokes. The purpose of this program is usually to capture usernames and passwords for various accounts. This program has network access, and the text file created from the keystrokes is then sent to the hacker that used the program. This hacker now has access to all of the information you typed since the program began to run.

Sending Personal Information over an Employer's Network

Information sent over a network can be viewed by the owner of that network. Employees may believe that information they send over the network is private, but that is actually not the case. An employer can view the information being sent over their network at any time. If an employee is accessing personal email, banking sites, or other personal information, then that information is visible to the employer. Making such information available to IT workers or consultants at your employer or school is an unnecessary risk and is never advised. It is even more risky to send personal information over public Wi-Fi, other people's Wi-Fi, or Wi-Fi that isn't password-protected.

Hackers

A **white hat hacker** (or simply white hat) is one who attempts to hack into computer systems for the purpose of testing the security of the systems rather than for malicious purposes. White hat hackers are often cybersecurity experts who have been hired by organizations to perform this testing. A company may wish to test the integrity of its network, so it may hire a white hat hacker to attempt to penetrate the system. In some cases, companies even hire former **black hat hackers**—people who hack into systems with malicious intent. Hackers who are hired for white hat work may perform **penetration testing**, where cyberattacks are used with the permission of the company. White hat hackers may also analyze the company's software for vulnerabilities, or they may try various tactics such as phishing without ordinary employees knowing.

Network Security Preventative Measures

Most people who have been using computers for a long time are familiar with the threat that viruses pose. However, even experienced computer users may not be careful about preventing viruses, or they may not know how to protect against viruses. Because of this, operating systems increasingly include antivirus components, warning messages for potentially dangerous actions, and frequent security patches in the form of automatic updates.

Beyond the protections that contemporary operating systems provide, users can also prevent attacks by obtaining antivirus or antimalware software. Such software suites may include a database of **virus definitions**, which are used for identifying dangerous files by matching file characteristics with those in the database. For these virus-scanning programs to be effective, they must be kept updated, and scans must be run regularly. Antimalware packages may include various other tools, such as web browser plugins that detect dangerous sites, attachments, links, and permission requests.

Finally, users can protect themselves by understanding that clicking links, opening attachments, visiting websites, and plugging in removable storage (such as USB flash drives) are all actions that could result in a malware infection. With this knowledge in mind, users can implement a few best practices, such as the following:

- never using a personal flash drive in a public computer
- never using another person's flash drive or a flash drive that was found
- using bookmarks or a search engine instead of manually typing web addresses
- checking to see where a link leads before clicking on it
- never allowing a program to run unless the source is trusted
- never connecting to an unprotected network
- never opening an email attachment without knowing what it is and who it is from

Strong Passwords

A **strong password** is a password that is unlikely to be guessed by a human or a computer program. Though calculating the likelihood of a password being guessed is a matter of some debate, a few broad guidelines for creating strong passwords can still be identified.

- One of the easiest and most important factors is password length. A widely agreed upon minimum password length is eight characters. But in general, the longer a password is, the better.
- Second, a combination of uppercase letters, lowercase letters, and numbers is generally ideal. However, be aware that complexity is considered less effective than length. Furthermore, because certain letters ("e" for example) and special characters ("!" for example) are used much more often than others, these characters may be easier for a program to guess.
- Third, a strong password does not contain any information that could be uniquely linked to the person who created it. Therefore, it is best to completely avoid names of family members or coworkers, street addresses you have lived at, phone numbers you have had, your date of birth, and other such information.
- Finally, never use the same password for more than one account. Even a very strong password will not be beneficial if you use it for more than one account, because if the password is ever hacked, it will almost certainly be tried for other accounts you own.

Firewalls

A **firewall** is a security program or hardware device that analyzes all data that comes into or goes out of a network. The firewall can be used to block certain types of traffic based on security rules. You can think of your

IP address as the address of your house, and the ports on your network as the rooms in your house. Each program sends information using these ports so that the router knows where it came from. A person may be allowed to come into your house but may not be allowed into all rooms in the house. It is a firewall's job to allow or deny access to information once it has arrived at your IP address, and let it flow through to the correct port. Certain ports are dedicated to specific types of information, so if a firewall detects something out of the ordinary, it will block that information or let the network owner make a choice about allowing access.

Antivirus Programs

An **antivirus program** is used to detect and remove viruses on a computer. It does this by keeping a virus database that can compare parts of your computer with known patterns shown by computer viruses. If a pattern is found, the program is flagged and a process is started to remove the infected code. Because new viruses are created all of the time and old ones can be modified, it is very important keep your antivirus program updated on your computer, or your system risks being infected by the newest threats.

Network Filtering Software

Network filtering software is used to limit access to certain parts of the network. The main reasons it is used is to prevent under-aged users from accessing inappropriate material, and prevent employees from accessing sites that reduce productivity or contribute to a hostile work environment. These filters work by spotting words and patterns that fit a specified set of rules about what should be off limits. Administrators of the system can also input their own sites and keywords that should be avoided.

Identifying Malicious Attacks by Analyzing Network Traffic Data

There are many tools available today that can analyze network traffic data on numerous levels. Some tools even go all the way down to the packet level, providing specific information and statistics about individual packets being passed over the network. By constantly monitoring this data, network professionals are able to get good baselines of what normal traffic looks like across their networks. In the event of a malicious attack, the traffic across the network may suddenly spike. This spike would trigger the network team to begin a deeper dive into the data and determine the cause of the spike. This investigation can assist in identifying an attack sooner than would be possible without traffic analysis. This allows the network team to respond quickly, reducing the effects of the attack.

Encrypting Data Sent over the Internet

Encrypting data that is sent over the Internet is a necessary precaution to prevent data from being seen by unauthorized users. Encryption is the process of changing data in such a way that it cannot be read without the proper digital "key." The process of decryption—retranslating the data back into usable form—can only be done using the key. However, the process of encrypting (and decrypting) data takes time, and in some cases it also increases the amount of data that must be sent over the Internet. Thus, encrypted data takes more time to send than unencrypted data. Despite this inconvenience, encryption is a necessary part of sharing information over a medium that is as open as the Internet. The trade-off is one where quickness and simplicity in data transmission are sacrificed for security.

Public key encryption is used to help ensure the privacy of people's credit card and banking information when shopping online at an e-commerce site. It uses two cryptographic keys, one that is public and another that is private. In a real-world example, lets picture two people who want to send information to each other in a box with a lock on it. The receiver (person 2) can purchase a lock with a combination, open it, and send it over to person 1, who wants to send the message. This lock acts as the public key, as it is sent to the other person and everyone who looks at it has access to it. Person 1 can then lock their message with the lock that was sent to them from person 2. Lastly, person 1 can send the locked box to person 2. Since person 2 purchased the lock in the first place, they have the combination and can open it. This combination is the private key and is needed to decrypt the message.

Chapter Quiz

Ready to see how well you retained what you just read? Scan the QR code to go directly to the chapter quiz interface for this study guide. If you're using a computer, simply visit the online resources page at **mometrix.com/resources719/oaecompsci** and click the Chapter Quizzes link.

Impacts of Computing and Learning Environments

Transform passive reading into active learning! After immersing yourself in this chapter, put your comprehension to the test by taking a quiz. The insights you gained will stay with you longer this way. Scan the QR code to go directly to the chapter quiz interface for this study guide. If you're using a computer, simply visit the online resources page at **mometrix.com/resources719/oaecompsci** and click the Chapter Quizzes link.

Impact of, Obstacles to, and Effects of Computing

Using Computers to Showcase Creativity

While computers are often recognized as tools that are based in logic and calculation, there are many creative uses for computers. Video game design requires stories to be written, characters to be designed, and game rules to be established. Animation and 3D modeling have been used to create movies and TV series that exist entirely in a computer-generated world. Digital music and digital music editing have changed the way musicians compose music. In addition, the advent of the Internet has allowed ordinary people to create their own video content or stream live to audiences they could never have reached otherwise.

Using Computers to Solve Problems

Using a computer to solve a problem has many benefits. One benefit is the speed of computers. Because computers can do many billions of calculations per second, they are able to solve problems quickly. Math- and logic-based problems are very easy for computers to solve. Another benefit is access to information. Computers generally have ready access to the largest collection of information in the world, the Internet. They can use this information for research purposes and to answer any question that is cataloged online. A third benefit is computers' ability to simulate different situations. Computers can run simulations of scenarios that would be difficult or impossible to simulate otherwise. For example, before building a skyscraper, planners could construct it virtually with a computer, allowing for various tests, such as structural integrity tests to determine if the building would be able to withstand natural disasters.

Collaboration

Benefits to Software Development

As the old saying goes, "Two heads are better than one." This also holds true in the computer science world. **Collaboration** between developers generally leads to better algorithms, more efficient code, and shorter development cycles. Collaboration brings together the collective experience of everyone in the group, not just a single person. Also, feedback from one individual can spark an idea in another person that may lead to a breakthrough solution. It is very difficult for a single person to get to this level of innovation alone, no matter how skilled that person may be. Collaboration and discussion generally lead the group to better solutions.

Options for Remote Collaboration

Modern technology offers many different opportunities for collaboration, even when team members are not physically located in the same office. A couple of the simplest ways to collaborate are phone conversations and instant message conversations. Collaborating this way requires almost no overhead, as this technology is readily available and already used by many people in their personal lives. Today, even video messaging is readily available through software like Google Meet, Zoom, and Microsoft Teams. More formal videoconferencing technology is also used. A product such as Cisco's Telepresence allows the meeting attendees to feel as if they are all in the same room together. These products make it very easy to collaborate with team members who are in any number of remote locations.

Increasing Collaboration Among Teams

While collaboration has been an industry buzzword for a few years now, it really is more than just that. Collaboration between team members almost always leads to better end products. Many companies today are completely redesigning their office spaces in an attempt to increase collaboration among their employees. Open floor plans are the new norm, with many offices creating spaces specifically for collaboration—whether ordinary team communication or specific purposes like idea generation or problem solving. Cubicles are becoming less common, with shared office spaces becoming increasingly popular. Some employers are even adding entertainment like ping pong tables and foosball tables to foster a culture of teamwork.

Collaboration Between Developers and Business Users

Collaboration between software developers is very important today due to the rapidly changing nature of this field. Things are changing so quickly that it is imperative for a developer to stay up to date on the most recent trends in the industry. One way to do this is through collaboration with other developers. Developers can share the latest trends, industry best practices, and other information with each other. In addition to collaborating with other developers, it is also a good idea for developers to collaborate with business users. Collaboration with business users can allow a developer to gain valuable insight into the way that a system is used. This can be very beneficial for a developer when planning for features and enhancements.

Using Computers to Foster Innovation

The main reason computers are so helpful with innovation is because they foster communication while providing access to, and sharing of, information. It is through this sharing of information that new ideas can form. In addition, because the medium allows for manipulation of data at a speed that has never been seen before in history, these ideas can come to fruition much faster, and problems related to the creation of the innovation can also be solved much more quickly. Also, because computers are becoming more and more accessible, regular people who have innovative ideas can more easily translate ideas into reality.

Computing Bias

Computing bias is when new technologies reflect existing human biases due to the way that the software is written. This software has biases directly written into the algorithms, sometimes without programmers even realizing they are doing it. These biases can be found at almost every level of development. Programmers need to be cognizant of bias in algorithms used in all types of computing innovations, as they are the first line of defense in combating perpetuated human biases. An example of a computing bias would be a credit score algorithm including race as a factor that either increases or decreases the score.

ADA and Computer Science

The **Americans with Disabilities Act** (ADA) is a law that was passed in 1990 to prohibit discrimination against people with disabilities. It attempts to give people with disabilities the same opportunities and access as people without disabilities. This applies to computer science because developers must consider accessibility issues when designing applications or websites. At the end of 2017, Congress decided not to move forward with the requirement that websites meet certain accessibility standards, but some courts have ruled that websites that invite the public (such as large retailers) must meet certain standards. For example, videos need caption options for the hearing impaired, and people with vision impairments need the ability to make the font on a site larger while still retaining the same layout of the site.

Spoken Language Requirements

Computer science is a field that spans across the globe, regardless of the language an individual speaks. Computer programming requires certain critical thinking skills, but it does not require an individual to speak or read a certain language. As computer applications are programmed, they are converted by the computer into **machine language** that is readable by the computer itself. All computers use machine language, and all programs are eventually converted into machine language as they are compiled. Computer science concepts can be taught in a person's native language. As a matter of fact, many programming services today are performed for companies in the United States by providers working in countries where English is not the primary spoken language. Application requirements are passed off to programmers, and programmers are able to develop solutions whether they speak English or not.

Attracting More Women and Minorities

Computer science is a field that has traditionally not been entered by many women or minorities. It is important to engage women and minorities early in their school careers to get them excited about the computer science field. Exposure to the field at younger ages can promote an enthusiasm that continues as students get older. Women and minorities may be motivated to pursue computer science careers if they are made aware of the career paths that are available for people with strong computer science backgrounds. Additionally, showing them that the computer science field typically has jobs that pay very well can build excitement about careers in the field. While great strides have been made in recent years in this area, work must continue to be done to attract even more women and minorities into computer science.

The Digital Divide

There are five main factors that are responsible for **the digital divide**.

1. **Community**: Could be something as large as a country or as small as a rural town. Some communities do not, as a whole, have access to computers or the Internet, either because the infrastructure does not exist or because computers have not been part of the community's culture.
2. **Income and Educational Attainment:** Those on a low income may not be able to afford a computer or Internet access. Likewise, those who never gain the ability to use computers will not be able to take advantage of technology.
3. **Age** is another factor, because as people get older, they are less likely to learn to use technology. Learning computer technology is also more difficult for people who did not grow up using computers is one form or another, and therefore did not have computers naturally become part of their lives.
4. **Disabilities**: People who are blind or unable to use keyboards are at a great disadvantage when it comes to technology that is built for people who can both see and use a keyboard.
5. **Language Barrier**: The number of languages that software or websites are available in continues to grow, but there are still some programs without multilingual support, as well as many that provide only a limited number of languages.

Bridging the Digital Divide

One way to bridge the digital divide for people with low income and education is to make technology accessible for them in the community, free of charge. Easy access to technology at libraries and community centers would provide use of technology to a large group of people. However, providing access is only one piece of the puzzle. There could also be free classes available to help to educate these groups. As people learn more about computers and technology, they can pass this knowledge on to their friends and family members.

Health and Safety Effects of Computer Technology

While technology has brought about many positive changes to society as a whole, there are also some negative effects to human health and safety. Mental issues stemming from being "overly connected" include narcissism, depression, cognitive losses, and the expectation of instant gratification in other parts of that person's life. In addition, many social issues also present themselves, including a sense of isolation and deficits in social skills. These social damages especially affect children who are often in their social developmental stages. Physical health can also be affected by computer use, including hearing loss, neck strain, vision problems, and issues related to being in a seated position too long.

Social Impact of Cell Phones Used by Children

Young people and children having personal cell phones is becoming more and more common. This has a significant impact socially. Having a cell phone is becoming a status symbol for younger kids, and children whose parents cannot afford a cell phone for them can sometimes be left out of social circles that exist mainly online in social media. In addition, giving a child access to a phone presents other societal risks such as viewing or posting inappropriate material on the Internet. Adding online etiquette education in school curricula is one important step toward preparing children to take cell phone and Internet use seriously.

Effect of Computer Science on the Retail Industry

One industry that has been dramatically affected by computer science is the retail industry. Think back to the way that purchases were made a decade ago versus how purchases are made today. Back then, most purchases were made at a "**brick and mortar**" (i.e., physical) retail store. The customer went to the store, searched through the available inventory, and then made a purchase. Today, a huge portion of retail sales are made online. With fast and convenient shipping options, online shopping is made very easy for consumers. Furthermore, shoppers can search quickly for items across multiple retailers, often finding better deals than they would be able to get otherwise. Some other examples of industries that have been affected by computer science are banking, entertainment, and medicine.

Effects of Science, Culture, and Commerce on Technological Innovation

Science usually breeds technological innovation because new technologies become available based on new scientific discoveries. Culture and commerce tend to direct where these new discoveries are used, as cultural and commercial needs drive what is created. So, when scientists discover ways to create technology, cultural and commercial groups tend to find niches where this technology can be applied.

Intellectual Property and Ethics in Computing

Software Licenses

Software licenses, also known as **license agreements**, limit the uses of a program. For instance, a **single-user license** prevents multiple simultaneous users. A **multiple-user license**, on the other hand, enables more than one user at the same time. Often, companies will purchase a multiple-user license to cover all the employees in an office. The price of a multiple-user license generally depends on the projected number of users. A site license, meanwhile, permits the program to be used in a certain location. If a site license is obtained for an office, for instance, all the people in that office can use the software. A concurrent-use license permits multiple copies of a program to be run at the same time. The price of a concurrent-use license generally depends on the number of copies required.

EULA

An **end-user license agreement** (EULA) appears when newly-installed software is run for the first time. It requires the user to confirm agreement with the license terms by pressing a button. Unless the user agrees with the license terms, the program will not run. By pressing the button that indicates agreement, the user enters into a legal contract with the software publisher. Any failure to observe the terms of the agreement can make the user liable. Typically, the EULA includes the limitations of the license and the terms of the warranty.

Open-Source Software

Open-source software, of which Linux is perhaps the best example, can be modified by its users. The source code of the software is available so that programmers can alter, adjust, or tinker with it. Linux is protected by copyright and is not in the public domain, but it can be legally adjusted by any of its users. Because Linux is complex, making useful changes requires extensive knowledge. Regardless, the program must be accompanied by the source code, even though the program itself is compiled when distributed. Open-source software may be covered by a Berkeley Software Distribution license—better known as a **BSD license**—or a **general public license** (GPL), the latter of which is stricter.

Software Copyrights

A **software copyright** safeguards ownership of a program and restricts the rights of non-owners to alter and distribute the program. A consumer who purchases a piece of software does not have the right to sell copies but is permitted to install the program and make a backup copy. Moreover, purchasers are allowed to copy sections of software for use in a teaching situation. For instance, computer science professors can use sections of software to illustrate principles of programming. The copyright notice on a piece of software typically appears in the form of the copyright symbol followed by the year (e.g., ©2010), though the absence of this notice does not preclude copyright protection.

Creative Commons Licenses

Use of a **Creative Commons** license allows work to be distributed under different terms. Creative Commons licenses come in various types; the likely best type for sharing a work of art for use but not for editing would be **CC BY-ND**. This license allows for the distribution of work as long as credit is given and also as long as the original work is not changed. In other words, other people can use the work of art in any projects that they see fit, but the work of art will maintain its original likeness and credit will be given to the original creator.

Advantages of Using CC BY and CC0

CC0 is the Creative Commons license that places the creative work in the public domain. This means that anyone can use it and modify it without giving credit to the original creator. **CC BY** has the same rules as CC0 except with the additional rule that the original creator must be given credit for their creative work. This giving of credit, also known as attribution, is the main motivator for using CC BY rather than CC0—so that even if the author doesn't profit from the work, they can at least become better known if the work becomes widely used. CC0 is commonly used once attribution is no longer particularly relevant. For example, graphics or characters for a hit game from 20 years ago are no longer being used in a profitable way. The author might choose to place a CC0 license on these pieces of art, enabling fans of the franchise to create their own games or content based on these characters without fear of legal action.

Digital Plagiarism

Digital plagiarism is when a project or idea is directly copied from an online source without giving credit to that source. It can be avoided by paraphrasing or by reading the text and then using it as the basis for your own ideas. If it is necessary to use information directly from a website, be sure to cite them as a source when using text directly from the article. Often, digital plagiarism can be combated through education, because many people commit plagiarism without fully knowing that they are doing so.

Piracy

Computer Software **Piracy** is the use of copyrighted software without licensed access. This usually occurs by making illegal copies of games, books, movies, or music. In addition, streaming any of these digital media without authorization is also unlawful. It is illegal because by making unlawful reproductions of digital media, the companies do not earn any revenue. The person pirating is in effect stealing from the profits of those companies. Using pirated software can result in file corruption or even serious legal consequences. In addition, many programs that have been modified to work without valid serial keys include embedded malware that will be installed on the host system along with the pirated software.

Internet Safety

Electronic Communications and Privacy Act

The **Electronic Communications and Privacy Act** is a statute passed in 1986 which prevents government from listening in or copying electronic data by computer under certain circumstances. The initial act that was created in 1968 only covered the interception of conversations using land line telephones. Due to the expansion of technological communications which now includes digital data, updates were necessary. The Act is broken down into three sections, or "Titles":

- **Title I** "prohibits the interception of any wire, oral, or electronic communication, and prohibits illegally obtained communications as evidence".
- **Title II** "protects the privacy of the contents of files stored by service providers".
- **Title III** "requires government entities to obtain a court order in order to install devices that capture dialed numbers and related information from outgoing calls for a targeted individual".

Children's Online Privacy Protection Act

The **Children's Online Privacy Protection Act** protects the privacy of all children aged 12 and below. It does this by asking for parental consent whenever personal information is collected about the under-aged users. The Act was written and passed in response to companies who were targeting children and collecting personal information about them without notifying the parents. A website operator must comply with six main requirements of the Act. This includes a privacy policy that explains how information is obtained from the user, as well as the necessity of parental consent before collecting personal information from anyone 12 years or younger. In addition, an explanation of what information is collected on the children must be provided, along with the right to delete information at any time.

Acceptable Use Policies

An **acceptable use policy** is a document stating how people can use a particular network, including the internet. Before users obtain access to the network, they must agree to the terms of this policy. Most organizations have an acceptable use policy, including educational institutions, companies, and even some public Wi-Fi hot-spots. Many of these agreements include specifications such as avoiding violating the law, hacking, sending spam or junk mail, or crashing websites. The benefits of having an acceptable use policy include preventing cyber security threats, ensuring users are not doing anything illegal on your network that you may be responsible for, and making sure that the users of the network are focusing on productivity and not using any sites that are not directly related to the work or studies that are acceptable at the workplace or institution.

Ethical and Legal Responsibilities of Using Social Media

Social media is one of the most recent ways to communicate with a large audience quickly and easily. Sometimes, because of how easy it is to post and how many people a single post can reach, things can be said that are unethical or even illegal. To avoid this, avoid misrepresentation in the promotion of services and products as well as the listing of credentials. Making product claims such as, "works for everyone, guaranteed!" is not an evidence-based claim and misrepresents the product. Also, stating that you are the "best doctor in the city" is a baseless claim of credentials.

Data Mining

Data mining is the process of acquiring data, analyzing that data, and then extracting useful information from it. The data is often used to solve problems, determine patterns, or find new opportunities for a particular business. For users, data mining can be positive. By extracting data that is meaningful to a particular user, that person can connect with new and exciting products that are personalized for them. This means they may see advertising they are more likely to enjoy, and find new products that they would like to buy but wouldn't have known about otherwise. The negative impact of data mining for users is that mined data can sometimes be misused or even stolen. A major problem with this is that consumers may not even know which data are being mined and which had been stolen or misused. It is for this reason that it is important for all users of an online service to read the terms of service before accessing and using a site.

History of Computing

ARPANET

ARPANET, or **Advanced Research Projects Agency Network**, was invented in 1969 for academic and research purposes. Paul Baran developed the idea for packet switching, which allowed data to be sent quickly over vast distances without a direct connection between the source and destination. Instead, messages were passed from one computer to another on a huge mesh network. On January 1, 1983, ARPANET officially converted to the TCP/IP standard. Most recognize this day as the birth of the internet.

Creator of the First Website

Scientist Tim Berners-Lee not only created the first website, but also three bedrock technologies of the today's internet. First, **Hypertext Markup Language** (HTML) is the language of web pages, describing how pages are to be displayed, often through the use of links. Next, he created **Hyper Text Transfer Protocol** (HTTP), which was the set of rules for sending websites over networks. Lastly, he created **Uniform Resource Locators** (URL), which allowed users to easily find pages online using web addresses. To bring all of these tools together in a useful package, he also devised a basic browser as well as web server software.

Impact of Bill Gates and Steve Jobs

Bill Gates and Steve Jobs met in the late 1970s. Jobs had developed the Apple computer along with Steve Wozniak but wanted to use Gates' software on it. Gates built a spreadsheet program (Excel), a word processing program (Word), and a simple programming language (BASIC). Gates and his company Microsoft also wrote software for IBM, and there were many similarities between Microsoft's Windows operating system (released in 1985) and the one being developed at Apple, as each used a Graphical User Interface (GUI). At this point their relationship turned into a rivalry, and each spent many years working to outdo each other. With great rivalry came great innovation, and the two were able to make some of the most innovative hardware and software that is still being built upon to this day.

Homebrew Computer Club

The **Homebrew Computer Club** was established in 1975 in Menlo Park, California. It was a group of hobbyist electronics enthusiasts who came together to share information, trade circuits and other computer parts, and design personal computers using various DIY methods. It is significant because it started the idea of the home computer and paved the way for many DIY kit computers such as the "Altair", hailed as the first of its kind. Steve Wozniak frequented the meetings and has stated that it gave him the idea to create the Apple I computer, often hailed as the world's first "ready out of the box" home personal computer.

Diverse Student Populations

Understanding Students' Diverse Backgrounds and Needs

Self-Education

Educating oneself on students' diverse backgrounds and needs enhances one's overall understanding of their students and creates a culturally sensitive, accepting classroom environment tailored to students' individual needs. There are several avenues through which teachers should educate themselves in an effort to build an accepting and respectful classroom climate. Communication is key for learning about diversities; thus, it is important for teachers to foster and maintain positive communications with students' families to deepen understanding of cultures, beliefs, lifestyles, and needs that exist within their classrooms. This could include learning some language of students with different cultural backgrounds, attending family nights at school, or participating in social events within their students' communities to integrate themselves into the culture. Furthermore, teachers can learn more about their students' backgrounds and needs through gaining an understanding of student differences, incorporating these diversities into the curriculum, and encouraging students to participate in learning by sharing aspects of their lives with the class.

Teaching, Learning, and Classroom Climate Benefits

A deep understanding of students' diverse backgrounds and needs provides multiple benefits for teaching, learning, and overall classroom climate. Knowledge of students' diversities allows teachers to understand the individual needs and abilities of their students and tailor instruction accordingly to maximize student development and achievement. Additionally, it allows teachers to know which authentic materials to incorporate in lessons and instructions to best create an engaging, relevant, and respectful learning experience that fosters student interest in learning and promotes success. Furthermore, by enhancing understanding of students' diverse backgrounds and needs, teachers consequently begin to model an attitude of inclusivity, acceptance, and respect for differences, which is then reflected by students and achieves a positive, welcoming classroom climate that promotes diversity.

Implications for Teaching, Learning, and Assessment in Diverse Classrooms

In any classroom, a teacher will encounter a wide range of variances among individual students that inevitably will influence teaching, learning, and assessment. Diversities in ethnicity, gender, language background, and learning exceptionality will likely exist simultaneously in a single classroom. Educators must be prepared to teach to these diversities while concurrently teaching students the value and importance of diversity. The curriculum and classroom environment must be adjusted to meet individual student needs and create an **inclusive**, **respectful**, and **equitable** environment that welcomes differences and allows for success in learning. This begins with the teacher developing an understanding of the unique diversities that exist within their students and using this knowledge to **differentiate** curriculum, materials, activities, and assessments in such a way that students of all needs, interests, backgrounds, and abilities feel encouraged and included. Furthermore, the teacher must understand how to instill appropriate supports to accommodate the diverse needs of students and how to modify the classroom environment in such a way that is reflective of the diversity of the students.

Considerations for Teaching in Diverse Classrooms

Ethnically Diverse Classrooms

As society becomes increasingly diverse, teachers will certainly encounter classrooms with students of multiple ethnicities. Thus, to create an accepting and respectful classroom environment that allows for success in learning for all students, there are several factors to consider. Teachers must educate themselves on the various ethnicities within their classroom. This includes being mindful of the **social norms, values, beliefs, traditions,** and **lifestyles** of different ethnic groups and learning to communicate with students and families in a respectful, culturally sensitive manner. Additionally, teachers must make a conscious effort to incorporate aspects of each ethnicity into the curriculum, activities, and classroom environment to create an inclusive atmosphere that teaches the acceptance, respect for, and celebration of differences. Teachers must be **culturally competent** and ensure that all materials are accurate, relevant, authentic, and portray the different ethnicities within the classroom in a respectful, unbiased manner. Furthermore, teachers must consider how their own ethnicity impacts their teaching style and interactions with students, how they may be perceived by other ethnic groups, and how to respond in a manner that fosters respect and inclusivity.

Gender-Diverse Classrooms

When approaching a gender-diverse classroom, teachers need to consider their perceptions and expectations of different genders as well as their interactions with different genders. Teachers should also consider how the classroom environment and materials portray gender differences. Teachers must work to eliminate possible stereotypical beliefs so that all students feel respected, accepted, and encouraged to participate. Furthermore, teachers must consider how their behavior acts as a model for how students perceive gender roles and should act in a way that eliminates gender divisiveness. Teachers should use gender-neutral language when addressing students and ensure that all students receive equal attention. Teachers must maintain equal academic and behavioral expectations between genders and be sure to equally praise and discipline students so that neither gender feels superior or inferior to another. Regarding curriculum and classroom materials, teachers must ensure that the classroom environment encourages equal participation in, access to, and choice of all activities and procedures. Activities and materials should provide equal opportunities and foster collaboration between genders. Furthermore, teachers must ensure that curriculum materials avoid gender stereotypes and highlight each gender equally in order to create an accepting and respectful learning environment that provides equal opportunities for students of all genders to develop their individual identities and abilities.

Linguistically Diverse Classrooms

In a **linguistically diverse** classroom, teachers must consider how to effectively demonstrate value for students' native languages while simultaneously supporting the development of necessary language skills to thrive in the school setting. By accepting and encouraging students to use their native languages, teachers can establish an inclusive learning environment that celebrates linguistic differences and encourages students to want to build upon their language skills. Through this, teachers create an equitable learning environment that allows for academic success. To develop English language skills, teachers must first consider each student's language ability, level of exposure to English prior to entering the classroom, and the level of language learning support each student has at home. Teachers can then implement effective instructional strategies and supports to modify curriculum in a way that addresses students' language needs. Teachers must also consider the implications of the classroom environment on language acquisition. By creating an atmosphere that encourages language acquisition through **literacy-rich resources** and **cooperative learning**, teachers promote the use of language skills and ultimately provide opportunities for success for all students.

Linguistic Supports and Instructional Strategies for English Language Proficiency

Incorporating a variety of linguistic aids and instructional strategies is beneficial in supporting ELL students of varying levels of English language proficiency. **Visual representations** to accompany instruction, such as posters, charts, pictures, slide shows, videos, tables, or anchor charts, are valuable in providing clarification and reference while promoting vocabulary acquisition. When delivering instruction, **body language** such as hand gestures, eye contact, and movement to mimic verbal directions and explanations can provide clarification to enhance understanding. These students may also require **translation devices** for clarification, an interpreter to help with understanding instructions and new concepts, alternate assignments with simplified language, or **individualized instruction** from an ESL teacher. Frequently checking for understanding and providing clarification as necessary throughout instruction are necessary to ensuring ELL students understand learning materials, instructions, and assessments. In addition, creating a print- and literacy-rich environment is valuable in promoting English language acquisition. This can be done by including word walls for new vocabulary, reading materials that vary in complexity, labels, and opportunities for speaking, reading, and writing within instruction.

Learning Disabilities and Other Exceptionalities

In a classroom where learning disabilities and exceptionalities are present, teachers must consider accommodations for students of various learning needs while fostering an atmosphere of respect and acceptance. Teachers must understand the individual learning needs of each student and differentiate instruction accordingly to create an equitable and inclusive learning atmosphere. For **learning disabled** students, teachers must consider accommodations that allow for inclusion in all areas of curriculum and instruction. Such considerations may include extended work time, individualized instruction, and cooperative learning activities to ensure that learning disabled students are provided the necessary supports to achieve academic success. For students with other exceptionalities, such as **gifted and talented** students, teachers need to consider ways to provide challenging and stimulating opportunities for expansion and enrichment of curriculum. Furthermore, teachers must be aware of their own interactions with students in order to demonstrate and encourage respect and acceptance among students. By providing supports for individual student success, teachers can effectively highlight students' strengths and teach students to accept and celebrate differences in learning abilities.

Instructional Techniques

Implementing Multiple Instructional Techniques to Maximize Student Learning

Incorporating multiple instructional techniques into the classroom maximizes student learning by enhancing intellectual involvement and overall engagement. When instructional material is presented through a variety of means, it facilitates an **active learning** environment in which students' interest is captured and they are motivated to participate in learning. Varying teaching strategies stimulates engagement and fosters achievement by encouraging students to actively participate in their own learning and implement critical thinking skills to consider information more deeply. Students' understanding is strengthened when content is presented in different ways through various instructional techniques by providing them with multiple frames of reference for making connections and internalizing new concepts. In addition, utilizing multiple instructional techniques allows the teacher to effectively **differentiate instruction** to access multiple learning styles and address individual student needs to ensure understanding and enhance the overall learning process.

Instructional Strategies to Differentiate Instruction

Implementing a variety of strategies for differentiation helps to ensure that instruction appeals to students' varying learning styles and needs. By incorporating **multiple modalities** into direct instruction, such as visual representations, written directions, video or audio clips, songs, graphs, or mnemonic devices, teachers can differentiate the presentation of new concepts and information. Using strategies to differentiate instructional activities is also beneficial in diversifying the learning experience. By providing opportunities for **independent, collaborative**, and **hands-on** learning, teachers can ensure that learning is accessible and engaging to all students. In addition, learning activities should allow for a degree of flexibility in order to appeal to students' varying needs and preferences. Activities such as task cards, educational technology resources, and learning stations provide this **flexibility** and allow for a student-directed experience in which students can choose to learn in the way that best suits their needs. Similarly, assigning open-ended projects as summative assessments allows for a degree of **student-choice**, thus differentiating the method in which students demonstrate their understanding.

Varying the Teacher and Student Roles in the Instructional Process

Varying the roles of the teacher and students as an instructional technique is beneficial in creating an engaging, dynamic classroom environment that maximizes learning. When different roles are implemented, instruction is diversified, thus stimulating student interest and engagement. In addition, certain teacher and student roles are most applicable and effective in specific learning situations. When teachers acknowledge this and understand when to adopt and assign particular roles, they can effectively deliver instruction in a way that deepens student understanding and fosters success in learning. In presenting new content, directions, or modeling new skills, for example, the roles of **lecturer** and student **observer** are effective. In hands-on learning situations, students can take on the role of **active participant** while the teacher acts as a **facilitator** to create a student-centered and engaging learning environment in which students are given ownership over their own learning. Such variation enhances intellectual involvement by promoting critical thinking and problem-solving skills through self-directed learning. Skillfully assigning different roles throughout the learning process also allows the teacher to effectively address students' individual learning needs and preferences to promote engagement and enhance the learning experience.

Fostering Intellectual Involvement and Engagement

Effective instruction includes a variety of strategies for fostering intellectual involvement and engagement to promote academic success. Presenting instruction using various approaches provides multiple avenues for learning new content, thus ensuring and strengthening student understanding to facilitate achievement. In addition, diversifying instructional strategies creates variety in the classroom that effectively stimulates students' interest and motivation to engage in learning. Strategies such as **cooperative learning, discussion**, and **self-directed opportunities** encourage active student participation that enhances intellectual involvement by allowing students to build on background knowledge, deepen understanding by exploring others' perspectives, and take ownership over their own learning. This ultimately increases student engagement and motivation for success in learning. Similarly, incorporating **inquiry**, **problem-solving**, and **project-based** strategies promotes curiosity in learning, creativity, and the development of critical thinking skills that stimulate intellectual participation and engagement to create a productive learning environment. Implementing **digital resources** and media throughout instruction is integral in enhancing academic success by making learning relevant, interesting, and differentiated to accommodate various learning needs. At the end of a lesson or activity, allowing students the opportunity to reflect is a valuable strategy in increasing intellectual involvement, retainment, and academic success by facilitating personal connections with learning to build understanding.

Actively Engaging Students by Incorporating Discussion into Instruction

Classroom discussion is a valuable instructional technique in engaging students throughout the learning process. When teachers skillfully pose higher-level questions in discussions, they establish an active learning environment in which students are encouraged and motivated to participate, thus enhancing overall engagement. Effective discussions prompt students to become **intellectually invested** in instruction by promoting the use of **critical** and **higher-order thinking** skills to consider information more deeply and devise creative solutions to problems. In addition, discussions stimulate engagement by providing students the opportunity to express their own thoughts and reasoning regarding a given topic to establish a sense of ownership over their learning. Furthermore, discussions foster a collaborative learning environment that actively engages students by prompting them to understand others' perspectives, consider alternative approaches, and build on one another's experiences to make deeper connections to learning.

Promoting Student Inquiry

The promotion of inquiry is a valuable instructional technique in enhancing student engagement and intellectual involvement. In an **inquiry-based** learning environment, students are encouraged to explore instructional material and devise their own conclusions or solutions to problems. This increases the effectiveness of the learning process by providing students with a sense of agency over their own learning. In addition, implementing this strategy fosters curiosity, self-motivation, and active participation, as it allows for hands-on, **student-led** learning that increases overall engagement. Incorporating inquiry into the classroom stimulates critical and higher-order thinking skills as students construct their own understanding by interacting with learning materials, analyzing their findings, and synthesizing their learning to create new conclusions, results, and responses. To effectively incorporate inquiry into the learning process, the teacher must provide several opportunities for self-directed learning, project-based learning, and student choice to stimulate curiosity. Questions must be open-ended, and students must be encouraged to hypothesize, predict, and experiment in their learning. The teacher must be flexible in instruction to allow space and opportunity for exploration and allow time for reflection and extended learning opportunities to facilitate further inquiry.

Incorporating Problem-Solving into Instruction

Providing opportunities for creative problem solving within instruction effectively creates an engaging and successful learning experience. Students become more **intellectually involved** when encouraged to actively participate in learning and utilize **critical thinking skills** to test hypotheses, analyze results, and devise creative solutions to problems. This hands-on, **student-directed** approach promotes success in learning by allowing students to interact with learning materials as they seek answers to complex ideas and problems in an engaging environment. Problem-solving enables students to make deeper connections to their learning to enhance understanding, as this strategy prompts them to employ and develop background knowledge. In addition, problem-solving activities allow for collaborative learning in which students can actively engage with peers to build on one another's knowledge and experience, thus enhancing successful learning.

Intellectual Involvement, Active Student Engagement, and Success in Learning

A productive learning environment is composed intellectually involved students that are actively engaged in successful learning. A strong correlation exists between **intellectual involvement**, **active student engagement**, and **success in learning**, and each component is necessary for effective instruction. Effective instruction consists of challenging students based on their abilities and teaching them to think deeply about new ideas and concepts. This ultimately encourages students' intellectual involvement, as it prompts them to utilize their critical thinking skills to build on their background knowledge, consider alternative perspectives, and synthesize their learning to devise creative solutions. When students are intellectually involved in instruction, they become more personally invested and engaged, as learning becomes relevant, interesting, and challenging. Engaged students are active participants in their learning, thus enhancing their overall productivity and academic success.

Effectively Structuring Lessons

When developing instruction, it is imperative that the teacher is knowledgeable on how to effectively structure lessons to maximize student engagement and success. Each lesson must include a clear **objective** and explicitly state the process for achieving it. To initiate engagement, effective lessons begin with an **opening**, or "warm-up," activity to introduce a new topic, diagnose student understanding, and activate prior knowledge. Instruction of new material must be delivered through a variety of teaching strategies that are consciously tailored to students' individual learning needs to enhance participation and ensure comprehension. Direct instruction should be followed by **active learning** activities with clear directions and procedures to allow students to practice new concepts and skills. Throughout a successful lesson, the teacher checks frequently for understanding and comprehension by conducting a variety of **formative assessments** and adjusts instruction as necessary. Including **closure** activities is essential to successful learning, as it gives students the opportunity to reflect, process information, make connections, and demonstrate comprehension. In structuring lessons effectively according to students' learning needs, the teacher establishes a focused and engaging learning environment that promotes academic success.

Example of a Daily Lesson Plan Structure

Flexible Instructional Groupings

Flexible instructional groupings provide the teacher and students with a versatile, engaging environment for successful learning. Skillfully grouping students allows for productive, cooperative learning opportunities in which individual strengths are enhanced and necessary support is provided, thus enhancing motivation and engagement. When working in groups, students' understanding of instruction is strengthened, as they are able to learn and build upon one another's background knowledge, perspectives, and abilities. Instructional groups can include students of the **same** or **varied abilities** depending on the learning objective and task to increase productivity and provide scaffolding as necessary for support. This strategy is effective in enabling the teacher to **differentiate** instruction and adjust groups as needed to accommodate varying learning styles, abilities, and interests to maximize engagement and success in learning.

Effective Pacing of Lessons and Importance of Flexibility to Students' Needs

Effective pacing is imperative to focused and engaging instruction. Teachers must be conscientious of the pace of their instruction and ensure that it is reflective of their students' learning needs and sustains their attention. Instruction that is delivered too quickly results in confusion and discouragement, whereas if instruction is too slow, students will lose interest and become disengaged. A well-paced lesson states clear learning goals and objectives while clearly outlining the means to achieve them to elicit student motivation. The teacher must consider the most **efficient** and **engaging** instructional strategies for presenting new material to establish a steady pace and maintain it by incorporating smooth **transitions** from one activity to the next. It is important that teachers are conscious of the rate of instruction throughout all stages of learning while maintaining **flexibility** in pacing in order to be responsive to their students. As individual students have different learning needs and processing times, they may require a faster or slower rate of instruction to understand new concepts and remain engaged in learning. Frequent checks for understanding and reflection activities are essential strategies in determining if the pace of instruction must be adjusted to accommodate students' needs.

Connecting Content to Students' Prior Knowledge and Experiences

Implementing effective instructional strategies for connecting content to students' prior knowledge and experiences enhances the relevancy of learning and fosters deeper connections that strengthen understanding. To achieve this, teachers must educate themselves on students' backgrounds, experiences, communities, and interests to determine what is important and interesting to them. With this knowledge in mind, teachers can successfully locate and implement **authentic materials** into instruction to enhance relevancy. Additionally, encouraging students to bring materials to class that reflect their backgrounds and including these materials in instruction makes learning relevant by allowing students to make **personal connections** to content. Instructional strategies such as brainstorming, KWL charts, prereading, and anticipation guides allow the teacher to determine what students know prior to learning a new concept, thus enabling them to connect content to students' background knowledge in a relevant way. Incorporating digital resources further enhances relevancy in learning. Teachers can locate videos or audio clips that relate to instruction and reflect students' background experiences and interests. Using digital resources to introduce a new concept is a valuable strategy in developing students' **schema** on a topic to build prior knowledge and make learning meaningful by fostering connections.

Making Learning Relevant and Meaningful

For learning to be relevant and meaningful, it is essential that teachers present content in a way that connects with students' **prior knowledge** and experiences. When students are able to apply new ideas and information to what they already know through effective instructional techniques, it facilitates strong **personal connections** that make learning relevant and meaningful. In addition, personal connections and **relevancy** are strengthened when teachers consciously incorporate materials to reflect students' individual backgrounds and experiences in instruction. Linking content to students' background experiences enables them to relate instruction to real-world situations, thus establishing a sense of purpose for learning by making it applicable to their lives. Intentionally connecting content with students' prior knowledge and experiences enhances the effectiveness of the instructional process and fosters positive attitudes toward learning.

Enhancing Student Engagement and Success in Learning

Engaging instruction employs a variety of instructional strategies and materials to create a relevant, meaningful, and successful learning experience. Effective content establishes a clear and applicable purpose for instruction that increases student participation in the learning process. Presenting relevant and meaningful content enhances understanding and engagement by enabling students to create real-world, **personal connections** to learning based upon their own backgrounds and experiences. In addition, when instruction is tailored to reflect students' unique interests and preferences, content becomes more appealing and students' willingness to learn is enhanced. When students can perceive content through their own frames of reference with instructional materials that reflect their unique differences, they are able to effectively internalize and relate information to their lives, thus increasing engagement. Engaged learning ultimately facilitates academic success in that when students are motivated to learn, they demonstrate positive attitudes toward learning and are more likely to actively participate.

Adapting Instruction to Individual Needs

Evaluating Activities and Materials to Meet Learning Needs

The careful selection of instructional activities and materials is integral to accommodating students' varying characteristics and needs. When evaluating the appropriateness of activities and materials, several considerations must be made. Teachers must consider whether activities and materials align with state and district **academic standards**. Teachers must also evaluate the quality and effectiveness of the activities and materials in supporting students' unique differences as they achieve learning goals and objectives. All materials and activities must be **developmentally appropriate** across domains yet adaptable to individual students' learning needs. In addition, they must be challenging yet feasible for student achievement relative to students' grade levels and abilities to promote engagement and the development of critical and **higher-order thinking** skills. Teachers must evaluate activities and materials for versatility to allow for student choice and differentiation in order to address varying characteristics and needs. Teachers must also ensure that activities and materials are accurate, **culturally sensitive**, and reflective of students' diversities to foster an inclusive learning environment that promotes engagement.

Instructional Resources and Technologies

The implementation of varied instructional resources and technologies is highly valuable in supporting student engagement and achievement. Effective use of resources and technologies requires teachers to evaluate their appropriateness in addressing students' individual characteristics and learning needs for academic success. Teachers must be attuned to students' unique differences in order to seek high quality technologies and resources that address their students' needs and support the achievement of learning goals and objectives. Technologies and resources must be **accurate**, **comprehensible**, easily **accessible** to students, and **relevant** to the curriculum and the development of particular skills. Teachers must also consider the grade-level and **developmental appropriateness** of technologies and resources as well as their adaptability to allow for differentiation. Effective technologies and resources are interactive, engaging, and multifaceted to allow for varying levels of complexity based on students' abilities. This allows teachers to provide appropriate challenges while diversifying instruction to appeal to varied characteristics and learning needs, thus fostering an engaging environment that supports success in learning for all students.

Adapting Activities and Materials to Meet Individual Characteristics and Needs

In effective instruction, activities and materials are adapted to accommodate students' individual characteristics and needs. Teachers must be attuned to students' unique differences and understand how to adjust activities and materials accordingly to facilitate academic success and growth. To achieve this, teachers must incorporate a **variety** of activities and materials that appeal to all styles of learners. Activities and materials should provide **student choice** for engagement in learning and demonstration of understanding. By differentiating instruction, teachers can effectively scaffold activities and materials to provide supports as necessary as well as include extensions or alternate activities for enrichment. **Chunking** instruction, allowing extra time as necessary, and accompanying activities and materials with aids such as graphic organizers, visual representations, and anticipation guides further differentiates learning to accommodate students' learning characteristics and needs. Conducting **formative assessments** provides teachers with valuable feedback regarding student understanding and engagement, thus allowing them to modify and adjust the complexity of activities and materials as necessary to adapt to varied characteristics and learning differences.

Instructional Resources and Technologies

When teachers understand students' individual characteristics and needs, they can adapt instructional resources and technologies accordingly to maximize learning. To do so effectively, the teacher must incorporate a diverse array of **multifaceted** resources and technologies that support and enhance learning through a variety of methods. This ensures that varying learning needs are met, as students of all learning styles are provided with several avenues for building and strengthening understanding. Additionally, the teacher can adapt resources and technologies to accommodate individual students by **varying the complexity** to provide challenges, support, and opportunities for enrichment based on ability level. Supplementing technologies and resources with **scaffolds**, such as extra time, visual representations, or opportunities for collaborative learning, further enables the teacher to adapt to individual learning needs. When effectively implemented and adapted to students' characteristics and needs, instructional technologies and resources serve as valuable tools for differentiating curriculum to enhance the learning experience.

Materials and Resources

Materials and Resources That Enhance Student Learning and Engagement

Instructional Materials and Resources

The careful selection of instructional materials and resources for lesson plans is an integral component of enhancing student engagement and the overall learning experience. Lesson materials should be relevant to students' interests so as to facilitate personal connections to learning and ultimately, deepen understanding. In building positive relationships with students by educating themselves on students' backgrounds and interests, teachers can effectively locate and implement varied instructional materials and resources that are relevant to students and foster motivation for learning. Additionally, interactive materials, such as manipulatives or other hands-on learning resources, enhance learning and engagement through encouraging participation. Similarly, cooperative learning materials encourage student participation and engagement through fostering collaboration. Teachers can also enhance learning experiences through incorporating authentic materials that are relevant to instruction such as maps, brochures, historical documents, or similar materials that enhance student engagement and learning.

Technological Resources

Technology is integrated in nearly every aspect of life as a tool to enhance and assist in daily activities. This notion also applies in the classroom, as technological resources are an excellent method of increasing student engagement and interest, supporting students in their individual learning needs, and enhancing learning. The use of computers, tablets, smartphones, and other technological resources serve to improve understanding of classroom instruction, foster relevancy and personal connections, and scaffold instruction to address diverse learning styles and needs. Additionally, teachers have myriad digital resources available in the form of interactive websites, videos clips, and apps that can be implemented to enrich lessons and increase development across all subject areas. Often, these resources accommodate students' individual learning needs through providing increasingly challenging activities based on individual skill level, and the teacher can utilize these resources to tailor instruction to address individual student needs. Technological resources can also add authenticity to learning experiences, making them more engaging and enhancing student learning. Virtual field trips or science experiments can provide real-world connections to instruction by recreating authentic learning experiences without students having to leave the classroom.

Community Resources

Community resources are beneficial in enriching instruction to foster engagement and enhance student learning. They provide students the opportunity to connect and apply what they learn in the classroom with the real world. This ultimately makes learning more authentic, as students are able to see the relevancy of what they are learning. This enhances learning by making it more engaging. Through field trips, teachers can incorporate community resources such as museums, art exhibits, science centers, and even local areas such as parks or historical sites into curriculum to accompany material learned in class. Additionally, if access to field trips is limited, teachers can take advantage of community outreach programs that bring learning experiences to classrooms. Reaching out to members of the community that are relevant to topics being covered in class, such as scientists or local historians, can be beneficial in allowing students to understand how what they are learning is applicable outside of the classroom. Locating and implementing community resources enhances student learning and engagement through making learning authentic, relevant, and applicable in the real world.

Developmentally Appropriate Materials and Resources

To create engaging and effective learning experiences, instructional materials and resources must be developmentally appropriate. Teachers must have a solid understanding of the general cognitive, physical, social, and emotional developmental levels of their students as well as individual differences in skills and abilities to properly select developmentally appropriate materials. The age and developmental level appropriateness of instructional resources can be determined by considering the material's size, height, and level of difficulty for students. Whether materials accommodate individual differences in skill level, ability, or interest can be determined by their versatility. If a resource can be used in multiple ways, it will appeal to a variety of learning needs and interests and support development across domains. Developmentally appropriate materials are reflective and considerate of students' diversities. Teachers can determine this by using their knowledge of students' backgrounds to select materials that incorporate and are sensitive to their students' cultural differences to support development by fostering personal connections to learning.

Chapter Quiz

Ready to see how well you retained what you just read? Scan the QR code to go directly to the chapter quiz interface for this study guide. If you're using a computer, simply visit the online resources page at **mometrix.com/resources719/oaecompsci** and click the Chapter Quizzes link.

OAE Practice Test

Want to take this practice test in an online interactive format?
Check out the online resources page, which includes interactive practice questions and much more: **mometrix.com/resources719/oaecompsci**

1. A teacher is writing code to add up all the grades for a given class and determine the class average. The grades are stored in an array named `grades[]`. Read the following code and determine what code should replace `/* missing code */` so that the code satisfies its given purpose.

```
float average ← 0
float total ← 0
for(int i ← 0; i < grades.length; i ← i + 1)
      /* missing code */
end for
print average
```

a.
```
total ← total + grades[i]
average ← total / grades.length
```

b.
```
total ← grades[i]
average ← total / grades.length
```

c.
```
average ← total / grades.length
```

d.
```
average ← total / (grades.length + 1)
```

2. Which of the following is an example of simulation and modeling?

a. printing out a multiplication table for 1 through 10
b. displaying a list of the top ten baby names of the year
c. using baseball statistics to predict this year's World Series winner
d. determining the dimensions of a box given its length, width, and height

3. Josh wants to determine how many quarters a vending machine will give him when he purchases an item. This vending machine will always use the least number of coins as change. For example, when he purchases an item that is $1.65, he will insert $2 and will receive $0.35 in change. Of that change, one coin will be a quarter.

Here are some variables that Josh set up so far:

```
int change                //a positive integer representing the
                          //  number of cents given
int quarters ← 0          //the number of quarters to give
```

Which component of code will be a helpful addition to his program?

a.
```
if(change ≥ 25)
      quarters ← quarters + 1
end if
```
b.
```
quarters ← change % 25
```
c.
```
quarters ← change / 25
```
d.
```
if(change - 25 > 0)
      quarters ← quarters + 1
end if
```

4. Which of the following is a benefit of inheritance in object-oriented programming?

a. A subclass is dependent on its parent class.
b. Inherited functions work faster than normal functions.
c. One object can contain another object.
d. Code redundancy is reduced.

5. A robot has a light sensor that detects whether an object placed in front of it is mostly white or mostly black, using an output range from 1 to 100, where everything 50 or under is mostly white, and everything from 51 to 100 is mostly black. Which of the following transformations of data would NOT make the data more readable?

a. Removing values greater than 100
b. Replacing values from 1 to 50 with "white" and replacing values from 51 to 100 with "black"
c. Rounding decimals to the nearest integer
d. Removing values less than 1

6. A certain small file type has a maximum size of 7 bytes and 3 bits. If the file is currently 3 bytes and 5 bits, how many more bits can be stored as part of the file?

a. 30 bits
b. 38 bits
c. 3 bits
d. 62 bits

7. Consider the array below.

```
int[] values ← [1, 4, 8, 10, 11, 16]
```

Using a binary search, how many comparisons will it take to find the value 11?

a. two
b. three
c. four
d. six

8. An elderly couple lives far away from their grandchildren in a senior living facility. They would love to have an easy way to talk to and see them but have never used a computer before. Which of the following would be the best permanent solution to this problem? They should ________.

a. Be provided a laptop with a webcam
b. Move closer to their grandchildren
c. Attend classes on how to use a computer
d. Go to a neighbor's house and use their computer

9. In the internet address www.google.com/mail, which of the following indicates the name of the third-level domain?

a. www
b. google
c. com
d. mail

10. What is a common unintended consequence of protecting intellectual property through patents and copyrights?

a. Companies must develop completely new ideas.
b. Competition is reduced, possibly creating monopolies.
c. Companies may not always know that they are acting illegally.
d. Customers do not know which companies own certain intellectual property.

11. Ernest is upgrading his internet connection. He wants to make sure that he can stream 1080p HD video without stuttering. Which of the following internet speeds is the minimum necessary?

a. 20 Mbps
b. 5 Mbps
c. 1 Mbps
d. 100 Kbps

12. Consider the array below.

```
int[] nums ← [4, 6, 9, 11, 22]
```

Using a linear search, how many comparisons will it take to find the value 22?

a. two
b. three
c. four
d. five

13. Which of the following is an example of the IoT (internet of things) technology?

a. a Wi-Fi-enabled thermostat
b. a public USB charging station
c. a coffee maker with a timer switch
d. a cell phone that can send text messages

14. What should replace `/*missing code*/` so that the `for` loop becomes non-halting?

```
/* missing code */
    print "Hi there!"
end for
```

a. `for(int i ← 10; i > 0; i ← i - 1)`
b. `for(int i ← 0; i < 10; i ← i + 1)`
c. `for(int i ← 10; i < 10; i ← i + 1)`

d. `for(int i ← 0; i < 10; i ← i - 1)`

15. Customers trying to reach a certain florist's website are unable to reach that site. It is later found that one of their competitors was unethically sending a flood of traffic to the site in order to prevent anyone from reaching it. This type of attack is known as which of the following?

a. a DoS attack
b. a malware attack
c. an IP flood attack
d. an SSL attack

16. A company wants to set up a system where its employees can access their files from anywhere as long as they have an internet connection. Which of the following should the company use?

a. hard disk storage
b. cloud-based storage
c. flash drive storage
d. LAN storage

17. A program is used to determine how many people in a group are senior citizens, when "senior citizen" is defined as anyone 65 or more years old. The ages have already been entered into an array named `input`**, which contains 3 values. The current code is below.**

```
int[] input ← [45, 80, 37]
if(input[0] ≥ 65)
        seniors ← seniors + 1
end if
if(input[1] ≥ 65)
        seniors ← seniors + 1
end if
if(input[2] ≥ 65)
        seniors ← seniors + 1
end if
```

Which choice would be the best code to achieve the same result using iteration?

a.
```
while(count ≤ 3)
if(input[count] ≥ 65)
        seniors ← seniors + 1
end if
end while
```
b.
```
while(count < 3)
if(input[count] ≥ 65)
        seniors ← seniors + 1
end if
end while
```
c.
```
int count ← 0
while(count ≤ 3)
if(input[count] ≥ 65)
        seniors ← seniors + 1
end if
        count ← count + 1
end while
```
d.
```
int count ← 0
while(count < 3)
if(input[count] ≥ 65)
        seniors ← seniors + 1
end if
        count ← count + 1
end while
```

18. Ping pong balls are often used in generating numbers for the lottery. When a number pops up in the machine, this number can be categorized as _________.

a. pseudorandom
b. random
c. deterministic
d. static

19. How should teachers arrange classroom furnishings and materials to create supportive climates?

a. Arrangements should not let students feel too comfortable.
b. Arrangements should discourage dialogue among students.
c. Arrangements should keep students from owning the room.
d. Arrangements should support collaboration among students.

20. Examine the following diagram.

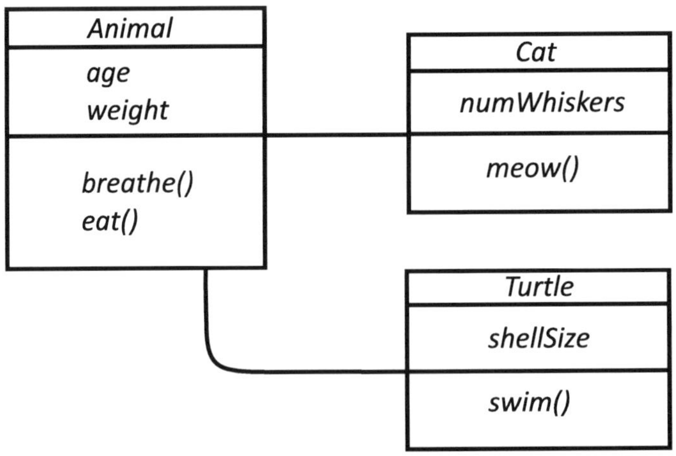

Which of the following is an example of an instance variable?

a. `Animal`
b. `breathe()`
c. `shellSize`
d. `Turtle`

21. James was creating a program to make colored shapes. He has three different shapes to choose from: square, triangle, and circle. He has three different colors to choose from: blue, green, and red. One of his methods looks like this:

```
void greenCircle()
      print "green"
      print "circle"
end greenCircle
```

He realized that if he continued to code this way, he would need nine different methods to make all the different types. How could he generalize the information so that he would need only one method?

a. Using parameters
b. It is not possible to generalize
c. Using a loop
d. Using return values

22. Mary has a stopwatch that only counts the number of seconds that have elapsed during a certain period of time. She wants to create a program that will tell her how many hours, minutes, and seconds have elapsed, instead of only showing the total number of seconds. She writes the following code:

```
1       String showTime(int totalSeconds)
2       int hours ← 0
3       int minutes ← 0
4       int seconds ← 0
5
6       seconds ← totalSeconds % 60
7       hours ← totalSeconds / 60
8       minutes ← hours / 60
```

Lines 6 through 8 are not working correctly. Rework the statements and variables to make the code correctly implement Mary's idea.

a.
```
seconds ← totalSeconds % 60
minutes ← totalSeconds / 60
hours ← totalSeconds % 3600
```
b.
```
seconds ← totalSeconds % 60
minutes ← totalSeconds / 3600
minutes ← minutes % 60
hours ← totalSeconds / 3600
```
c.
```
seconds ← totalSeconds % 60
minutes ← totalSeconds % 3600
minutes ← minutes / 60
hours ← totalSeconds / 3600
```
d.
```
seconds ← totalSeconds / 60
minutes ← totalSeconds / 3600
hours ← totalHours / 60
```

23. Which of the following is an example of bad documentation practice?

a. leaving brief comments within the code
b. adding images to documentation
c. describing classes and methods
d. giving variables arbitrary names

24. In computer storage, a _____ is a unit of measurement equal to 2^{40} bytes.

a. megabyte
b. gigabyte
c. terabyte
d. petabyte

25. Which programming construct is the following code an example of?

```
if(num > 4)
        print num
end if
```

a. Sequence
b. Selection
c. Iteration
d. Recursion

26. Penelope begins typing an essay for her English class. At one point during her writing, she notices that she has written exactly 2,048 characters. How much space are these characters taking up on her computer if she is writing in a plain text document?

a. 1 KB
b. 2 KB
c. 3 KB
d. 4 KB

27. How can teachers establish positive, productive learning environments for students whose developmental levels vary within the same classroom?

a. Observe levels/types of children's play and provide only activities matching these.
b. Give older elementary and middle school students high school-type collaboration.
c. Do not expect new preschoolers sharing, but do model, encourage, and reward it.
d. Confine productive learning environments in high school classes to the classrooms.

28. A sequence of statements in binary that is generated by compiling is called _________.

a. source code
b. object code
c. script code
d. Boolean code

29. Jason has a program that allows the user to enter the number of hours they have exercised in the past year. It currently has a dropdown list that contains the values "1 to 10", "11 to 20", and "21+". He wants to make his program more specific, so he will replace the dropdown list with a textbox. What must he include in his code with this change?

a. a check to ensure the number entered is negative
b. a check to ensure the number entered is positive
c. a check to see if the number entered is an integer
d. a check to see if the number entered is between 1 and 21

30. Examine the code below:

```
int x ← 0
int y ← 0

for(int i ← 0; i < 0; i ← i + 1)
       x ← x + 1
end for

int j ← 0
do
       y ← y + 1
       j ← j + 1
while (j < 0)
```

What are the values of x and y after the code executes?

a. x is 0 and y is 0
b. x is 1 and y is 1
c. x is 1 and y is 0
d. x is 0 and y is 1

31. A dog owner designed an automatic dog feeder. When the dog pushes a button, an electronic signal triggers a motor to open a hatch and drop a treat into the dog's bowl. The dog only knows that when he pushes the button, he gets a treat. In computer science this concept is known as ________.

a. Abstraction
b. Inheritance
c. Polymorphism
d. Aliasing

32. Jack notices that pages he has visited before but that have not changed load faster in his browser than pages he has never visited. Why is this?

a. The pages are saved in cache memory.
b. The pages have been bookmarked.
c. The browser automatically downloads visited pages faster.
d. The ISP allows faster download speeds for users for pages they visit repeatedly.

33. A farmer has been using a computer program to calculate the total cost of sod in rectangular areas on his farm. Sod costs $1.49 per square foot. In one part of his program, he is determining the cost to cover a rectangle that is 50 by 100 feet, so he uses this code below.

```
float totalCost ← 1.49 * 100 * 50
```

In yet another area, he needs to cover 25 by 30 feet with sod, so he uses the code below.

```
float totalCost ← 1.49 * 25 * 30
```

In order to make his code more reusable, he should use ________.

a. a for-loop that loops through all the areas the farmer needs to calculate
b. an if statement that changes the algorithm based on parameters
c. a while-loop that continues as long as there is at least one more item to calculate
d. a function that has cost, length, and width passed in as parameters

34. In the following recursive algorithm, which is the base case?

```
int doWork(int num)
        if(num ≤ 0)
                return 0
        else if(num > 100)
                return 2 + doWork(num - 1)
        else if(num > 50)
                return 1 + doWork(num - 1)
        else
                return doWork(num - 1)
end doWork
```

a.
```
else if(num > 100)
    return 2 + doWork(num - 1)
```

b.
```
else if(num > 50)
    return 1 + doWork(num - 1)
```

c.
```
if(num ≤ 0)
    return 0
```

d.
```
else
    return doWork(num - 1)
```

35. What expression is `not(a < 4 and b > 3)` equivalent to?

a. `(a ≥ 4 and b ≤ 3)`
b. `(a > 4 and b < 3)`
c. `(a ≥ 4 or b ≤ 3)`
d. `(a > 4 or b < 3)`

36. Consider the `if` statement below.

```
if(cost ≥ 100)
      print "free shipping"
else if(cost ≥ 50)
      print "$5 shipping"
else
      print "$10 shipping"
end if
```

Which of the following is the smallest set of input values that will sufficiently test all cases?

a. 101, 100, 75, 50, 25
b. 150, 75, 25
c. 200
d. 101, 102, 51, 52, 40, 41

37. Which of the following communication mediums allows for the fastest transmission of data?

a. CAT-5
b. fiber-optic
c. coaxial
d. twisted pair

38. In the context of decomposing a problem, which is NOT an example of an actor?

a. users
b. devices
c. goals
d. clients and servers

39. Which of the following is NOT a means by which a consumer provides data that companies may collect?

a. writing an email
b. saving a text file locally
c. using social media sites
d. filling out online surveys

40. Which is NOT a legal method that companies use to gather information on users?

a. Monitoring your social media
b. Tracking you on public Wi-Fi
c. Reading documents saved on your local hard drive
d. Tracking you on apps you've downloaded

41. Which of the following is an example of uncrackable encryption based on the current limits of computing power?

a. AES-256 encryption
b. Caesar cipher encryption
c. random substitution encryption
d. the Enigma machine's encryption

42. One of the most well-known tests in computer science is the Turing test. This test determines __________.

a. If an algorithm is the most efficient solution
b. If an AI is believable
c. The time it takes for a process to complete
d. If a network exists

43. Convert 35_{10} to octal.

a. 43
b. 40
c. 41
d. 42

44. A carnival game consists of a wheel with three sections of unequal sizes. The section labeled "LOSE" has a 95 percent chance of being selected. The section labeled "CANDY" has a 4 percent chance of being selected. The section labeled "GRAND PRIZE" has a 1 percent chance of being selected. Consider the code below, which simulates this game.

```
//random() returns a random integer between 1 and 100

int playGame()
   int rand ← random()
         if(rand > 5)
               print "LOSE"
         else if(rand > 1)
               print "CANDY"
         /*missing code*/
   end if
end playGame
```

Which statements below could replace `/*missing code*/` **so that the simulation runs as intended?**

```
I.     else
             print "GRAND PRIZE"
II.    else if(rand > 0)
             print "GRAND PRIZE"
III.   else if (random() < 2)
             print "GRAND PRIZE"
```

a. I, II, and III
b. I and II
c. III only
d. II and III

45. Trace the following program and decide which of the following operations best represents the calculation that will take place.

```
int[] list ← [1, 7, 2, 8, 6]
int sum ← 0
for(i ← 1; i < 4; i ← i + 1)
      sum ← sum + list[i]
end for
print sum
```

a. 7 + 2 + 8
b. 7 + 2 + 8 + 6
c. 1 + 7 + 2
d. 1 + 7 + 2 + 8 + 6

46. Which of the following is a benefit of using cloud-based data storage instead of local storage?

a. faster data access
b. increased security
c. easier expansion of capacity
d. physical access to files

47. Which of the following is NOT a valid debugging technique?

a. Using print statements to print out current values
b. Using watch points
c. Recompiling the program
d. Changing the input

48. Which of the following is the defining feature of a cluster computer system?

a. It relies on redundant storage disks.
b. It uses a battery and can be held in the hand.
c. It consists of many computers working together.
d. It allows many users to compute on the same server.

49. How many bits does it take to store the number A_{16}?

a. one
b. two
c. three
d. four

50. Which of the following feedback methods is uniquely available for code that has been released in an alpha version?

a. code review
b. end user review
c. peer review
d. ad hoc review

51. Which of the following is a reason to write original code instead of using a library?

a. Writing original code is more convenient.
b. Writing original code is less time consuming.
c. Original code is more likely to be bug-free.
d. Original code is better suited to unique purposes.

52. A certain game uses the following method to determine how many damage points to assign. The variable `sword` is a string representing the current type of sword, and `strength` is an integer representing the strength of the swing as a value from 1 to 4.

```
int diceRoll()          //returns a random integer from 1 to 6
int determineDamage(String sword, int strength)
    if(sword == "fire")
        return 2 * diceRoll() * strength
    else if(sword == "ice")
        return 3 * diceRoll() * strength
    else if(sword == "diamond")
        return 4 * diceRoll() * strength
    end if
end determineDamage
```

Which of the following calls to `determineDamage` could produce a value of 24?

I. `determineDamage("fire", 4)`
II. `determineDamage("ice", 4)`
III. `determineDamage("diamond", 1)`

a. I and II
b. II and III
c. I and III
d. I, II, and III

53. Barry wrote a program and realized that he needed to find the sum of the integers in an array. He also realized he needed to do this same operation many times in his program, so he wrote the following method:

```
int sumArray(int[] a, int size)
    int sum ← 0
    for(int i ← 0; i < size; i ← i + 1)
        sum ← sum + a[i]
    end for
end sumArray
```

Programming in this way is an example of ________.

a. Extensibility
b. Modifiability
c. Reusability
d. Testability

54. A high school robotics team sends the signals below to their robot to control it.

0 forward
1 backward
2 pivot left
3 pivot right

They are worried about other teams picking up their signals to determine how to complete the challenges, so they have encrypted their signals. Below is their decryption key.

```
(input - 2) % 4
```

What actions will the robot take if they send the encrypted commands below to their robot?

```
7, 9, 18, 4
```

a. pivot right, backward, pivot left, forward
b. backward, pivot right, forward, forward
c. backward, pivot right, forward, pivot left
d. pivot right, backward, pivot left, pivot left

55. What is a data breach?

a. any use or viewing of files without permission
b. any action that violates a company's security policies
c. any violation of the Department of Homeland Security's privacy policies and procedures
d. any observable occurrence in a system or network that has negative consequences

56. Consider the recursive algorithm below.

```
1    int process(int x)
2    if (x == 0)
3         return 1
4    else
5         return x + process(x - 2)
6    end if
7    end process
```

What change must be made to the recursive algorithm so that it will not cause infinite recursion when `process` **is called with a value of 9?**

a. replace line 5 with **`return`** `x + process(x - 4)`
b. replace line 2 with **`if`**`(x ≤ 0)`
c. replace line 2 with **`if`**`(x == -2)`
d. replace line 5 with **`return`** `x + process(x + 2)`

57. John looked out his window on a snowy day and decided to record the snowfall every hour. He developed the following chart in which Hour represents the hour that he took the measurement and Total represents the total snow accumulation up to that point.

Hour	1	2	3	4	5	6
Total	2	3	5	6	8	9

He decided to write code to predict what the totals would be if it kept snowing in the same pattern.

```
for(int i ← 1; i ≤ hour; i ← i + 1)
     /* missing code */
end for
```

Which statement(s) could replace `/* missing code */` **so that his program represents the snowfall totals correctly based on the chart?**

a.
```
if(i % 2 == 1)
   total ← total + 1
else
   total ← total + 2
```

b.
```
if(hour == 1)
   total ← 2
else
   total ← 2 * hour - 1
```

c.
```
if(hour == 1)
   total ← 2
else
   total ← hour + 1
```

d.
```
if(i % 2 == 0)
   total ← total + 1
else
   total ← total + 2
```

58. Given the following code:

```
//substring method: this method returns a string from start to end
- 1
//String substring(int start, int end)

1      void strings(String s)
2            String foo ← ""
3            for(int i ← 0; i < s.length; i ← i + 1)
4                  foo ← foo + s.substring(i, i + 1)+ "!"
5            end for
6            print foo
7      end strings
```

If this method was called with the following code,

```
strings("hello")
```

the result would be `h!e!l!l!o!`

What would be the output if we swapped line 4 with the following code?

```
foo ← s.substring(i, i + 1) + "!" + foo
```

a. `h!e!l!l!o!`
b. `!h!e!l!l!o`
c. `!o!l!l!e!h`
d. `o!l!l!e!h!`

59. Elizabeth created a comic and wants to share it on the internet under the Creative Commons license. Which of the following conditions is required of all Creative Commons licenses and must be followed by anyone wanting to use Elizabeth's work?

a. No derivatives
b. Share alike
c. Noncommercial
d. Attribution

60. An amusement park uses three sensors on an old roller coaster. One sensor measures the speed, another measures g-force, and the last measures vibration. When they build a newer roller coaster, they use a total of six sensors.

Based on this information, which of the following is NOT true?

a. The newer roller coaster has more data to process.
b. The newer roller coaster's speed data will be more accurate.
c. More sensors could be added to the old roller coaster to increase data accuracy.
d. All the data can be used for diagnostic purposes.

61. Which of the following is a programming paradigm that allows the programmer to assert a desired result and does not address how to achieve the result?

a. imperative
b. object oriented
c. procedural
d. declarative

62. Given the following code:

```
/*
random() is a function that will return a decimal value x, where x
is 0 ≤ x < 1.
floor() is a function that rounds the decimal value down to the
nearest lower integer value.
*/

int result ← floor(random() * 4 + 66)
```

Which of the following numbers is a possible value of `result`**?**

a. 70
b. 4
c. 66
d. 67.5

63. Which of the following is NOT a good practice to incorporate for students who have difficulty finishing routine assignments?

a. The teacher should teach self-discipline about staying on task.
b. The teacher should avoid incorporating games into the materials because they might add too much time to the task.
c. The teacher should remove segments of the task, such as requiring the student to copy word problems before calculating the answer.
d. The teacher should divide the task into segments and allow the student to work on the parts throughout the day.

64. Which of the following is NOT terminology that directly relates to object-oriented programming?

a. Class
b. Inheritance
c. Polymorphism
d. Syntax

65. Which of the following is NOT an example of an obstacle to equal access computing?

a. race
b. gender
c. age
d. name

66. Which of the following problems would be best solved using a heuristic approach?

a. determining the total number of purchases made on a website on any given day
b. determining the average number of points a player made per game in a basketball season
c. determining the best streets to turn down to get to a destination while driving
d. determining the largest number in an array

67. Which of the following could NOT be protected by a copyright?

a. Computer code
b. An original painting
c. The idea for a better toaster
d. The blueprint of a house

68. Use the following code to answer the question.

```
int firstNum ← 15
double secondNum ← 2.0
int thirdNum ← 2
double firstAnswer ← 0.0
double secondAnswer ← 0.0

firstAnswer ← firstNum / secondNum
secondAnswer ← firstNum / thirdNum
```

Which of the following statements are true?

a. `firstAnswer > secondAnswer`
b. `secondAnswer > firstAnswer`
c. `firstAnswer = secondAnswer`
d. The code will result in an error.

69. The Botany Association is writing a program to simulate a rose, a daffodil, and a pansy in order to compare how much carbon dioxide each flower converts to oxygen over an equal period. Which of the following will NOT be a user input?

a. the amount of oxygen in the air when the simulation begins
b. the amount of carbon dioxide in the air when the simulation begins
c. the amount of oxygen in the air when the simulation ends
d. the type of flower currently being simulated

70. Which of the following is an IP address NOT useful for?

a. sending information
b. receiving information
c. identifying a physical location
d. decrypting information

71. Consider the algorithm below.

1. **int** total ← 10
2. **int** result ← 0

```
3     result ← total / 3
4     print result
```

Which of the following could replace line 3 and give the same result?

a.
```
while(total > 0)
      total ← total - 3
      result ← result + 1
end while
```

b.
```
while(total > 2)
      total ← total - 3
      result ← result + 1
end while
```

c.
```
while(total < 0)
      total ← total - 3
      result ← result + 1
end while
```

d.
```
while(total < 2)
        total ← total - 3
        result ← result + 1
end while
```

72. Stephanie's credit score is bad, but she wants to get a lower rate for an automobile loan she is applying for. Her roommate, Patricia, has excellent credit. So during Stephanie's online application, she uses Patricia's social security number. Which of the following best describes Stephanie's actions?

a. piracy
b. identity theft
c. phishing
d. hacking

73. Which of the following is an example of citizen science?

a. A small team of researchers analyzing the bird population in a town.
b. A scientist analyzing DNA samples in her free time.
c. Hikers logging into a global app to report bear sightings.
d. Social media internally keeping track of user opinions about global warming.

74. A certain professor grades tests where scores fall between 0 and 100 inclusively. A score of 0 to 50 is "below average," a score of 51 to 79 is "average," and a score of 80 to 100 is "above average." Below is the code that she is using print the grades based on the scores.

```
//precondition: 0 ≤ score ≤ 100
if(score ≥ 0 and score ≤ 50)
      print "below average"
end if
if(score ≥ 51 and score ≤ 79)
      print "average"
end if
if(score ≥ 80 and score ≤ 100)
      print "above average"
end if
```

Which of the following code segments would still give the correct output and be the most efficient use of code?

a.
```
if(score ≥ 0 and score ≤ 50)
      print "below average"
else if(score ≥ 51 and score ≤ 79)
      print "average"
else
      print "above average"
end if
```
b.
```
if(score ≥ 80 and score ≤ 100)
      print "above average"
else if(score ≥ 51 and score ≤ 79)
      print "average"
else
      print "below average"
end if
```
c.
```
if(score ≤ 100)
      print "above average"
else if(score ≤ 79)
      print "average"
else
      print "below average"
end if
```
d.
```
if(score ≤ 50)
      print "below average"
else if(score ≤ 79)
      print "average"
else
      print "above average"
end if
```

75. The strategy of having two methods with the same name in the same class but with different parameters is called _________.

a. overloading
b. overriding
c. overwriting
d. overstating

76. Which of the following is an example of abstraction?

a. When I press the gas pedal, the car moves.
b. When I move the tip of a pencil across the surface of a paper, I write.
c. When I throw a ball in the air, it comes back down.
d. When I walk in the rain, I get wet.

77. Prior to school beginning every August, a second-grade teacher builds a daily schedule for his classroom. What is the best explanation for why he chooses to create this schedule?

a. Children learn best from teacher-centered activities
b. Children learn best when they are provided structure and consistency
c. Children have diverse backgrounds and family lives
d. Parents frequently request this information

78. In a database, which of the following is equivalent to the term "record"?

a. Table
b. Row
c. Column
d. Interface

79. What is most true about the relationship of teaching and classroom management?

a. Teacher management decisions are more complex when instruction is more demanding.
b. Encouraging student responsibility changes student behavior without affecting content.
c. When students solve novel problems and create products, teacher decisions are simpler.
d. Teachers focus on helping students meet academic demands instead of social demands.

80. Which of the following is an example of an ethical use of computers?

a. using your friend's Netflix account as your primary source of digital entertainment
b. connecting to a neighbor's password-free Wi-Fi without permission
c. using an image that has a creative commons license on your website without credit
d. using your library card to access an online library in another city and borrowing an e-book

81. Which of the following is NOT a common operating system task?

a. memory management
b. internet management
c. storage management
d. device management

82. Many cars today have sensors used to alert the driver to the presence of cars in neighboring lanes. On cars equipped with these sensors, each side mirror on the car may have a light that turns on when there is a car within the sensor's range in the lane on that side of the car. The typical range of such a sensor is from just behind the car (on the right or left) to the side mirror itself—an area that includes what is sometimes known as the driver's "blind spot."

Imagine you are writing the program for one of these cars. You want to use a variable to store a value that indicates whether the light should be on or off. Which datatype would be best to use?

a. integer
b. string
c. float
d. Boolean

83. Which of the following is the lowest layer in the OSI model?

a. application
b. session
c. presentation
d. physical

84. The New York City subway system captures the following data on a particular route. The subway train's maximum speed is 55 miles per hour.

Day	Distance	Time
1	500 miles	1 hour
2	0 miles	0 hours
3	150 miles	3 hours

A program attempts to compute the average speed of the train for each day by dividing the distance traveled by the time it took to travel that distance. Which of the following statements is true given this scenario?

I. Either the calculation for Day 1 will cause an error, or the sensor information is invalid.
II. Either the calculation for Day 2 will cause an error, or the sensor information is invalid.
III. Either the calculation for Day 3 will cause an error, or the sensor information is invalid.

a. I only
b. II only
c. I and II
d. I, II, and III

85. A physical security strategy for a building may involve a guard at the door who allows only those with the correct security clearance to enter. A(n) _____ is much like a digital version of this concept, as it lets only particular traffic through to a computer or network.

a. antivirus suite
b. virtual private network
c. firewall
d. protocol

86. What does the following method do?

```
//precondition: num is greater than or equal to 0.
int mystery(int num)
      if(num > 10)
            return num % 10
      else
            return num
end mystery
```

The previous method accepts a number and then returns the _______.

a. Tens place value
b. Ones place value
c. Number divided by 10
d. 10 percent of the number

87. How do IP protocols provide redundancy?

a. They reroute packets if a route becomes unavailable.
b. They use alternate destination addresses.
c. They receive from multiple inbound addresses.
d. They send all packets in triplicate.

88. Which of the following is a reason programmers should always document their code well?

a. The code will not work without good documentation.
b. Certain development methods require it.
c. Clarifying what the code does is often helpful.
d. Some error messages are related to improper documentation.

89. Katie is designing a video game in which you can drive a car. Currently, people who are testing her game say that the driving feels too easy to control, as the car does not go off the road no matter what speed it is traveling. Which of the following will make the controls more realistic?

a. Increasing the processing power of the computer
b. Increasing the number of variables simulated
c. Decreasing the input lag
d. Decreasing the data

90. The following is a recursive function. Identify the equivalent iterative algorithm.

```
int doCalculation(int x)
        if(x == 0)
                return 0
        else
                return x + doCalculation(x - 1)
        end if
end doCalculation
```

a.
```
int doCalculation(int x)
    int sum ← 0
    while(x < 0)
        sum ← sum + x
        x ← x - 1
    end while
    return sum
end doCalculation
```

b.
```
int doCalculation(int x)
    int sum ← 0
    while(x > 0)
        sum ← sum + x
        x ← x - 1
    end while
    return sum
end doCalculation
```

c.
```
int doCalculation(int x)
   int sum ← 0
   while(x < 0)
      sum ← sum + x
      x ← x - 1
   end while
   return x
end doCalculation
```

d.
```
int doCalculation(int x)
   int sum ← 0
   while(x > 0)
      sum ← sum + x
      x ← x - 1
   end while
   return x
end doCalculation
```

91. Which of the following wireless systems was developed first?

a. text messaging
b. Wi-Fi
c. cellular networks
d. Bluetooth

92. Which of the following is NOT a factor that may prevent a computer from solving a problem?

a. time
b. storage space
c. cost
d. an infinite loop

93. The use of code in a step-wise procedure to develop applications is called _________.

a. object-oriented programming
b. procedural programming
c. functional programming
d. low-level programming

94. A sensor on a piece of machinery has a valid range of values from 5.5 to 10, inclusive. Which is a correct data validation statement to determine when to display an error?

a.
```
if(input < 5.5 or input > 10)
   print "Error"
end if
```

b.
```
if(input ≥ 5.5 and input ≤ 10)
   print "Error"
end if
```

c.
```
if(input ≤ 5.5 or input ≥ 10)
   print "Error"
end if
```

d.
```
if(input > 5.5 and input < 10)
   print "Error"
end if
```

95. Which of the following is NOT a benefit of open data?

a. Predicting changes in real time
b. Promoting progress and innovation
c. Encouraging public education
d. Helping maintain copyrighted information

96. A college student is doing a study on people's bodyweight. Which of the following is an appropriate data collection method for the study?

a. installing a weight sensor at the door of a supermarket
b. asking a doctor to provide patient records for use in the study
c. setting up a booth on campus and asking people to participate
d. emailing people and asking them to self-report their weight

97. John wants to animate a character in a video game. To do this, he needs to create a walking animation. There are many parts to this animation, so he decides to start with just making the character's leg move. This is an example of ________.

a. Structural breakdown
b. Abstraction
c. Decomposition
d. Top-down design

98. Some code will be run using these variables:

```
int[] a ← [4, 8, 2, 7, 9, 12]
int sum ← 0

//code to be replaced
for(i ← 0; i < 6; i ← i + 1)
      sum ← sum + a[i]
end for
print sum
//end code to be replaced
```

Which of the following code segments can replace the code so that it will still have the same output?

a.
```
for(i ← 5; i < 0; i ← i - 1)
      sum ← sum + a[i]
end for
print sum
```
b.
```
for(i ← 0; i ≤ 6; i ← i + 1)
      sum ← sum + a[i]
end for
print sum
```
c.
```
int i ← 5
while(i ≥ 0)
      sum ← sum + a[i]
      i ← i - 1
end while
print sum
```
d.
```
int i ← 0
while(i ≤ 6)
      sum ← sum + a[i]
      i ← i + 1
end while
print sum
```

99. Consider the recursive function below.

```
int factorial(int x)
if(x == 1)
      return 1
else
      /*missing code*/
end if
end factorial
```

Which of the following should replace `/*missing code*/` so that the `factorial` function correctly calculates the factorial of a positive integer greater than 1?

a. `return x * factorial(x)`
b. `return x * factorial(x + 1)`
c. `return x * factorial(x - 1)`
d. `return x * factorial(x * x)`

100. In the following recursive algorithm, which part is the recursive call?

```
1    int start(int a)
2    if(a == 10)
3         return a
4    else
5         return a + start(a + 1)
6    end if
7    end start
```

a. line 1
b. line 2
c. line 3
d. line 5

101. Which of the following is NOT an example of a detrimental effect of smartphones on the health of their users?

a. heart conditions
b. insomnia
c. sedentary lifestyles
d. addiction

102. Sarah wants the newest video game but doesn't have enough money to pay for it. She searches the internet and finds a site where she can download the game for free. She feels she is not hurting anyone if she downloads it because she is just copying the software. If she downloads it, she is _________.

a. Game cracking
b. Software pirating
c. Ethically hacking
d. Social engineering

103. An amusement park ride allows visitors to line up ahead of time. As is usual for lines, the person who gets in line first gets to ride first, followed by the next person in line, etc. The line does not have a set length and can get larger or smaller depending on the number of waiting visitors. The best data structure to simulate the line is a(n) __________.

a. stack
b. queue
c. map
d. array

104. Which form of teacher body language is most likely to promote misbehavior in class?

a. The teacher looks students directly in the eye when speaking.
b. The teacher speaks in a calm but assertive tone.
c. The teacher stands with his or her back straight and head held high.
d. The teacher keeps his or her eyes focused on a book and speaks very softly.

105. A company that develops original software code wants to make sure that their intellectual property is protected. Which of the following can be used to do so?

a. a trade secret
b. a copyright
c. a patent
d. a trademark

106. After the following calculation, what is the value of the variable `myNum`?

```
int myNum ← 5
myNum ← 4 + myNum % 2 * 6
```

a. 10
b. 6
c. 11
d. 24

107. In binary measurement, 1 kilobyte (KB) is equal to how many bytes?

a. 1,024
b. 1,000
c. 1,000,000
d. 1,024,000

108. Nadia wants to log in to her favorite social media site. When she types in her username and password, it is compared to the values stored in the site's database. If they match, she is allowed access to her account. This is an example of:

a. data validation
b. data verification
c. data mining
d. data encryption

109. A school wants to use spreadsheet software to display information about the percentage of students who are getting As, Bs, Cs, Ds, or Fs in a computer science class. Which of the following graphs would be the best to represent this data so that you can easily see the percentage of students in relation to the whole?

a. Bar graph
b. Pie chart
c. Line graph
d. Scatter plot

110. Consider the following library documentation.

```
/* This method returns a string where start is the index of the
first character to be returned, and end is the index of the last
character to be returned, with all other characters in between also
being returned. */

String substring(String s, int start, int end)
```

If `substring("pizza", 2, 3)` is called, what string will be returned?

a. zz
b. iz
c. za
d. pi

111. Which of the following is an appropriate use of randomization in a program?

a. randomizing the address associated with a particular user
b. randomizing the number of items a person ordered at a pizzeria
c. randomizing the amount of change to give back in a vending machine
d. randomizing the number of bonus points you get in a video game for finishing a level

112. American Standard Code for Information Interchange (ASCII) is a great example of data _______.

a. encryption
b. hashing
c. encoding
d. transferring

113. Jason and Chloe are playing a card game. During each turn they can add a card to the discard pile, or they can remove a card from the top of the discard pile. Which data structure would be best if we were trying to implement this aspect of the game in a program?

a. Queue
b. Stack
c. Map
d. Array

114. Look at the following procedures:

```
void firstProcedure(int x, int y)
       x ← x - y
       y ← secondProcedure(x, y)
       print x
       print y
end firstProcedure

int secondProcedure(int a, int b)
       if(a ≥ b)
              return a
         else
              return b
       end if
end secondProcedure
```

What will be the output of the call to `firstProcedure(-5, -3)`**?**

a. 2, 2
b. -2, -2
c. -5, -3
d. -3, -5

115. Sonia wants to buy some apples. Apples are $0.30 each, so she uses the following equation to calculate the cost.

```
float cost ← numApples * 0.30
```

This equation is _________.

a. linear
b. exponential
c. quadratic
d. logarithmic

116. A programmer was tasked with creating classes for objects representing items in a grocery store. Which of the following is a correct hierarchy from low to high?

a. carton, egg, dairy section, store
b. store, carton, dairy section, egg
c. egg, carton, dairy section, store
d. store, dairy section, carton, egg

117. Jerry is writing a program to fill boxes of donuts. At the end of the day, Jerry gets to eat any donuts that do not fit into a box, so he wants to find an easy way to determine how many donuts will not fit. Each box has a capacity of six donuts, represented by `int BOX_SIZE`. The total number of donuts baked for the day is inputted as `totalDonuts`. Jerry's current code is below.

```
int determineLeftover(int totalDonuts)
      int BOX_SIZE ← 6
      return totalDonuts % BOX_SIZE
end determineLeftover
```

Jerry realizes that the compiler he is using does not recognize the % operator. What can Jerry replace `return totalDonuts % BOX_SIZE` with in order to get the same result?

a. `return totalDonuts - BOX_SIZE`
b. `return totalDonuts / BOX_SIZE - BOX_SIZE`
c. `return totalDonuts - (totalDonuts / BOX_SIZE) * BOX_SIZE`
d. `return totalDonuts - (totalDonuts / BOX_SIZE)`

118. Vehicles in a parade drive by in a certain order. A car is at the front of the parade and is followed by a motorcycle. The vehicle types then continue alternating. Cars have four wheels and motorcycles have two. The following is a recursive method to calculate how many wheels in total there will be in the parade. Will it return the correct answer as written?

```
1    int wheels(int vehicles)
2         if(vehicles % 2 == 1)
3              return 4 + wheels(vehicles - 1)
4         else if(vehicles % 2 == 0)
5              return 2 + wheels(vehicles - 1)
6         else
7              return 0
8         end else
9    end wheels
```

a. Yes, no changes to be made.
b. No, line 1 should say `if(vehicles % 2 == 0)`.
c. No, line 5 should say `return 2 + wheels(vehicles)`.
d. No, the method will recurse indefinitely.

119. Which of the following is NOT a benefit of using an integrated development environment (IDE)?

a. automatic error corrections
b. increased efficiency
c. possibility for collaboration
d. readily available debugging tools

120. Sarah is trying to program a robot to navigate a maze. She has implemented a simple programming interface in which different colors represent the actions the robot can take.

Blue: move one space in the direction the robot is currently facing
Red: rotate clockwise one quarter-turn
Orange: rotate counterclockwise one quarter-turn

If Sarah's robot is currently facing east, which set of commands will allow her robot to be two squares north of her current position, given that there are no obstacles in sight?

a. Red, Blue, Blue
b. Orange, Orange, Blue, Blue
c. Blue, Red, Red, Blue, Orange, Blue, Blue
d. Blue, Orange, Orange, Blue, Red, Blue, Blue

121. Which of the following computing environments offers the most security?

a. local
b. wide-area network
c. local-area network
d. the cloud

122. James is designing a program in which players get to move twice as many spaces on the game board every time a six is rolled on a die. A random integer is generated when `random()` is called.

```
int roll ← random()
if(random() == 6)
        spaces ← roll * 2
else
        spaces ← roll
end if
return spaces
```

Which of the following statements about the code is true?

a. The code will run as James expects.
b. James should have returned the `roll` variable instead of the `spaces` variable.
c. The condition should read `if(roll == 6)`.
d. `spaces ← roll * 2` should be replaced with `roll ← roll * 2`.

123. Which of the following statements is correct regarding digital signatures?

a. They do not rely on the signer keeping their private key secret.
b. They utilize symmetric cryptography to encrypt messages.
c. They guarantee that a message has not been altered while in transit.
d. They provide privacy to the sender of the message.

124. Which of the following is NOT a type of empirical evidence?

a. qualitative evidence
b. quantitative evidence
c. theoretical evidence
d. experimental evidence

125. Consider the code segment below.

```
if(weather == "rain" and temperature > 50)
        print "bring umbrella"
else
        if (temperature < 25)
                print "too cold"
        else if (temperature < 35)
                print "a bit chilly"
        else
                print "not too bad"
        end if
end if
```

If the string `weather` has the value "rain" and the integer `temperature` is 30, what will the output be?

a. not too bad
b. a bit chilly
c. too cold
d. bring umbrella

Answer Key and Explanations

1. A: In order to get the average of the grades, sum the grades, adding each grade to `total` as the loop executes. When that is completed, get the average by dividing the total sum by the number of grades in the array.

2. C: The computer application of modeling and simulation involves using a computer to build a mathematical model that accounts for certain parameters of the real-life object or activity. Often, predictions can be made from these simulations, with multiple simulations giving different results. Answer choices A, B, and D will always give the same results, as they are just presentations of facts or of computations based on facts.

3. C: The division operator, when used with integers, returns the whole number portion of the quotient. Therefore, using this operator on the change variable, which contains the number of cents, will return the number of 25-cent portions of the total number of cents. None of the other choices would count the number of quarters.

4. D: Thanks to inheritance, code that already exists can simply be reused, reducing redundancy. Subclasses being dependent on their parent classes (A) is actually a disadvantage, because care must be taken to remember that any changes to the parent class will affect the subclass as well. Inherited functions (B) actually work slower than normal functions. One object can contain another object (C) because of composition, not because of inheritance.

5. C: Rounding decimals to the nearest integer. Rounding decimals to integers does not make them more readable in this example, as you will still have to figure out if the resulting value is both within the acceptable range and if it should be interpreted as black or white. Removing values less than 1 and greater than 100 gets rid of values that are outside of the acceptable range, so this makes sense. Replacing values from 1 to 50 with white and 51 to 100 with black also makes sense because it will be easier to read which objects are black and which are white.

6. A: Since there are 8 bits in a byte, the maximum size of the file is $7 \times 8 + 3 = 59$ bits. The current size is $3 \times 8 + 5 = 29$ bits. Therefore, we can calculate the remaining number of bits by subtracting 29 from 59, giving us 30 bits.

7. A: Every binary search starts at the center element of the array being searched and approximately halves the list every time. Since the number of elements in this list is even, this binary search will first look at 8 (the third value) since it is the lower index of the two middle indexes. The value 8 is not the target, so the search continues with the remaining range. The value 8 and everything to its left is discarded, and the center element of the remaining range (10, 11, 16) is checked. The middle value in the range now being searched is 11, the target value. Thus, it will take two comparisons to find 11 using a binary search in this array.

8. C: Attend classes on how to use computers. Many older people have never needed a computer and have therefore been left behind when it comes to technology. Educating them is the best way to have them become technologically self-sufficient. Just sending them a laptop does not help them, since they wouldn't know how to use it. Moving closer to their grandchildren may not be possible and is overcompensating for a problem that can be solved with an easier solution. Going to a neighbor's house to use their computer may work a few times but relying on someone else for something that can be learned is not the best option.

9. A: The first-level domain name is "com". The second-level domain name is "google". The "mail" portion of the address is the name of a folder that is accessed at the domain www.google.com.

10. B: By protecting intellectual property, laws may also create an environment where monopolies easily form, as potential competitors have either no access or restricted access to the ideas that the market leader has protected. Companies developing their own new ideas (A) is beneficial, so this answer choice would not make sense. Companies are required to determine whether or not other companies have protected their intellectual property, so ignorance of the laws (C) cannot itself be considered a drawback. Finally, customers are not directly affected by knowing or not knowing which companies own certain intellectual property, so answer choice D is not correct.

11. B: The minimum necessary speed for streaming 1080p HD video is 5 megabits per second (Mbps). A speed of 100 Kbps is poor by modern standards, though it is about double the speed of a dial-up connection.

12. D: A linear search starts from the left of the array and compares the searched value with each element in order. Because 22 is the fifth element, it will take five comparisons.

13. A: The term "internet of things," or simply "IoT," refers collectively to all the everyday devices that can connect to the internet in order to send and receive information. Generally this internet connection is an aid to the functionality, usefulness, or convenience of the device. Some common examples of IoT technology are Wi-Fi-enabled thermostats, smart TVs, DVR-equipped set-top boxes, and smart refrigerators.

14. D: `for(int i ← 0; i < 10; i ← i - 1)`. This loop runs infinitely, or in other words, is non-halting. The variable `i` starts at 0 and subtracts 1 each time, so the end condition of `i` becoming at least 10 will never be met. Both answers A and B run to completion, while C never runs at all.

15. A: When a massive flood of superfluous requests are made in order to prevent users from reaching a server, it is known as a denial of service (or DoS) attack.

16. B: Cloud-based storage allows users to access their data from anywhere they have access to the internet, which is what the company wants. Hard disk storage (A) and flash drive storage (C) are both types of local storage, meaning the data would only be on particular machine. Choice D is local area network (LAN) storage, which is the storing of files on a network that exists inside a relatively small physical area. This would allow employees to access their files on a server in, for example, the same building. But a LAN by itself would not allow employees access from anywhere.

17. D: The `count` variable must be first initialized to 0. Choice A and choice B do not include a declaration of `count`. Once it is declared and set to 0, it can be used to check the values at each of the three indexes in `input`: `input[0]`, `input[1]`, and `input[2]`. The loop in choice C would continue until `count` was incremented to 3, but 3 is not an index in `input`. Choice D declares `count`, sets `count` to 0, and stops looping when `count` reaches 3, so it is the correct answer.

18. B: Ping pong balls in a lottery machine give a truly random number, because the ball that pops up is not based on any predetermined value. Pseudorandom numbers (A) are generated based on a seed value and therefore are not truly random. Deterministic numbers (C) have a predetermined value that is based on an event or equation. Static numbers (D) stay the same.

19. D: To create supportive classroom climates, teachers should arrange the furniture and materials to promote student comfort (A), dialogue (B), ownership (C), and collaboration (D).

20. C: `shellSize`. Instance variables are variables within classes. `Animal` and `Turtle` are classes, while `breathe` is a class method.

21. A: Using parameters. By using parameters for the color and the type, James could use a series of conditional statements based on those two parameters to print out the correct information.

22. C: We start by determining the number of seconds the stopwatch will display by getting the remainder of `totalseconds` divided by 60. Calculating the number of minutes to display requires two operations: first finding the remainder of `totalseconds` divided by 3600, then dividing that remainder by 60. To determine the number of hours to display, we simply divide `totalseconds` by 3600. As an example, let `totalseconds` be equal to 9,237.

$$\text{seconds} = 9237 \% 60 = 57$$
$$\text{minutes} = \frac{9237 \% 3600}{60} = \frac{2037}{60} = 33$$
$$\text{hours} = \frac{9237}{3600} = 2$$

Thus, the stopwatch would display 2 hours, 33 minutes, and 57 seconds.

23. D: Part of good documentation is giving variables suitable names. For example, if a variable represents the number of students in a classroom, `numStudents` would be a better variable name than `x`. If the variable names reflect the purposes of the variables, the code will be not only more readable but easier to understand in context.

24. C: When counting bytes, each prefix before "byte" represents a different multiple of 10 as the exponent of 2. From small to large, 2^0 bytes is 1 byte, 2^{10} bytes is 1 kilobyte, 2^{20} bytes is 1 megabyte, 2^{30} bytes is one gigabyte, 2^{40} bytes is one terabyte, and 2^{50} bytes is one petabyte.

25. B: Selection. A selection structure, otherwise known as an if statement or decision statement, allows the computer to run certain pieces of code only if a Boolean expression is true. Sequence refers to the order in which code is executed. Iteration is more commonly known as using a loop structure, in which code is repeated until some Boolean condition is met. Recursion refers to a method that repeatedly calls itself until a base case is true.

26. B: In plain text, each character takes up 1 byte. There are 2^{10} bytes (or 1,024 bytes) in 1 kilobyte (KB), so there are 2,048 bytes in 2 KB. As Penelope has 2,048 characters in her paper thus far, the text file contains 2,048 bytes, or 2 KB, in characters.

27. C: Preschool is a time in life in which students are highly likely to be at different developmental levels in the same classroom. Instead of expecting students to share, as might be above their current developmental skill level, teachers should promote sharing with modeling, encouraging, and rewarding sharing. Considering developmental levels for positive classroom environments, teachers can observe children's levels/types of play (unoccupied, independent, onlooker, parallel, associative, cooperative) and offer them not only matching activities (A), but also experiences at the next higher levels/types. Teachers must remember that older elementary and middle school students have not developed the social interaction skills of high school students, and accordingly guide them in peer collaboration (B). They should not expect new preschoolers to share, but instead should model, encourage, and reward sharing (C). For high school students, teachers can extend learning environments beyond classrooms (D) to surrounding communities, including service projects.

28. B: Object code is the sequence of binary statements that is generated by a compiler. It is usually specific to the current system architecture. For example, a Windows-based computer could not read object code intended for a Mac-based computer. Source code (A) is program code written in a programming language, and it must be compiled in order to run. Script code (C), or scripts, are series of instructions that are interpreted at runtime rather than compiled. Boolean (D) is not a type of code. In programming, the term "Boolean" most often refers to variables of the Boolean datatype, which can only be two different values ("true" or "false").

29. B: Because he will make the input more open-ended, Jason must now include some data validation to ensure that the user does not input invalid data. It's not possible to exercise a negative number of hours, so a check to ensure the number entered is positive would be the most appropriate. It isn't necessarily an issue if the number entered is a decimal or outside the range of 1 to 21.

30. D: `x` is 0 and `y` is 1. A **`for`** loop is a pretest loop, meaning the condition is tested first, and then the code within it is executed only if the condition is true. Since 0 is not less than 0, the very first time the loop executes, the condition is false, and the code does not execute. This maintains the value of `x` as 0. A **`do while`** loop is a posttest loop, meaning that the condition is tested after the code runs. This means that the code will run at least once, even if the condition is false, and in this case the condition is also false. However, before getting there, the value of `y` is increased by one, resulting in `y` containing the value 1.

31. A: Abstraction. Abstraction is reducing complexity through the removal of details. The dog does not know, or care, about the inner workings of the dog feeder. His input is the press of the button, and the output is the dog treat; the mechanics behind it are hidden. Inheritance is when one object takes on characteristics of another object, usually in object-oriented programming. Polymorphism is the capability of one object to represent many objects. Aliasing is when an object has different names that all point to the same memory address.

32. A: To save time, browsers keep graphics and text that they download. This data is stored in cache memory. This way, if the user visits a page again, the browser will not need to download all the page's content a second time. This functionality saves time and other resources. Bookmarking functionality (B) saves time for the user by allowing them to customize which pages they can access without having to remember a URL or use a search engine, but it does not affect load speeds. Cache memory helps to avoid downloads (choices C and D) that are actually unnecessary.

33. D: Using a function is the best way to reuse code that follows a specific algorithm. The algorithm could be replaced with `float totalCost ← cost * length * width`, and these variables could be entered as parameters.

34. C: `if (num ≤ 0) return 0`. The base case is the case that does not call itself and ends the recursion. Since it returns 0, the recursive calls will end here, and the recursion will unwind.

35. C: When distributing the **`not`** unary operator, all relational operators are flipped: **`and`** becomes **`or`**, > becomes ≤, and < becomes ≥.

36. A: When testing conditional statements, you must always test a value within the range and also at the endpoint(s). In choice A, 101 is a value within the range, 100 is at the endpoint for that range, 75 is in the second range, 50 is at the endpoint of the second range, and 25 doesn't satisfy either of the conditions, so it tests the else portion.

37. B: Fiber-optic cables transmit data as a stream of light that flows through fibers. This is faster than the electrical signals that flow through the other three types of cables mentioned.

38. C: Goals are not possible actors in the process of decomposing a problem. The term "actor" refers to external entities that the system must interact with. Because goals are not an external entity, they are not considered actors.

39. B: Since the text file is saved locally, the information it contains is not available for companies to collect. Social media, surveys, and emails all can be used by the company who owns them to mine for data that can then be used for advertising purposes, for example.

40. C: Reading documents saved on your local hard drive. It is illegal for companies to access and read documents stored locally on your personal computer. Answer A is legal, as every social media site that you sign up for requires you to sign a terms of service document that allows the company to monitor you. Answer B is also legal because many stores provide public Wi-Fi in order to collect information on the current shoppers. Answer D is legal as well. Similar to social media, apps can receive data about you while you are using the app, and some even do so in the background.

41. A: It would take today's computers millions of years to crack 256-bit encryption. Therefore, this encryption is used to send secure information over the internet, for example.

42. B: If an AI is believable. Alan Turing was a computer science pioneer who developed a test to determine a computer's ability to mimic human intelligence. The test is administered by a human typing through a computer. They will either be communicating with another human or a computer, and it is up to that person to determine which it is.

43. A: The since the octal numeral system is base 8, converting a number in base 10 to octal can be achieved by repeated division by 8. Start by dividing 35 by 8. The result is 4, with a remainder of 3. Then divide 4 by 8. The result is 0, with a remainder of 4. Since we have reached 0, we can now arrange the remainders in reverse order of how we got them. This yields the answer, 43.

44. B: I and II. The statement in III is incorrect because it calls `random()` again in the `if` statement. Unless by chance the same number between 1 and 100 is generated, this will result in a different value being compared during this statement. For example, if at the beginning of the program `random()` generates a 1, then at else if statement in III, `random()` would be called again, most likely resulting in a value different from 1. In such a case, nothing would be printed. The statements in I and II will both provide the intended results, with I being the more efficient choice. The third comparison is not necessary; if `rand` is not greater than 5 and not greater than 1, it can only be 1, as 1 is the minimum.

45. A: The for-loop will begin at index 1, which is 7. So it will add 7 to `sum`. On the next iteration, it will increment `i`, and since `i` will still be less than 4, it will add the value at that index to `sum`. It will continue until the index is equal to 4. Thus it will add `int[1]`, `int[2]`, and `int[3]`, or 7, 2, and 8.

46. C: With cloud-based data storage, data is stored on a company's server. Expanding capacity is as easy as upgrading to a plan that offers more storage. In order to increase local storage, a purchase of a hard drive, solid-state drive, or other storage medium would be necessary. Some mobile devices do not have expandable storage, and an entirely new device would be necessary in these cases. The other three answer choices are benefits of local storage.

47. C: Recompiling the program. Recompiling the program without any changes will not give you different results and will not help you determine any errors in the program. Using print statements will allow you to see the values of variables at different points in the program, and similarly, watch points will show you those values in the debugger. Changing the input may also help because certain inputs may produce errors while others may not.

48. C: Though a cluster is viewed as a single system, it utilizes networking to aggregate the computing power of many computers to work together on extremely large computing tasks. Some computers do have redundant storage disks running in parallel (A), but this is not an attribute of cluster computer systems specifically. Hand-held computers (B) have had many forms, but are different from cluster computer systems. Today, it is easy to compute on the same server as other users (D), though in the past this was the function of workstations.

49. D: As the hexadecimal numbering system, or hex, is base 16, and 16 is equal to 2^4, we know that it will take a combination of four base-2 numbers, or four bits, to store the hex number A.

50. B: Once code is released in an initial version like an alpha, it is possible to collect end user feedback. The code is no longer in-house and may now be reviewed by the people who will be using it. Each of the review types in the other answers choices can be conducted well before release.

51. D: Using library code is more convenient (A) and less time consuming (B). Library code is also much more likely to be bug-free, having been tested by many sources. However, if you need code for a unique purpose, there may be no library functions that can directly replace your original code. In such cases, you have no choice but to write your own code

52. D: I, II, and III. Because `diceRoll()` is always a value between 1 and 6, we only need to determine whether 1 through 6 can be a factor of 24 given the two other factors, which are the integer corresponding to `sword` and the value of `strength`. The set of arguments in I can return a value of 24 if `diceRoll()` returns a value of 3, since $2 \times 3 \times 4 = 24$. The set of arguments in II can return a value of 24 if `diceRoll()` returns a value of 2, since $3 \times 2 \times 4 = 24$. The set of arguments in III can return a value of 24 if `diceRoll()` returns a value of 6, since $4 \times 6 \times 1 = 24$.

53. C: Reusability. Since Barry is using the code in multiple areas of his program, it is a better idea to create a method than to repeat the same code in each different area. Extensibility refers to the ability of a program to be extended and built on. An example of this is when one class inherits the capabilities of another. Modifiability is the ability for a system to be easily modified when necessary. Testability is the ability for a program to be broken down into easily testable parts.

54. C: The robot will move backward, pivot right, move forward, and pivot left. Using the first input of 7 as an example, we subtract 2 from the input value to get 5. Then the modulus operator gives us the remainder after the integer division of 5 / 4, which is 1. This value maps to the command to move backward. The same procedure for the remaining inputs gives us the commands for pivot right, move forward, and pivot left. Note that for the last input, 4 - 2 gives us 2, and 2 % 4 gives us 2 as the remainder, as 4 goes into 2 zero times, with a remainder of 2.

55. A: Viewing or using files without permission is considered a data breach, no matter how minor the activity is. Many company data breaches happen due to database security flaws and can affect millions of people. A violation of a company's security policy (B) is called a "security incident." A violation of the Department of Homeland Security's privacy policies and procedures (C) is called a "privacy incident." An observable occurrence in a system or network that has negative consequences (D) is referred to as an "adverse event."

56. B: Because 9 is odd, and because we are subtracting 2 from `x` each time, eventually `x` will be passed in with a value that is less than 0, and it will never equal 0. Therefore, the base case `x == 0` would never run. By setting it to `x ≤ 0`, recursion will stop as soon as `x` is passed in with a value less than 0. Choices A and C have the same problem as the original algorithm; `x` will pass over all even numbers—including 0—if its initial value is odd. In choice D, `x` would increase in value each time, so recursion would be infinite for any initial value of `x` greater than 0.

57. D: Every odd hour the total increases by 2, and every even hour the total increases by 1. In order to determine the even and odd hour, use the modulus (%) operator. The modulus operator determines the remainder after one number is divided by another. An even number divided by 2 will have 0 as the remainder, and an odd number divided by 2 will have 1 as the remainder. Therefore, use a decision statement to determine if the number is even or odd and then add the correct value. Answer A is incorrect because it adds 1 when the result of `i % 2` is 1, meaning it is odd, and adds 2 otherwise. This is the opposite of the requirement. Answer B works for hours 1, 2, and 3 but breaks down for any hour after that. Answer C works for hours 1 and 2 but also breaks down after that.

58. D: `o!l!l!e!h!`. By moving the concatenation of the `foo` variable to the end, you will reverse the inputted word. Since the "!" was not moved, it will still be placed after each individual character that is concatenated to the string.

59. D: Attribution. Attribution is required by all Creative Commons licenses and requires the user to attribute the source and link to the original if any changes were permissible. *No derivatives* is a condition that may be added that states that the original art must not be changed in any way. *Share alike* means that any work that was derived from the original needs to be shared under the same license as the original. *Noncommercial* means the work cannot be used for commercial purposes.

60. B: The newer roller coaster's speed data will not necessarily be more accurate. Although the new roller coaster has more sensors, the question does not specify how many sensors will be used for each measurement. In other words, it is possible that only one sensor is still used for speed, while three sensors might be used for g-force and two sensors for vibration. But it is certainly true that there will be more data to process for the new roller coaster (A). Furthermore, we have no reason to think that no sensors could be added to the old roller coaster to improve data accuracy (C), or that any of the data gathered from the sensors would be useless for diagnostics.

61. D: There are two main programming paradigms: imperative and declarative. Imperative languages include object-oriented programming and procedural programming. These types of languages require the programmer to provide instructions to the computer on how to achieve desired results. Declarative programming is not concerned with how the computer is achieving the results, but it requires the programmer to clearly define what those results are.

62. C: Because `random()` returns a number where $0 \leq x < 1$, multiplying both endpoints by 4 results in $0 \leq x < 4$. Adding 66 to these endpoints gives $66 \leq x < 70$. Therefore, 70 and 4 (choices A and B) are out of bounds of this equation. Though 67.5 is inside the range, the `floor` function will round this down to 67, the closest integer that is less than 67.5. Therefore choice D is not a possible value of `result`.

63. B: It helps students to stick to a task if the task is made more fun by adding novelty to it through games or personal interest materials. For students who have difficulty staying with and completing routine tasks, the teacher can employ certain strategies that will encourage the child to stick with the work. One way is to explain to the students about the importance of remaining on-task and monitoring oneself. Another way is to eliminate any part of the routine that really isn't necessary, such as copying sentences. Still another way is to break up the task into smaller time commitments. In this way, the student doesn't get too bored before being allowed to go to something else, but he or she is nonetheless required to come back in a timely manner to finish.

64. D: Syntax. Syntax refers to the rules of a programming language and does not directly relate to object-oriented programming. Classes are the basis of object-oriented programming because they are used to create instances of objects. Inheritance refers to one class inheriting the properties of another. Polymorphism refers to one object being represented as another object in the current context.

65. D: Race, gender, and age are all obstacles to equal access computing, whereas name itself is not.

66. C: A heuristic approach is used mainly when an approximate answer is acceptable because efficiency is key. This is often the case when an answer is needed quickly because conditions are changing in real time. For example, if a person were driving (as in answer choice C), they would likely prefer to be given a "good guess" at the best route very quickly, as the alternative is to receive the perfect path but only after a relatively long wait. If the calculation takes even a little bit too long, it will no longer be valid, because the driver will have already passed that route.

67. C: The idea for a better toaster. Copyright only protects tangible items and original works, and an idea is not tangible. A painting is the most tangible of all, so that can be copyrighted. A blueprint for a house is a tangible plan for something to be created. Computer code, while not physical in itself, does represent the creation of a computer program.

68. A: `firstAnswer > secondAnswer`. When an integer is divided by another integer, the decimal portion is truncated, or dropped, from the number. Therefore $15/2 = 7$. When there is at least one decimal value in the division problem, decimal division occurs, resulting in a decimal answer: $15/2.0 = 7.5$. Therefore, `firstAnswer` is larger than `secondAnswer`.

69. C: The program is to determine how much carbon dioxide is converted to oxygen by each of three flower types. In order to run such a simulation, a user would have to input the starting amounts of oxygen and carbon dioxide. Therefore, choices A and B are not correct. A user would also need to specify the type of flower being simulated, so choice D is not correct. Before the simulation has been run, it is impossible to know how much oxygen will be in the air at the end of the simulation, so this will not be a user input.

70. D: An IP address is used to send and receive information over the internet (A and B). It can also be used to identify the physical location that it is associated with (C). However, an IP address by itself does not enable decryption of encrypted information.

71. B: This choice will continue to subtract 3 from the original number until the that number is 2 or less. Meanwhile, for each subtraction of 3, it increments `result`, yielding the same answer as performing integer division using `10 / 3`. The result in both cases is 3, which the remainder of 1 being discarded.

72. B: Identity theft is when someone uses someone else's personal information without their permission. It is unethical as well as illegal.

73. C: Hikers logging into a global app to report bear sightings. Citizen science uses the collective strength of a community to collect and analyze data. A small team of researchers could not collect the same amount of data about a particular topic that a large community could. A single scientist also could not go through as much information as the population at large. Social media keeping track of user opinions is not scientific research because it is opinion-based and done without people knowing it is being done.

74. D: This is the most efficient use of code among the choices. The if statements only test for the upper limits of the first two ranges, which is possible because the whole if statement structure works in a cascading fashion wherein the lowest range is checked first, then the middle range is checked, and finally any score that doesn't fit into those two ranges is assumed to fit in the highest range. Although choice C is similar, because it begins with the highest range, every valid input will result in the output "above average." Choices A and B both contain code that would work. However, they are less efficient because they both needlessly check the upper and lower limits of two ranges.

75. A: Overloading (or more formally "function overloading") is the practice of writing different functions with the same name and distinguishing them only by their expected parameters. This allows similar methods to be called using the same function name while ensuring that the function appropriate for the context will be used. Overriding (B) (or "method overriding") is a feature of object-oriented programming languages wherein, if a child class has one of the same methods as the parent class, the child class method takes precedence. Overwriting (C) is the process of writing data directly in the place of existing data, effectively erasing the existing data. "Overstating" is not a standard term in programming.

76. A: When a person presses the gas pedal of a car, there are many things that go on inside the car to make it move. This is an example of abstraction because these inner workings are hidden from the driver; the driver only sees the result of the car moving. None of the other choices represent abstractions. In each case, the effect results directly from the cause, with no hidden processes.

77. B: Children, especially at younger ages, learn best when they feel secure and can know what to expect. By creating a daily schedule, the students are provided with stability, which helps make the students feel comfortable and safe while in his classroom. This allows the students the opportunity to learn, ask questions, and flourish because they do not have to wonder what to expect when they enter the classroom. Providing the students with consistency can greatly help development.

78. B: Row. In a database, each row is a record because it represents one specific group of data.

79. A: When instruction is more demanding—e.g., when students are asked to solve novel problems and create products—teacher decisions are not simpler (C) but more complex. When teachers encourage student responsibility, both teachers and students approach and understand instructional content differently (B). Teachers must not only help students meet academic demands for comprehension and manipulation of subject content, but also help them meet social demands (D) for effective demonstration of their content knowledge in interactions with others.

80. D: It is ethical to use your library card to access an online library in another city and borrow an e-book. Using your friend's Netflix account without paying for your own (A) and connecting to a neighbor's Wi-Fi without permission (B) are both unethical. You can use an image that has a creative commons license on your website; however, it would be unethical to use it in on your website without credit (C), as this would suggest it is an original image.

81. B: The operating system (OS) manages memory, devices, and storage on the local system. It does not manage the internet as a whole. Other things the OS manages include the CPU, any applications, and user interface devices.

82. D: A Boolean variable can hold only two possible values, "true" and "false". Because the sensor will determine that either there is a car in the next lane or there is not a car in the next lane, and because the light must be either on or off, a Boolean variable will be the logical choice, as it likewise can only be one way or the other. Each of the other choices will be less efficient because it will have many possible values, and, though these values will not be used, the variable will take up more memory than a Boolean variable would.

83. D: The seven layers of the OSI model from top to bottom are application, presentation, session, transport, network, data link, and physical.

84. C: Statement I is true because the sensor information for Day 1 must be invalid. The maximum speed of the subway train is 55 mph, and dividing 500 miles by 1 hour gives 500 mph. This means there must have been an error in the sensor information. Statement II is true because the data for Day 2 indicates that the train traveled 0 miles in 0 hours. This data is not necessarily invalid, as it is possible that the train did not run at all that day. However, the program will divide 0 by 0 to determine the speed. The division by zero will result in an error. Day 3's data seems possible, and because 150 / 3 is 50, the resulting average speed is well within the maximum speed of 55 mph.

85. C: A firewall is a security system, typically a physical device, that filters the traffic going into or coming out of a network based on the specifications of the firewall's owner. A firewall would be used by an organization that needs to keep a network secure. Antivirus suites (A) are software packages that include a scanner to analyze files to see if they contain any malware. They may also include applications to monitor network traffic to a computer. A virtual private network (B) is also software. It enables the creation of private networks that use the public internet for connectivity. A protocol (D) is a system of rules that allows computers to interact over communication networks.

86. B: Ones place value. When you use the modulus operator (%) it returns the remainder after division. Since `num % 10` returns the remainder after dividing the number by 10, this will result in the ones place value of the number.

87. A: Redundancy in IP protocols is provided by the ability to reroute packets as needed given which routes are available, among many possibilities.

88. C: One of the reasons why programmers should document their code well is to clarify what the code actually does. This saves time and potential confusion when others read the code, and it can serve as a much-needed reminder for the programmer if they need to access their code later on, after they've forgotten about it. Documentation is not required for the code to compile (choices A and D). In fact, the compiler completely ignores all comments. Documentation might be required by a method of development (B), but such a requirement would not be a reason to document well all the time.

89. B: Increasing the number of variables simulated. If the car is sticking to the road too much, the simulation needs more information to determine the correct physics based on factors such as the car's speed, trajectory, tires, and weight. This requires an increase in the number of variables in the simulation.

90. B: The recursive function sums up all the numbers and returns that sum. The `while` loop in this selection also does that. With each iteration, `x` is added to a sum value and decreased by 1. Once the value is 0, the loop ends, and the sum is returned.

91. C: The first commercial cellular networks become available in the 1970s, although they were very expensive to use at the time. Text messaging (A) is officially considered to have been invented in 1992, but it did not catch on until later. Wireless networking had been in development for many years, but the protocol that Wi-Fi uses was not released until 1991, and the Wi-Fi mark came even later, in 1999. Bluetooth was invented in 1989, but it did not become commercially used until ten years later.

92. C: The cost of computer components is not a direct factor that will prevent a computer from solving a problem. No computer component costs an infinite amount of money. Time (A) is a factor because the problem may take an infinite amount of time. Some problems may also involve an infinite amount of space (B). Also, if a computer is ever caught in an infinite loop, it will never stop and will therefore never solve the problem.

93. B: Procedural programming is based on procedure calls. Object-oriented programming relies on the concepts of classes and objects. Functional programming is the process of building software by composing functions. Low-level programming is writing machine language—code that is directly executed by the CPU—or writing in a programming language that is not far removed from machine language.

94. A: Since the system has a valid range from 5.5 to 10, inclusive, the invalid range is when it is less than 5.5 or greater than 10.

95. D: Helping maintain copyrighted information. Data that is open to the public has many benefits, such as allowing for better simulations and predicting changes to climate in real time; promoting innovation through use of publicly available datasets; and allowing the public to be educated about statistics they may not normally have access to. Open data does not, however, help maintain copyrighted information because the purpose of open data is to freely spread information.

96. C: The highest quality, ethically obtained data will come from weighing consenting participants directly. Installing a weight sensor (A) would not be particularly helpful because the data would be detached from all identifying information. It would also be unethical and likely illegal for a doctor to release medical records for this purpose, and it would thus be inappropriate to make such a request (B). Email lists (D) can be obtained through various methods, but there is only a slim chance that enough potential participants would respond to an email with correct information or at all.

97. C: Decomposition. Decomposition is the process of breaking down large problems into smaller ones. Before John can make the character have a full walk cycle, he first needs to do a simpler task, which is making his character move its leg.

98. C: This loop begins with `i` being equal to 5, the maximum index in the array. It then decrements this value by 1 each time the loop runs, and includes all of the integers until 0, inclusively. The loop will still traverse the entire array and sum up all values within it, and will merely be counting down from 5 through 0 instead of counting up from 0 through 5.

99. C: The base case of this recursive function is when `x` is 1. For a positive integer greater than 1, the value of `x` will need to decrement each time the function runs, until it reaches 1 and the recursion ends. Choice C is the only one that subtracts 1 from `x` each time, so it is the correct choice.

100. D: Line 5 is the recursive call because it is the part of the function where the function calls itself.

101. A: Studies have shown that continual smartphone usage can lead to insomnia, addiction, and a sedentary lifestyle. No studies have reported heart conditions that are directly related to smartphone usage.

102. B: Software pirating. Software pirating is the illegal downloading or copying of software that the creator intended you to pay for. Game cracking is the act of breaking copyright protection algorithms in order for people to pirate and play games. Ethical hacking is trying to break into a company's computer system so that the company can fix any security flaws in that system. Social engineering is the process of deceiving individuals so that they divulge confidential information.

103. B: A queue is a first-in-first-out (FIFO) data structure that allows for changing lengths. Stacks (choice A) are last-in-first-out (LIFO).

104. D: The teacher who speaks softly and avoids making eye contact with students is less likely to command respect and obedience in the classroom. All three of the other answers represent assertive body language that is more likely to result in students responding well to the teacher. This includes looking students in the eye, speaking in a firm voice, and maintaining good posture.

105. B: Copyrights are used to protect original works of authorship, such as art, music, and software. Trade secrets (A) are used to protect private information that is necessary for a business to stay competitive. Patents (C) are used to protect innovations or discoveries. Trademarks (D) are used to protect the identity of a product or service through the use of branding (i.e., specific words, symbols, etc.).

106. A: 10. Because of order of operations, the modulus operator is calculated first, so $5 \% 2 = 1$. Then multiplication follows, giving $1 \times 6 = 6$. Lastly, addition by 4 gives the answer of 10.

107. A: Because binary is base 2, we can calculate the equivalent number of bytes equal to any larger unit (kilobyte, megabyte, etc.) by raising 2 to the appropriate power. One byte is $2^0 = 1$. One kilobyte is $2^{10} = 1{,}024$. Therefore, 1 KB is equal to 1,024 bytes.

108. B: Data verification is used to determine if data (in this case, Nadia's login credentials) is correct. Data validation (A) is a coding practice where checks are put in place to make sure inputted information meets the criteria that the program expects (for example, specifying a certain number of digits for a user-entered phone number, or prohibiting negative numbers being entered for a prompt that asks the user's number of pets). Data mining (C) is the activity of searching for and discovering patterns in large datasets. Data encryption (D) is the process of transforming data into a form that is only readable by those with the correct encryption key.

109. B: Pie chart. A pie chart is the best option when trying to visualize percentages of a whole population. A bar graph could show the percentages; however, it is difficult to see how each bar corresponds to the school population as a whole. A line graph and scatter plot work better for displaying two variable data sets. For example, a line graph would work well if the school were trying to display a graph of the number of students that were present each day of school for a year.

110. A: Since strings begin with index 0, and since we know based on the method documentation that this method will return the characters at positions 2 through 3, we can see that the method will return "`zz`".

111. D: Randomness is appropriate for bonus points in a video game because it adds an element of chance to the game. If you were to randomize an address associated with a user (choice A), the number of items a person ordered (choice B), or the amount of change a vending machine gives back (choice C), then in each case there would be no point in storing this data at all, since the data needs to be accurate in order to be useful.

112. C: In ASCII, each commonly used character (e.g., letters of the Roman alphabet, numbers, and certain special characters) is assigned a number between 0 and 127. This practice, of assigning characters a number code so that they can be used and interpreted by computers, is known as "encoding." Encryption (A) is a way of putting data in a format where it can only be read by someone with the key to reveal the format. Hashing (B) is a mathematical computation commonly used to check the validity of data. Transferring (D) is the process of moving data.

113. B: Stack. A stack follows the FILO, or first in last out structure. Since cards are "pushed" on to the top of the cards in the discard pile and "popped" off of the cards in the discard pile, this is the best structure to use. A queue is the opposite of a stack because it uses a FIFO, or first in first out structure. This works well to simulate, for instance, people lining up at a cash register. An array doesn't work well since its size is static, and a map is too complex for the situation.

114. B: -2, -2. The variable `x` is first replaced with -5-(-3), which is -2. Then `secondProcedure` is called with parameters `-2, -3`. Since `a` is greater than `b`, `a` is returned, so a value of -2 gets stored in `y`. Now both `x` and `y` are -2, giving the answer -2, -2.

115. A: Sonia's calculation is considered linear because it contains a constant and a first-order term (or a term whose exponent is 1). A quadratic calculation (C) would contain a variable that is raised to the power of 2 (e.g., x^2), while in an exponential method (B), the variable itself would be the exponent (e.g., 2^x). A logarithmic equation (D) would contain a logarithm (e.g., $\log_2 x$).

116. C: Since eggs are the smallest and simplest object in this hierarchy, we start from there. We can define the rest of the hierarchical relationship by working our way up the inheritance chain. Eggs are part of a carton. Cartons are found in the diary section. Dairy sections exist in grocery stores.

117. C: In regular mathematics, the formula in choice C would yield 0. However, `totalDonuts / BOX_SIZE` performs integer division because both variables are integers. If `totalDonuts` were 14 for example, the result would be 2. Then, we multiply this number by `BOX_SIZE`, giving us $2 \times 6 = 12$. Finally, we subtract this number from `totalDonuts` to get the number of remaining donuts. If `totalDonuts` is 14, then we accurately calculate that two donuts are left over: $14 - 12 = 2$.

118. D: No, the method will recurse indefinitely. Because the only possible outcomes of `vehicles % 2` are 0 and 1, the code will never execute the final `else` and stop running.

119. A: Although an IDE increases efficiency (B), allows for collaboration (C), and includes debugging tools (D), it does not automatically fix mistakes in code.

120. D: Blue, Orange, Orange, Blue, Red, Blue, Blue. The best way to solve this problem is to draw it out and refer to the programming interface that Sarah has created. These directions make the robot move one square east, then turn 180 degrees, move back to the starting position, face north, and then move north twice.

121. A: Local computing offers the most security because no information is sent across a network. All the information is physically stored with no way for anyone else to access it unless they are using that computer. Wide-area networks (WANs), local-area networks (LANs), and the cloud each involve at least a greater security risk than local computing only because they require information to be sent over a network.

122. C: The condition should read `if(roll == 6)`. The line that reads `if(random() == 6)` generates a new random number inside the conditional statement. Instead, use the number already generated in the previous line, which is stored inside the roll variable.

123. C: Digital signatures allow the receiver of a message to determine whether it is coming from a trusted source and whether it has been tampered with while in transit. Digital signatures do rely on the signer keeping their private key secret, because otherwise bad actors could impersonate them (A). They utilize asymmetric cryptography, not symmetric cryptography (B). Privacy is not a function of digital signatures – other types of encryption must be used for that purpose if desired (D).

124. C: Empirical evidence is evidence obtained by observation or experimentation. Qualitative (A), quantitative (B), and experimental (D) evidence all fall under that category. Theoretical evidence is evidence that is based on calculation, not on direct observation.

125. B: The condition in the first if statement is false, because although the string stored in `weather` is "rain", the value stored in `temperature` is not greater than 50. So the code in **`else`** will run. The condition in the next if-statement will also be false because `temperature` is not less than 25. However, the next condition will be true because `temperature` is less than 35, so "a bit chilly" will be printed, and the final **`else`** will be ignored.

Online Resources

Due to our efforts to try to keep this book to a manageable length, we've created a link that will give you access to all of your online resources:

mometrix.com/resources719/oaecompsci

It's Your Moment, Let's Celebrate It!

Share your story @mometrixtestpreparation